THE BUZZ ON™

WINE

Chris Sherman

LF LEBHAR-FRIEDMAN BOOKS
NEW YORK · CHICAGO · LOS ANGELES · LONDON · PARIS · TOKYO

The Buzz On Wine

Lebhar-Friedman Books
425 Park Avenue
New York, NY 10022

Published by Lebhar-Friedman Books
Lebhar-Friedman Books is a company of Lebhar-Friedman, Inc.

Printed in the United States of America

Library of Congress Cataloging-in-Publication Data

> Sherman, Chris (Christopher Barnes), 1947-
> The buzz on wine / Chris Sherman.
> p. cm
> Includes index.
> ISBN: 0-86730-817-6 (alk. paper)
> 1. Wine and wine making. I. Title
>
> TP548 .S542 2000
> 641.2'2--dc21   00-058362

Produced by Progressive Publishing
Editor: John Craddock; Creative Director: Nancy Lycan; Art Director: Peter Royland
Editorial Contributors: Michele Thomareas, Rusty Fischer, Justin Misik
Designers: Angela Connolly, Rena Bracey, Vivian Torres, William Setzer, Laurie Osborne, Lanette Fitzpatrick

Visit our Web site at lfbooks.com

THE BUZZ ON™

WINE

ACKNOWLEDGMENTS

The author dutifully wishes to thank Jack Cakebread (and the whole clan), Bernard Portet, Orville Magoon, Jill Davis, Sergio Traverso, Jim Fiolek, and Marcus and Anna Moller-Racke, who taught me 15 years ago about the sweat, passion, and intelligence that turn grapes into wine.

I am indebted to many others since then, longtime friends in the wine trade and hardworking people I will never know in fields and cellars around the world. Finally I must thank everyone with whom I've shared a glass of good wine and good conversation, especially my wife, Sandra.

We also wish to thank the following for their contributions to this book:

Esme Berg at Food and Wines From France; Jacquie Happ at Happs; Bonnie Siconolfi at Castello Banfi, Vinum Communications; Nina Zeiger at Organic Wine Company; Megghan Driscoll at Southcorp Wines; Andrea Dodson at Leeuwin Estate; Elisna Krige & Naas Erasmus at Distillers Corp. Ltd. & Michelle Armour at MMD; Mary Jo Chism at Dry Creek Vineyard; E. Thomas Costello at Sable Ridge Vineyards; Bertrand Denoune at Alsace-Willm; Ken Field at Blue Pyrenees Estate; Kathie Fowler at Joseph Phelps Vineyards; Stephanie Legiuron at Leclerc Briant; Alejandra Ramirez at Viña Montes; Johannes Selbach at Selbach-Oster; Jenny Stonier at Stonier's Winery; Mary Anne Tracy at Mantanzas Creek Winery; The German Wine Information Bureau; Antinori; Atlas Peak Vineyards; Bonny Doon; Bully Hill; Ca' del Solo; Cabrière Estate; Folonari; Golders Vineyard; Guenter Wittman; Kendall-Jackson & Stonestreet; Markham Vineyards; Michele Chiarlo; Mildara Blass Wines; R. H. Phillips; Ridge Vineyards; Rutherford Hill Winery; Silver Oak Cellars; Sterling Vineyards; Seven Peaks Winery; Villa Cerna; William Hill Winery; A. C. Noble at the Department of Viticulture and Enology at The University of California, Davis; and http://www.aboutwine.com.

THE BUZZ ON WINE

CONTENTS

WINE: A WET & WILD HISTORY

Hip America has become so wine conscious that we've run out of domestic vineyards to experiment with and have pushed up the sales levels of imported wines from countries as vastly different as France and Chile, Spain and Australia.

After all, dot-com millionaires and all of those young, day-trading lions working seventy hour weeks need something a little more acceptable than draft beer and stale pretzels to relax with after a long day (and night) at work. What better way to unwind with panache than to uncork a fine vintage from overseas? (Or just up the road from Silicon Valley, for that matter. Washington and Oregon—not to mention California—long ago entered the wine war as well.)

Yet it's not just the distance of the vineyard or the price of the bottle that makes drinking wine so appealing. After all, it's the whole lifestyle that goes along with it: The shiny corkscrew. The snooty waiter who crumples under your withering wine wit. The fancy labels and foreign-sounding words. The twist of the wrist when pouring. The stiff shoulders of the bottle. That gold-embossed, leather bound wine list that reads like the French edition of *War and Peace*. It's all so . . . civilized.

And yet, it's really not. A few grapes. Some dirty feet stomping them into glorified sour mash. Some oak barrels and a big spittoon. Where's the glamour in all of that? Nowhere, if all we were talking about was a few bottles of grape juice with a kick. But this is wine we're talking about. After all, if wine wasn't so cool, the phrase would read "The days of soda pop and roses."

For despite the technological revolution and the ever-expanding information superhighway,

wine is our link to history—in liquid form. Poured into every bottle, whether it's a $200 French Bordeaux or a domestic carafe of Turning Leaf circa, oh, let's say 2000; the proof is in the tasting. The first sip of wine, any wine, speaks volumes. And not just to the tongue, but to the brain, and even more important, the heart, as well. For the scientists, the tasters, the sommeliers, the vineyard owners, and even the grape pickers all have something to say: "Look how hard we worked, folks. Better yet, taste how hard we worked!"

A glass of wine isn't just a drink. It's an experience. A flashback to last year, or even last decade. It's history in a glass, but with an aftertaste of hope. Hope for next year's vintage, perhaps. It's your passport to exotic, foreign lands, whose soil, culture, and evolution sweep across your tongue with every sip.

It's history in the making, and it's making history with every press, crush, and vintage. So? Ready for your tour of all things vintage, vineyard, and vino? Right this way. Look out for that spittoon!

TOP-5 SIGNS YOU'RE NOT AN EXPERT ON WINE YET

5 You still think "Bordeaux" rhymes with "Gore-Tex."

4 Jug? Twist off? Box? So many choices…so little time.

3 You keep asking the liquor store clerk, "Does this come by the glass?"

2 No one wants to hear any more of your "alternate uses" for the corkscrew.

1 Your annual "Sangria and Slim Jim" dinner party.

1 ONE
JUST DRINK IT

You enjoy wine, or you think you might. You get a kick out of the brilliant color in the glass, like the smell of it, and savor the bright cheery taste and the smooth way it slides down your throat. It could be a liebfraumilch, a white zin, a Portuguese rosé, a glass of lambrusco on an imaginary trip to Italy, or a soft and easy California merlot. Doesn't matter.

What you don't enjoy is feeling a fool or a peasant when a waiter hands you a wine list that goes on for pages and pages with words you can't pronounce and prices you can't say without gulping. It's worse in a wine store where there are even more choices, and a clerk going on about malolactic fermentation, which you hope isn't contagious. In the liquor store there are almost as many labels, and no help at all. If you don't see a bottle you know, you grab the one with the nicest label and get out in a hurry. What a miserable state of affairs for something as fine as wine.

Wine is about enjoying, not about learning. Getting to know wine should be natural, not contrived. You didn't have to learn to eat, did you? Okay, maybe sushi took a little work, but steak, pizza, ice cream, chocolate?

FIRST, STUFF **YOU** SHOULD FORGET

I'LL **NEVER LEARN** ALL THESE NAMES

You don't need to learn them all, just the ones you like. Most wines are named for either the grape used to make them or the place where they were made. Get to know the names of the grapes first, like chardonnay and cabernet sauvignon. These are the names used most prominently on most U.S. wines, and those from other New World wineries in Australia, Chile, and South Africa and occasionally in certain parts of Europe.

Then you can move back to the Old World, where the wines are distinguished by place names, because wine has been made in a certain area for so long, its product and name are synonymous. In Burgundy, red wines are made from pinot noir; in Bordeaux they are made from a blend of grapes including cabernet sauvignon and merlot; knowing a wine is from the Saint-Émilion section of Bordeaux will tell you more specifically about the blend (heavy in merlot). Explore one country at a time (see Chapters 7–13), perhaps starting with France since it has the most distinct varieties.

Along the way you'll bump into a third form of naming, the proprietary or brand name, used throughout the world of wine from Blue Nun to Opus One to Cristal, which tells nothing about the grapes or the place, only an image the owner wants to present.

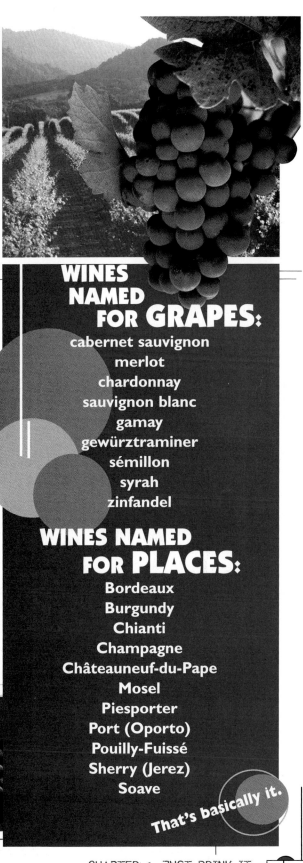

WINES NAMED FOR GRAPES:
cabernet sauvignon
merlot
chardonnay
sauvignon blanc
gamay
gewürztraminer
sémillon
syrah
zinfandel

WINES NAMED FOR PLACES:
Bordeaux
Burgundy
Chianti
Champagne
Châteauneuf-du-Pape
Mosel
Piesporter
Port (Oporto)
Pouilly-Fuissé
Sherry (Jerez)
Soave

That's basically it.

OKAY, BUT I JUST CAN'T KEEP TRACK OF ALL THE VINTAGES

You don't need to know how much it rained in Australia or whether the summer was too cold in Burgundy—yet. (See Chapter 6, "I'm Over the Edge and Must Know All.")

Weather does affect the quality and quantity of the grape harvests, especially in the cooler parts of Europe, but its effect on everyday wine drinking is minimal. New World vineyards have more consistent temperate weather. Improvements in technology have enabled good winemakers to survive bad vintages. Besides, in wine, the good really do die young: Most wine is drunk young; vintage variations matter little in most white wines, or in wines of any kind when they're young.

There's a bonus reason not to worry: We've been blessed with a string of strong vintages. Take 1985, if you want to remember one year for the next two decades. And just to make it easier, we have had by chance great vintages almost everywhere every five years since. File away 1985, 1990 and 1995. Now this isn't perfect. There was no '90 vintage in port and '95 was only very good, not great, in some countries. But this is a good start.

Like Bordeaux? Take the whole decade of the '80s, from 1981 to 1990, and you can barely go wrong (1984 and '87 were the weakest). In fact, 1988 through 1990 were vintage years in Bordeaux, Burgundy, and Germany. Things did slack off for a while but starting in 1994, better vintages showed up around the world and the first tastes make the 1995 and '96 vintages look the best of the decade. In California the entire decade of the 1990s has been remarkably good, with only 1993 slumping to a mere "very good" on most vintage charts. Don't sweat vintages until you start buying $40 bottles to lay down in your cellar for five years or more. Then it's important to buy good vintages.

1985
1990
1995

I CAN'T AFFORD TO SPEND A LOT OF MONEY

Who does when you can buy plenty of good wine for $10 to $12? Honest.

Sure, people pay $50 to $100 for the top growths from Bordeaux and Burgundy; big-deal Italian wines and California superstars are in the same price range. And the days when the "Fighting $5" varietals included surprisingly good cabernet sauvignon are pretty much over.

That leaves plenty of room to navigate in the wine shelves. Find your way around the less traveled corners of the wine world and less prestigious grapes, and you'll learn how to buy a good $10 bottle of wine. If you want to know how to buy a good bottle of wine for $100, just open your wallet.

You should realize that price *generally* reflects quality in wine. You may find a great $7 bottle that's as good as an overpriced $20 bottle, but there may be a good reason one bottle costs $10 or $20 more than another. The winery may have used better grapes from more expensive vineyards, made the wine more carefully, spent more on the barrels to age it, or waited longer to sell it, all of which make differences you can taste. Demand caused by advertising, supposed fame, or buzz about a high rating can force the price up higher than the quality merits, but if you ignore the hype, you can usually get your money's worth.

Today, the fight for inexpensive wine market share is being waged in new vineyards in southern France, Italy, Chile, and Australia; they've moved up a few dollars, but the results are better too.

"There are so many great wines out there at a good price. I mean, I'm talking $10, even below $10. . . . Very affordable prices that you can experiment with. Because obviously you can't go experiment on a $20 or $30 bottle of wine. No one can."

—Gina Gallo

Spend $10 to $15, however, and you can get good bottles from California, Australia, Italy, France, and Germany. Pop $20 to $30 and you can taste some of the finest wines from the New World, and get a taste of all but the most expensive from the Old.

TOP-5 BENEFITS TO BUYING WINE AT A CONVENIENCE STORE

5 With the change, you can buy a 6-pack and do some real drinkin'.

4 Friendly, attractive cashiers who always know what wine goes with Slim Jims.

3 Where else are you supposed to buy apple-flavored wine?

2 At least you'll never have to invest in one of those fancy corkscrew thingamajigs.

1 On your way out of the store you can steal a stack of newspapers to sleep under.

No **MYSTERY** TO THE **HISTORY**

NO ONE KNOWS WHO DISCOVERED WINE. NO ONE KNOWS WHO DISCOVERED PIZZA EITHER. SO WHAT?

The first grapes supposedly were grown in Persia; the Persians figured out how to make wine, which isn't *that* impressive, since grapes naturally turn into wine if they're crushed in a bucket with some water. Wine drinking spread to Egypt, and soon after, visiting Greeks on a loot-and-pillage fest picked up some carryout casks and vines and brought them home; the Greeks finally ran out of good ideas and gave way to the conquering Romans, who swilled wine big time. They also grew grapes on the sides of river banks, which proved to be a key point. Boats could be used to transport wine in quantity, and spread the juice even more. Roman Catholic Church officials were heavy

into wine and incorporated the grape-growing ritual as part of their 3,000-year progress plan. (Only 1,000 more years to go!)

At one point, the English almost cornered a piece of the wine market. They had a major real estate stake in France (a province called Bordeaux) and in 1372, England imported three million gallons of a wine called claret across the channel. That's six bottles per person for everyone in England, Wales, and Scotland. England lost Bordeaux in a dispute in 1453, but that's where the claret came from, and the Queen's land hasn't been the same since; the Brits turned to beer. Today, all table wine (cheap stuff) sold in Great Britain barely averages six bottles per person, same as the 14th century.

Flash ahead to the 17th century and the invention of corked bottles; aging wine, instead of sticking a spout in a barrel and having an all-day keg party, became an option. There are still bottles from the 1700s that are drinkable.

The New World

California produced about 8 million gallons a year in 1876; it produced 32 million gallons by 1900, but Prohibition virtually wiped out the wine business in California. Out of more than 200 vineyards that operated in the state before Prohibition, only 20 survived until 1933 when Prohibition was repealed.

CURRENT EVENTS

Today, California has more than 800 wineries, and the revolution in American winemaking has matured and spread from Napa Valley to all corners of California and the Northwest U.S.; almost every state, for better or for worse, has its own wineries. Americans are also diversifying into new and old grape varieties from the French Mediterranean and Italy. Everywhere, new brands are born almost weekly, and tired old names strive to improve quality and reassert their claim to prominence.

Australia has cast off its cheapie status and been recognized as a serious producer and innovator. Chile has quickly become a significant exporter, and its wines have come to prominence on lists, especially in New York City. South Africa has rejoined world trade, and New Zealand and Argentina look on enviously from the wings.

The Old World is changing too. In France, young entrepreneurs and old estates alike have expanded quality plantings into underutilized areas, exported more from Alsace and the Loire, and gone abroad to the U.S., Chile, and Australia. Radical change in Italy built a new tradition of fresh flavor and created whole new wines in Tuscany. Germany is struggling to modernize its appeal. Spain has emerged from its modern dark ages to be the greatest new source of quality wine. And a reawakened Eastern Europe may see its historic vineyards revive.

You already know this: The wine selections you face are more bewildering than ever. Through the miracle of modern transportation, all these thousands of labels are in your face in restaurants, wine stores, and supermarkets.

Relax. It's all wine.

One of the great peculiarities of wine occurred in what wine historians call (while holding their noses) *The New World*—as if three centuries of civilization (which includes inventing the Fender Stratocaster and shag carpet) don't count.

The Spanish brought European grapes to South America, and they've been merrily at it ever since, but in North America, wine growing got nowhere. A bug called phylloxera kept eating the roots. There was a native American grape plant, but its wine tasted more like vintage bug juice than vintage grape. The Old World got its comeuppance when the root-eating bug was accidentally imported in the 1860s and nearly destroyed the European wine crops. Someone eventually figured out that certain American grape roots weren't affected by the bug. Many of the grapes now grown in Europe were grafted onto American, aka *New World*, roots.

The delay in growing wine in the U.S. lasted about 200 years until California started to be settled.

REMEDIAL SCIENCE

Over a long summer a grape ripens, people go to the beach, frogs croak, baseball drones on and on, fish jump, and cotton grows high. It's in the summertime that the tart grape, high in acid, turns into a plump fruit, rich in sugar. When the crushed grapes ferment, yeast will turn the sugar into alcohol. That's the key: Grapes plus yeast equals wine. Then, as the wine ages, the slow exposure to oxygen will add the final touch.

Other fruits and honey can make wine, but they're no match for grapes. The grape is particularly suited to wine and has been cultivated primarily for that purpose for thousands of years. During that time grapes have evolved into thousands of varieties. The grapes that make fine wine are from the *vinifera* branch of the grape's family tree. The best have been singled out as the "noble" grapes.

You may already know many of them by name: merlot, zinfandel, chenin blanc, riesling, and so on. These wines are named for the grape variety (varietal in wine lingo) that produced them. Each varietal has characteristic flavors (pinot noir usually tastes of cherry and pepper), specific growing conditions, climate needs, etc.

THE ROCKIER THE BETTER

Unlike other farmers, grape growers do not want rich fertile soil for vineyards. Nor do they want great productivity. They have sought out the rockiest, most difficult sites for vineyards since Roman times, and they prize low yields so much that many wine laws, medieval and modern, strictly limit crop size. Many fine vineyards produce only two tons of grapes in an acre, which make about 100 cases of wine.

They do, however, want the grapes in that crop to ripen perfectly, so that they have the right amount of sugar. Achieving high sugar without losing the necessary acids is the goal of every grower.

You may have noticed that many famous wine regions are valleys. Many great vineyards are on the valley's hillsides to take advantage of the stony soil and the good drainage on the slopes. There are exceptions, however, in the fine flatland vineyards of Bordeaux and Napa.

Grape vines do need sun, soil, and water, but the mix is the key. Generally white grapes like cooler weather and less rich soil to create wine with higher acidity. Dark red grapes like it hotter, and can prosper in richer soils. But nothing is that simple in grape growing. Each grape needs different amounts of heat in particular times of the year; some can tolerate wide variations in temperatures; many can't.

> **What is terroir? This is a French expression relating to the uniqueness of a wine made from grapes grown on a certain plot of land. It encompasses the vine's complete growing environment, including climate, aspect, soil, altitude, etc., and the effect all this has on the wine's character.**

Warmth is determined by latitude, cloud cover, morning fog, length of days, heat-retaining properties of the soil, and elevation. And north is not always cooler than south. Thanks to maritime effects and wind patterns, the Carneros region at the far south of Napa and Sonoma in California is cooler than the upper valleys farther north. Santa Barbara, 300 miles south, can be just as cool. Even in the same part of a valley, vines on the west side receive early morning heat and more sun; those on the east less.

Grapes in the coolest vineyards are the most fragile, which is why the type of grape and weather are more critical in Germany or Champagne than in sunny California or Australia. They often do not get enough warmth to ripen until very late, when they may also run the risk of frost.

Soil is important for its physical characteristics more than its nutrients. "Look at this soil," the Bordelaise will say, beaming as they scoop up softball sized rocks from a vineyard. These stones force roots to dig deep to find water. The right kind of rocks or soil can hold the heat of a summer day and release it at night, like the slate vineyards along the Mosel. Cold clay can protect vines from too much heat. Near white soils reflect heat.

While the chemical make-up in the soil is less important, pinot noir and chardonnay do like the chalky limestone of Burgundy, and some minerals in the soil may add trace elements to wine. With a little practice you can actually taste the climate in a wine—the heat in husky reds from sunny climates, or the cool nights in a delicate white. Expert wine tasters can taste and smell Burgundy's limestone or the gravel of Bordeaux. Or so they say.

"Almost all fermented products include naturally formed sulfites. Wine is no exception. Most winemakers, myself included, add small amounts of sulfur. This protects the wine from oxidizing and going bad on you."

—John Williams, winemaker

But any gardener who has tried the same pepper plant in different corners of his plot will not be surprised that cabernet sauvignon grapes grown in France, the Napa Valley, and Australia are not the same. Nor is the cabernet sauvignon from Spring Mountain the same as the cabernet from Rutherford a few miles south in the Napa Valley.

While grapes need some water, rain at the wrong time can do terrible damage. Spring rains can "shatter" the blossoms in the early stages of grape formation. Fall rains swell the grapes and dilute the sugar and flavor. Hail is worse; it beats up buds, berries, flowers, or full-grown grapes. Now aren't you glad you don't have to grow the grapes yourself?

TO YOUR HEALTH

Sulfites: Sulfur has been a natural part of grapes and wine making (and other forms of food production) since the earliest times in Europe and in the New World. It was used in the vineyard to control fungus, used in the winery to clean equipment, and used in wine to control oxidation and fermentation.

However, a relatively small number of people, including asthmatics, are sensitive to the chemical, and most wines carry a warning that they contain sulfites. Most wineries around the world have cut down substantially on sulfite content and a few have eliminated it.

WINE DIARIES

WINO OF THE MONTH CLUB

You're a big girl now. (Or so you like to think.) You've got your own apartment. A nice car. A good job. Most of the plants you've purchased recently are still alive. A husband and kid (or even a date that lasted past 11 p.m.) might be nice, but you're young. (Besides, your cat loves you.)

Your stock portfolio is growing. Your blood pressure (at least according to the do-it-yourself machine down at the drugstore) is about where it should be. You're still relatively cellulite-free. And you've finally traded in your college stash of "alternative" CDs for some more "adult" music, like Garbage and Limp Bizkit.

But there's something … missing. Despite all of your recent strides in that lifelong struggle known as the rat race, you still don't feel entirely grown up. And it's not just your Wonder Woman underwear and Barbie slippers, either.

Rather, it's a certain lack of sophistication you've felt lately. Not at work, of course, where you can collate, kiss ass, and multi-task with the best of them. Not in relationships, where you're miles ahead of the boyfriend bell curve. Not in politics, either. (You watch C-Span, after all.) Not even in literature. (You also watch *Oprah*.)

No, your latent feelings of intoxication inadequacy are more "cocktail" than cosmic in nature. After all, your sorority girl, keg party days are long behind you. Your independent days of tossing back B-52s and Fuzzy Navels until last call at the local watering hole are likewise fading into distant memory. But yet you're not quite ready for that mid-life, scotch and water or martini after work phase of your life either.

As a result, you've recently come to the decision that, if you could just get a grasp on this whole wine issue, your life as an adult could officially begin. No more relying on overbearing dates to choose your cheap glass of chardonnay for you. No more getting ripped off when you're ordering it for yourself by going with the "expensive equals better" philosophy. No more sitting at the kid's table at Thanksgiving and Christmas just because you made the infantile faux pas of showing up at the door bearing a bow-bedecked bottle of Boysenberry Blush or Off-White Zinfandel.

"That's it," you decide after coffee one Sunday morning, your feeling of grape angst suddenly overwhelming you. "From this day forward, I will pledge to learn all that I possibly can about wine."

Coincidentally, among the remains of the Sunday edition scattered around your apartment, you happen to spot the "Food" section lying just so at your feet, as if some Ghost of Cocktails Past had placed it there just for you.

You lunge for it desperately, hoping against hope for a pullout

Although you had no idea how people were supposed to pay two hundred bucks without leaving the house to go to work, you dialed the handy number "GUD-GRAP" and forked over your credit card number like a good little girl who was soon to become a wine-wise woman.

And, just as the ad proclaimed, you heard a knock at your door one mid-week evening about a month later. There, in the hands of an impatient FedEx employee, who no doubt was looking forward to a little sauvignon sampling of his own after a long day in traffic, was the very first stop on your virtual vineyard tour!

The cardboard box, covered quite cleverly with reaching grapevines, gave way to a multitude of Styrofoam packing material followed by a handy "wine tasting" pamphlet and a buff colored certificate, complete with gold-embossed seal, announcing that you were now an official "Wine of the Month" Taste Tester. Not to mention, naturally, your first real bottle of wine. Ever.

section appropriately titled something simple and easy like, oh say, "Everything you always wanted to know about wine so that you could finally begin your adult life and stop feeling childish but were afraid to ask!"

Unfortunately, there was no such list. However, buried there in between ads for high-priced corkscrews and tours of France, you do spot an ad for a brand new concept, "Wines of the World."

A start-up company, Good Grapes, Inc., was offering, "for a limited time only," a 12-month tour of the world's finest vineyards, delivered right to your door at the beginning of each month, for a paltry $199. (A little pricey, yes, but downright "cheap" in comparison with first class tickets to Pouilly-Fuissé or Champagne.)

"Impress your friends," read the ad copy. "Delight your dates. Floor your family. Start your tour of the world's finest vineyards today, without ever leaving your house!"

Sure, you'd tossed back a few Seagram's wine coolers in your earlier days. And, being on the corporate bowling team, you'd suffered through a few glasses of the local bowling alley's best on occasion. But never before had you, in the privacy of your own home, held a bottle of primetime wine, purchased by you (for an exorbitant price, lest we forget), in your very own hands. It was enough to bring a tear to your eye. Almost.

Feeling nearly as proud as the day you paid off that pesky student loan, you unveiled the brand new corkscrew you'd purchased in anticipation of this day and, following the handy instructions in your pamphlet, opened your introductory bottle of Boise's Best Bordeaux.

Naturally, you had no idea that Idaho was such a big wine Mecca. Or a particularly "exotic" destination to begin one's tour of the world's wondrous wines, for that matter. But then, you couldn't even open a bottle of wine without a check list, so what did you know?

Letting the wine breathe, you unveil one of your new cobalt blue wine glasses for the occasion and fill it to the brim after an appropriate amount of time. (Two minutes ought to be enough, right?) And, without hesitation, you bring the glass firmly to your lips and taste the heady bouquet of Boise's Best.

"Hmm," you frown, realizing the inaccuracy of first impressions and taking another sip just to be sure your taste buds weren't teasing. "Not quite as bad as the bowling alley, not quite as good as Kool-Aid."

Corking the wine for better days (or your next gag gift), you wait impatiently for another whole month before yet another winded FedExer delivers your next bottle of wine. Opening it up without delay this time, you unveil a perky bottle of "Miami Merlot" complete with dancing palm trees on the label and a cork shaped like a Cuban cigar.

"What the …" you snort as you open it without ceremony and taste it without your usual two-minute warning. (Or special glass, for that matter.)

"Interesting," is about all you can say for a taste as tart as lemon, and an aftertaste as sour as lime.

As future months bring you alternating bottles of Compton Champagne, Pittsburgh Port, and Kalamazoo Chianti, you soon discover that the "world of wine" referred to in the deceiving newspaper ad was obviously limited.

Naturally, neither your education is enhanced nor your brain intoxicated by this domestic dirge. And, after repeated attempts to contact Good Grape, Inc.'s non-existent customer service department, you suffer through an entire year of corny names, cheesy labels, and too-cute corks before your "vineyard visa" is officially revoked.

"Imagine that," you exclaim as you empty your final bottle of Muncie Mosel into the kitchen sink, watching it eat away those unsightly rust stains that had defied any of the other cleaners you'd ever tried. "At least that wine was good for something."

Pronunciation KEY

Can You Say ... Chardonnay?

Well, of course you can. Chardonnay is the most popular white wine in the U.S. Could it be because it's one of the most easily pronounced wines? After all, you only have to remember the "sh" at the beginning and the rest is phonetic.

But what about those other wines; how in the world do you pronounce them? Well here's a pronunciation guide to some of those other words on the "multilingual" labels.

Now, first, try whispering some more white-wine names:
- **Gewürztraminer** (geh·verts´·trah·mee´·ner)
- **Riesling** (rees´·ling)
- **Sémillon** (sem·ee·yon´)
- **Viognier** (vee·ohn·yay´)

Then roll some reds across your tongue:
- **Cabernet Sauvignon** (cab·er·nay´ so·vin·yon´)
- **Merlot** (mur·low)
- **Pinot Noir** (pee·no n'wahr)
- **Sangiovese** (san·joh·vay´·say)

Learn some more:
- **French:** Appellation d'Origine Contrôlée (ah·pel·ah·s'yawn´ daw·ree·jeen´ con·troh·lay´)
- **Italian:** Denominazione di Origine Controllata (deh·noh·mee·nah·t'zee·oh´·neh dee oh·ree·jeen´·eh con·troh·lah´·tah)
- **Spanish:** Denominación de Origen (deh·noh·mee·nah·th'yon´ deh oh·ree·hen´)
- **German:** Qualitätswein mit Prädikat (kval·ee·tate's´·vine mit pray´·dee·kat)

Too much of a mouthful? That's okay. Look for these and just say *quality*, then remember their abbreviations: AOC, DOC (dock!), DO, and QmP.

2 BASIC TRAINING

You don't have to learn how to taste or "develop a palate." You already have one. And you're the expert: No one else has a better palate than you do for knowing your own tastes. You're the one who will swallow the wine (and pay for it).

If all red wines taste like cherries to you, fine; if you can't smell the asparagus someone else finds in a sauvignon blanc, fine. Never tasted black currants, gooseberries, or lychee in real life, let alone in a glass of wine, the way some wine experts describe them? Don't worry; nothing wrong with thinking a wine smells like bubblegum, or tastes like shoe polish; some do, and if that's how you remember a wine, fine.

Remember that professional tasters may like bitter tannins and high acids in a wine that will make it taste great in ten years, just not right now. Wine expert Kim Caffrey's caricature of the "one-nostril thing" captures the pretentious fussiness of wine tasting perfectly. After exaggerated glass swirling, she tilts her glass and head equally, and arches her nose as much as her eyebrow, takes a whiff, sips, gargles, and then issues a pronouncement. Classic "techno-bourgeois-elitist-yuppie-bore."

Besides, the taste of wine is no more mysterious than iced tea. Actually tea has the same elements: the sweetness of sugar, the tart acid of lemon, and the bitter tannin of the tea leaves. All must balance the way you like them to.

Yet there's a truth hidden behind the tasting myth. A good wine pleases the senses.

Looking at a glass of wine shouldn't take long, and it helps. After all, you'd take a glance at a soda to make sure there wasn't a bug in it. The spectrum of colors produced by red and white wines includes more natural shades and tints than the cosmetics industry can imagine. Look for garnet, ruby, brick red, deep purple, and blushing pink; in white wine you will see wheat straw, pale gold, sunshine yellow, honey, and amber.

Here are two other tasters' tricks to better appreciate a wine's color. Look straight down into the glass and see if you can see your finger or anything beneath it to judge how deep and opaque it is. Then tilt the glass and look at the rim, the thin edge of the wine against the glass. Its halo, like the penumbra around the moon during an eclipse, may let you isolate the faint contributing colors, whether the red has some blue in it, or maybe some yellow or brown.

Sheer pleasure of looking at wine is why wine lovers prefer clear stemware and ideally a plain white background to better enjoy the color.

"If a life of wine, women, and song gets too much, give up singing."

—Anonymous

To an experienced taster analyzing a wine, the eye provides clues about the origin and age of a wine as well as aesthetic enjoyment. Red grapes from hotter regions generally give deeper, darker color to wine. Better quality wines hold their color all the way to the rim, rather than turn watery. Wines also change color as they age. Red wines start out with a blue or purple tinge, and slowly mellow into warmer orange and brown tones over the decades; white wines deepen in color, turning gold and eventually copper.

Is it possible for a red wine and a white wine after one hundred years to approach the same color? Yes, somewhere around caramel.

SWIRL AND SNIFF

The nose gets a bad rap in wine tasting. It's accused of being snobbish, sniffy, and snooty when actually your nose is the most important instrument of what we call "taste." Nothing snobbish about the smell of fresh buttered popcorn, gardenias, fresh-cut grass, a steak on the grill, the elephant house at the zoo, your boyfriend's aftershave, a new car, or an old book. We can and do smell all these things to help recognize them; the brain has thousands of them on file.

A glass of wine is a great place to stop and smell the roses, or violets, or beets, or cinnamon, or bananas, or even cigar boxes. These aromas can all be found in wine, honest, although winemakers don't really toss pineapples in with the grape. Critics and snobs may announce their discoveries with bluster (see "Speak, or Shut Up, Please" later in this chapter), but the many varied smells can be very real byproducts of chemical compounds within the original grape, the fermented product, or the interaction with wood and oxygen. The "butter" you smell in some chardonnays is natural diacetyl, which is used as butter flavor in food.

Getting more out of the smell is the reason for some of the physical routine in wine tasting, but you don't have to ham it up. Start by filling the glass less than half full, then swirl the glass so that some of the wine mixes with the air and some clings to the glass. Let it fill the bowl of the glass with the distinct aromas. It's also why white wines are served cooler than reds; their more delicate aromas will disappear in heat.

You'll be surprised how many aromas you can distinguish. The aroma wheel developed at the University of California at Davis identifies almost one hundred possible wine aromas and then breaks them up into useful categories. Is the aroma more fruity than vegetative? Does it smell crisp like citrus, intense and tart like berries? Or is it sweet and lush like tropical fruits, mild and fresh like a tree fruit, or concentrated and musty like dried fruit? If it's tropical, is it like banana (vanilla and bubble gum), melon (sweet and peachy), or pineapple (with a hint of tartness)? Work your way around the wheel and you'll recognize all the smells, good and bad, from woody to soapy.

You don't have to dwell any further than to see if you like the smell, and if it's drinkable.

The aromas can, however, identify the grape, how the wine was made, and where. Cabernet sauvignon usually has notes of bell pepper or mint; riesling hints of peaches and apricots; and some sauvignon blancs and other white wines can have the unmistakable odor politely described as cat spray. Toastiness, vanilla, coconut, and wood flavors are indicators of the aging process and the age. High alcohol can often be smelled or sensed as pungent or a tickling heat, and may be a reflection of ripeness, which is often a product of a hot climate. Some aromas are no fun now or later, and they usually come from storage problems. The wine has been kept too hot, too long, or too poorly corked, so that too much oxygen has reached the wine prematurely. Don't bother smelling a cork (just look at it and feel it to make sure it's moist); do smell the wine, if there's a strong scent of cork, mold, vinegar, or sulfur, send it back.

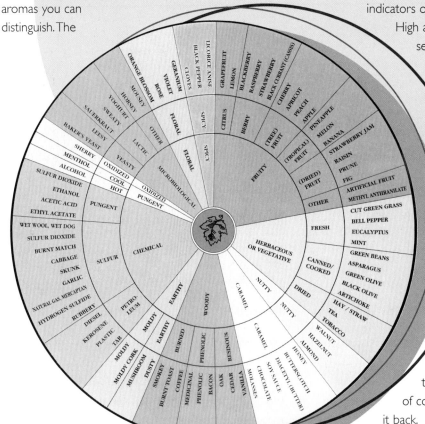

SIP
SIP SIP SIP **SIP** SIP
SIP SIP **SIP** SIP

sour bitter

sweet salt

Whew, let's have a drink. In real life, the sight and smell part of tasting won't take more than a minute or two; the goal is to put the wine in your mouth. That's where the final analysis will be made; the mouth will say whether you like it.

Most tasters sip a little wine into their mouths and then slosh it around. Their purpose is to expose the wine to the tastebuds, which have specialized locations:

• The tip of the tongue senses sweetness.

• The sides of the tongue pick up sour or acid flavors.

• The top of the tongue and roof of the mouth react to bitterness or dryness.

• Salt, rare in wine, is sensed on the front sides of the tongue.

It's also in the back of the mouth that the olfactory sense has a second chance to pick up smells, and in the mouth and the throat where wine registers on the sense of touch. The difference in weight and body of wines can be as obvious as those between nonfat milk and heavy cream. The texture can be luxuriously velvety, silky, raspy, or sluggish. Effervescence or tartness can make a wine refreshing or irritating, and too much dryness can make you recoil.

Swallow the wine and the taste continues in the finish—short, long, burning, or unforgettably good.

Ultimately they come together in a total sensation that you like. Or not. Did the wine look bright red, smell of cherries and strawberries, but had no flavor at all in the mouth, just tartness and a watery consistency? Shouldn't happen. A fine wine will keep all factors balanced.

SPIT IT OUT

When tasting more than two or three wines, some experts recommend not swallowing all the wine. Spitting is actually encouraged. Like baseball players, rodeo riders, and old guys in fleabag hotels, wine tasters spit freely. Alcohol will dull the palate and the senses. Leave the glasses on the table; you'll finish the one you liked.

SPEAK,
OR SHUT UP,
PLEASE

You don't have to say a word to anyone about the taste of a wine. Deciding whether you like it is more important. But do think about it a moment.

What was the best part? The aroma? The texture? You couldn't smell or taste anything there? You just didn't like it? Or you did?

It's your call. The key is to remember the wines you liked. The ones you didn't like? Forget 'em.

So figure out a system for remembering or recording wines you enjoy. Make a point to look at the bottle and read the label if that will help keep it in your mind. Or make a real note of it: Write down the name of a wine you liked, the grape, place, and producer. Put it on a card in your wallet, a spare page in your organizer, or a computer file, etc. You can get a fancy bound cellar book, or try to soak the labels off bottles if you want; the point is to remember so you can buy it again.

SIP AGAIN

One other thing. That wine you didn't like when you sipped it half an hour ago? Try it again. You'll be surprised how many wines, especially young red wines, open up after they've had some time in the glass.

TOP-5 SIGNS YOU'RE AT A BAD WINE TASTING

5.) Background music is a continuous loop of "Red, Red Wine."

4.) Crackers and cheese replaced with moon pies and pigs feet.

3.) All the other guests bring straws.

2.) Your host's unsettling habit of refilling the wine bottles from spittoons.

1.) Glasses of tequila to cleanse your palate between wines.

WINE DIARIES

THE WINE TASTING

Well, it's another Saturday morning and the race is on. Your best friend Dana takes the "Living" section, you take "Entertainment" and, thanks to empty coffee cups, not to mention emptier wallets, the two of you energetically scour the day's local cultural offerings for the best, and cheapest, thing to do in town.

"Hey, what about the 5th Annual Mincemeat Pie Eating Contest?" Dana asks.

"How do you feel about air shows?" you respond.

"I dunno, how do you feel about free Greek basket-weaving lessons?" Dana says.

"Midget wrestling?"

"Biblical scavenger hunt?"

"You up for a 5-K run to benefit unemployed mid-level managers?"

"How about a marriage retreat up at the Friends of Jupiter communal home?"

"There's a free seminar at the community college: Snakebites 101."

"Barber Shop Quartet Marathon?"

"Pig Calling Contest?"

"Soap Making Class?"

"The Hells Angels are giving a car wash."

"What about a Civil War reenactment?"

Frustrated, you pour another round of coffee and almost drop the cups when Dana screams in triumph: "I've got it, I've got it. The answer to our every Saturday need."

Imagining yet another outing to the Ocaloosa Swamp Flea Market and Munitions Show, you set her coffee down outside of a 3-foot kicking, jumping, and shouting radius and wait for the "bad" news. Surprisingly, there is none.

"You know that new French restaurant downtown?" asks Dana, barely able to contain herself. "Well, they're having a wine tasting today."

Pigs have 15,000 taste buds; hares have 12,000 and humans 10,000.

Conclusion? Take a pig to a wine tasting.

"Wow," you consider, mentally computing the $12 in your bank account. "Sounds good but … sounds expensive. I heard you need a gold card just to order appetizers at that place."

"Sure you do," she agrees. "But this is *free*. Free admission, free T-shirt, free crackers and cheese, and, best of all, all the free wine you can drink! And not the cheap stuff, either. This stuff's imported!"

"What?" you ask, snatching the paper out of her trembling hands and scanning the bold-printed ad for yourself. Sure enough, she was right. Obviously the new, snooty French eatery wasn't pulling in all the business it had expected and was in desperate need of a little free publicity.

"Whadya think?" Dana asks, checking her watch to see how much time was left before the early afternoon wine tasting.

"One hour to taste time!" you reply, racing her to the one bathroom in your apartment.

And, an hour later, right on time, you file side by side into the snooty French restaurant as the scent of ripe cheese and flowing French wine assails your Cheez-It and Budweiser acclimated nostrils.

Naturally, neither of you were quite sure what to wear and so you are severely underdressed, as Preppy after Ivy Leaguer wanders in wearing their Ferragamo shoes, crested blazers, complete Ralph Lauren ensembles, and tight-ass expressions.

"Is it just me?" whispers Dana as you fill out nametags and sign a fancy guest register complete with a feathered ball point pen, "Or do you feel like a bonafide Beauty School Dropout?"

"Can you say *Dukes of Hazzard*?" you agree, referring to your Levi and Gap getups.

"It said you get a free T-shirt," she explains. "I figured it would be like a Kiss concert, you know. Everybody wearing them over their clothes."

Unfortunately, you and Dana are the only ones wearing your too-large T-shirts as you stand awkwardly in the corner near the service bar listening to the master of ceremonies lecture on and on about pinot noirs and oaky noses.

The ringleader finally opens up the floor to the tasting as cliques excluding you and Dana meander about the dining room floor sampling Dixie cups (albeit fancy Dixie cups) half-full of reds, whites, ports, sherries, and champagnes.

Naturally, you and Dana grab a paper cup or two off each table and sip contentedly as you browse through the odorous cheese samplings and wafer thin, ritzy (*not* Ritz) crackers. Gossiping like teenagers, you enjoy the wines nonstop, and actually comment on one: "Whewww … that's a zinger!"

So you're surprised when, barely five minutes into the wine tasting, the supposedly upper crusters start spitting up into oversized silver chalices in the middle of each table. The poor saps.

"Gheez," says Dana. "I thought these types were heavy drinkers. All those cocktail parties and boozy benefits. They sure didn't last long."

"Oh, well," you commiserate, "more cheese for us!"

Toasting each other with your empty paper cups, you scour several other tables for more. Soon, however, the wine tasting feels much more like a wine "testing," as in … will you pass, or just plain pass out?

Surprisingly, those other wine spectators are still going strong.

"What's your secret?" you ask a forty-ish, Jackie Collins impersonator in the ladies room minutes later, while you hold Dana's hair as she upchucks $200 worth of fine wine and imported cheese into the nearest gaping piece of porcelain.

"For starters," sneers the plastic princess while reapplying her wine red lipstick, "we don't guzzle our wine like we're at a frat party. We spit it out in between samples to better sensitize our palates to the olfactory offerings being ensconced inside our sinus portals and taste bud receptacles."

"Well, that's no fun," Dana manages to mutter.

"Not quite as fun as projectile vomiting," says your snobby superior. "But we manage to eke out a smile or two before the day is done."

After you clean yourselves up and test yourselves for steadiness, you leave your ruined, yet free, T-shirts in the bathroom wastebasket and exit through the dishwasher's entrance.

"So," you reflect over the aspirin counter at the nearest pharmacy. "What will it be next: car wash or Biblical scavenger hunt?"

"I dunno," says Dana, the bouquet from her breath slightly less than nutty, much more than oaky. "I'm leaning toward a tobacco chewing contest. It's less tricky. You *know* you're not supposed to swallow that stuff."

TOP-5 SIGNS YOU DON'T BELONG AT A WINE TASTING

5.) You keep asking, "What *is* eating **Gilbert Grape** anyway?"

4.) Three words: **pull my cork.**

3.) You ask for a **"doggie bottle."**

2.) Your **monogrammed straw.**

1.) Your "Real Wine Tasters Swallow" T-shirt.

KNOWING THE GRAPE, READING THE LABEL

Of course you can read. But wine labels, while apparently a combination of random information and "art" scraped off some cathedral wall, are decipherable—with some help.

Using grape names instead of place names may not sound like a stroke of genius, but it is one of the most helpful contributions the New World has made to simplifying the enjoyment of wine. In the Old World, wines were simply known by the place from where they were made or shipped. The varieties of grapes used in each place were determined by weather and custom; certain red grapes grew better in France, while other grapes made wines in Italy. And the same grape made different wines in different places: the pinot noir wines of Burgundy, and the pinot noir of Champagne were not the same.

The place-naming tradition didn't work so well in the young nations filled with places that didn't even have names, let alone names that had been famous for wine for centuries. And thanks to modern technology, the New World is filled with places that can grow wine grapes, many still undiscovered.

Many of the words you already know from the labels of U.S. and Australian wines are the names of individual grapes that make different wines. Cabernet sauvignon, for instance, is a small blue-black grape. The name of the wine produced from this grape is eponymously named cabernet sauvignon. The merlot grape is more red and purple, larger, and has a thinner skin. Wine name: merlot. Chardonnay is a white grape; wine name—yep, chardonnay.

When the name of a grape variety is on a label, the wine is called a varietal, because it should have the characteristic flavor and body of a wine made from that variety of grape. Under U.S. law, 75 percent of the grapes in a varietal wine must be of that variety named. Some wines have 100 percent of the same grape; most will have some other kind of grape added for extra taste, aroma, or color.

AMERICAN LABELS

It is a part of wine life that there are lots of rules, and labels on American wines reflect the U.S. government's efforts to establish order and demand the truth from winemakers. U.S. wines have nine categories that must appear on the label:

Wine name: In the U.S., it's the grape: chardonnay, merlot, cabernet sauvignon, etc.

Brand name: The producer, generally, but can be a restaurant, store, etc., that contracted with a winery for a special label.

Bottler information: The name and address of the bottler; can be the producer and often is.

Estate-Bottled: If the producer owns or controls the vineyard, this phrase will appear.

Varietal: If you see one grape named on the bottle, the wine must be at least 75 percent of the variety of grape designated on the bottle.

Net contents: Usually 750 ml. (Often on the bottle.)

Contains Sulfites: Most wines have some. But some people, especially asthmatics, are sensitive to this compound, thus the warning, often on the back label.

SILVER OAK®

1993
ALEXANDER VALLEY

Cabernet Sauvignon

Cellared and bottled by SILVER OAK CELLARS
Oakville, Napa County, California
Alcohol 13.0% by Volume

Growing area: Sonoma Valley, Rutherford, etc. These are regulated by the government and can be as broad as "California" or as tiny as an individual vineyard.

Government warning: Health warning about the possible effects of alcohol, often on the back label.

EUROPEAN LABELS

Leave it to the Old World to have as many rules as possible to govern wine labels. The wine is so good it's worth the hassle, but finding consistency and logic in the French system in particular is difficult. It's a little like the Renault automobiles. They work, but no one is sure how.

Generally, the European labels have a place name on the label and an accompanying phrase that, to the informed person, indicates the quality of the wine.

The idea here is that if you know the place and the producer, you can figure out whether it has a good chance of being a good bottle of wine. It's this type of judgment call that keeps the wine experts in business.

Appellations of Origin are the first hurdles. They name where the wine is grown, but there's more to this than a name. There's a whole subset of categories, including the type of grape, the way the grape is grown, and how the wine is made. Of course, each country has its own set of requirements, thus leaving you stuck with having to learn the lingo on each country's label. But it's not impossible. Here's how it's done in France:

In 1932, the **Appellation d'Origine Contrôlée (AOC)** laws set minimum standards for each area in France that produced wine. The AOC strictly controls the origin, grape varieties and methods used, alcoholic strength, and quantity produced. If you see the AOC designation on the label, that's good. Obviously some regions are better than others, but this is a place to start.

Vin Délimité de Qualité Supérieure (VDQS): Second rank wines have been regulated in this category since 1945.

Vin de Pays: A category developed in 1973, which specifies origin but allows wide latitude in the grapes.

Vin de Consommation Courante: Drink it soon. Also called *vin ordinaire*.

The umbrella term for Old World countries that in essence try to grade their wines is Quality Wine Produced in a Specific Region (QWPSR). Thus, an AOC-designated wine from France is its QWPSR.

The label we show here is for France. Other countries' label translations appear in Chapters 8-13.

Here is what you can find on the French label. It isn't a bad rule of thumb that the more stuff there

is on the label, the better the wine, because the rules restrict what a producer can say about its product. Also, besides the AOC designation, look for the word "*cru*". This indicates that the wine came from a "classified" growth, meaning it's an exceptional wine.

Status: About 35 percent of the French wines have an AOC designation. Sometimes it will have the phrase "appellation contrôlée" or a variation, such as "Appellation Chambolle-Musigny 1er Cru Contrôlée."

Varietal: The kind of grape—merlot, chardonnay, cabernet sauvignon—is rarely mentioned. Usually all you can tell at first glance is if it is a white or a red. Only in the last few years have wineries in lesser regions named the grapes used largely in inexpensive wines for export.

Chateau Bottled/Domaine Bottled: Same as "estate bottled" on U.S. label.

Classified Growths: The *cru* designation isn't consistent from one wine growing region to another. Premier Cru is the top rank for Bordeaux; Grand Cru is the tops for Burgundy. If the word cru is on the label, it's a positive, although *cru* bourgeois is, well, pretty bourgeois.

Importer: Company that imports the wine to the U.S.

WINE DIARIES

CORKSCREW YOU (TAKE ONE)

This is it. I'm finally ready to do it. To take that big step into wine adulthood. To cross that line in the sand, and admit to the world that I'm no longer a simple beer guzzler or shot slammer but a bonafide wine connoisseur instead. To come out of the "Château closet," as it were. I've been putting it off for so long that by now, I can hardly believe that I'm actually going to do it.

What is it that I'm about to do, you ask, as I'm standing here outside the local Wine Warehouse easing my wheezing Tercel into a crowded parking space among the towering SUVs and gleaming convertibles?

Buy a corkscrew, silly. What did you think? After all, I've been making do with the little plastic number someone left behind in one of the kitchen drawers when I moved into my new apartment. You know the kind, where you unsheathe the screw and slide the index-finger size cap into the hole on top and use it to unscrew the cork? Yeah, like that *really* works. I've taken to buying a roll of paper towels at the same time I do a bottle of wine, just because I know there'll be so much cork left I'm bound to be doing some heavy straining.

"Wine improves with age. The older I get, the better I like it."
— ANONYMOUS

Anyway, I'm past all that now. I'm ready for the real thing. And so, in I go, whooshing my way through the automatic double doors and entering the magical world of the biggest wine store in town. Classical music soothes me as the smell of dusty green bottles and cigars from the corner humidor fill my nose.

Now, let's see. I'll just pass these reds here. Nope. Turn left at the whites. Not yet. On past the champagnes, the ports, the sherries, the cheese case, a tower of fancy crackers, those frilly vine-covered gift bags, and, what's *this*?

No corkscrews! Surely, you jest.

"Can I help you, sir?" asks a portly gentleman in a grape-covered apron bearing a nametag that says his name is Roger. "You seem to be having a little difficulty, and I couldn't help but notice you standing here in front of the jerked beef display and scratching your head. Are you perhaps in the wrong place? After all, you look like a beer drinker to me."

"I'm in exactly the right place, thank you very much," I huff, snatching a handful of gaily-wrapped meat snacks just for spite. "I just can't seem to find the corkscrew section."

"Ahh, allow me to assist you then," he offers, gesturing for me to follow him as he travels the length of the store before coming to a stop just in front of a gleaming glass case containing an odd assortment of futuristic-looking, metallic instruments obviously intended for the sole purpose of torture and mayhem.

"How odd," I comment, still straining my neck to glance around the store in search of the corkscrews. "I didn't know you sold guns here."

"Why sir," says Roger, rattling a set of keys large enough to make any prison warden smile with pride, "these are our finest selection of corkscrews."

And he's off! With that declaration, Roger proceeds to school me on the finer points of today's cornucopia of corkscrews:

"Now this," he smiles with pride, liberating a contraption that looks more like a leftover of the Spanish Inquisition than something I'd use to uncork a nice bottle of chardonnay, "is an heirloom-quality Laguiole. Now, that's pronounced la-gee-oal. 'Gee,' with a hard 'g,' of course. Notice the cutlery is expertly forged, stamped, honed, and burnished until it gleams, by artisans in the little mountain town by the same name in south central France.

"As a matter of fact, this is a fully functional, professional sommelier's corkscrew with a horn handle and a bottle opener-slash-blade that's serrated and shaped in a crescent to expertly cut foil. Indeed, this beauty comes in its own wooden box with peg-and-hole construction!"

"Wow," I whistle admiringly, watching Roger's

CORNUCOPIA of CORKSCREWS
(Which one do you use?)

Long Cork Waiter's Corkscrew

Two Prong Extractor

Corkex Extractor

Foil Remover

Cork Extractor

Uncorking Machine

Mezzaluna Waiter's Corkscrew

Wing Corkscrew

Beechwood Bistro Corkscrew

Power Corkscrew

"T" Corkscrew

Pulltap's Corkscrew

Boxwood Pocket Corkscrew

Rabbit Corkscrew

Plastic Pocket Corkscrew

King's Corkscrew

Picnic Corkscrew

Automatic Corkscrew, Gold Plated

Wing Corkscrew, Auger Worm

Vintner's Corkscrew

Waiter's Corkscrew with Straight Blade

Pullparrot Waiter's Corkscrew

Puigpull Corkscrew

eyes gleam with excitement. "Now, what's that baby gonna set me back?"

"A mere hundred and sixty dollars, sir," says Roger proudly. With a straight face, no less!

"What?" I cry. "And does it come with a case of Dom Perignon?"

"But sir," cries Roger, reluctantly re-shelving his sommelier's special. "It's made in France."

Seeing my hesitance, Roger considers several of the other encased corkscrews and liberates one that looks similar to something I saw zooming across my big screen TV when I was flipping by the Sci-Fi Channel last night. With two silver-tipped "wings" extending forward and a cylindrical center, it looks ready for lift-off at any moment.

"Since you obviously have no interest in the classics," Roger huffs, "might I interest you in a rather recent development in the captivating world of corkscrews: The Lever Model LXV Series. Now, the LXV is the finest screw-pull that the Wine Warehouse has to offer. It works like a bar mounted corkscrew, only this model is portable. Simply insert the very tip of the worm in the cork, close the arms, and pressure does the rest."

"I have to put a worm in there each time I use it?" I ask, scratching my head. "What is it, like some kind of alcoholic Pez dispenser?"

"Oh, I'm sorry," Roger condescends. "The *worm* is the screw, in wine speak. Now, shall I ring this up? After all, it comes in a gift box, with its own foil cutter and replacement worm, err, screw."

When I stand patiently for what seems like minutes, my expression boldly asking, "How much?" without an answer, I finally have to ask, "How much?" out loud. "$145," he answers, eyes on his feet to better avoid my reaction.

When he does look back up, a simple shake of my

head forces Roger back into the corkscrew case, where he returns with a jet-black piece of molded plastic shaped just like Captain Kirk's phaser, complete with a powerful point on the end.

"How about air-injection?" he asks, pointing the gun/corkscrew at me menacingly.

"Maybe," I shrug. "But how do you use that thing?"

"First," instructs Roger, "you push the hollow needle through the cork. Then use the plunger to inject air into the bottle, forcing the cork upward. On second thought, this method is only recommended for older wine bottles, as old corks may become spongy through the center and provide less of a grip for a standard corkscrew. Now that I think of it, you look like a strictly TV commercial bottle of wine drinker yourself."

With that, Roger sneers and pulls out a shiny silver contraption that looks like one of Inspector Gadget's retractable arms, with a zig-zag construction of interlacing levers and pulleys.

"Now," says Roger, turning the top handle and

slowly extending the collapsible contraption, "this model is known as the Zig-Zag and, while not the most aesthetically pleasing corkscrew I've offered you, it's bound to be about the most fun you'll ever have opening a bottle of wine. And, this should interest you, it only costs twenty-five dollars!"

"Nice," I murmur unconvincingly, leaning past the zig-zag and peering into the case to see a series of related corkscrews that look more like squids than corkscrews at all. Not to mention they were constructed of sturdy plastic with rich, vibrant colors resembling the latest series of iMacs.

"Oh, yes," Roger sighs, seeing me admire the candy-colored corkscrews. "*Those*. Well, if you must know, those are rather new models from the Zyliss company of Switzerland, redesigned to accommodate the newfangled flanged bottle rims. While they do have a Teflon worm, their cylindrical frame is plastic and flanged inside to grip the cork. As you can see, they are offered in opaque white or cheery translucent red, green, or blue. Priced to move, they sell for a meager twenty-four dollars."

"Flashy," I say, still hesitating to spend more on my corkscrew than I've yet to spend on a good bottle of wine. "But what about that little number there in the corner, with the two prongs sticking out?"

"You don't want that, sir," Roger admits, shaking his head. "In theory, these worm-less corkscrews are great. You ease the prongs between the cork and the bottle, then simply push down and pull up."

"Sounds great," I smile.

"Sure it does," Roger groans. "But if I had a dollar for every customer who came in complaining that all it did was push the cork down into the bottle, I could retire early and run the entire chain of Wine Warehouses from my château in the hilly vineyards of France."

Frustrated, and nearing the end of Roger's corkscrew class, I notice a familiar looking number in the very back of the case, crowded out by the flashier models with their shiny silver, extending zig zags, and telescoping arms.

"I'll take that," I announce, pointing to the old-fashioned Swiss-army knife gizmo with the "worm" tucked under the top and a foil-cutter curled at the end like a snaggletooth's toe. "How much?"

TOP-5 SIGNS YOU'RE READY FOR A NEW CORKSCREW

5.) You're getting a little **tired of** pouring your wine through a **strainer.**

4.) The **hammer** and the **ice pick** just aren't working as well as they used to.

3.) White? **No.** Red? **No.** Twist off? **Yes!**

2.) Sawing off bottle tops has actually become an option.

1.) Those crunchy things inside your wine glass aren't ice cubes.

"Sir," Roger warns. "I strongly recommend one of the finer models we discussed. Why, this corkscrew is strictly for the odd-bottle-of-wine-on-a-Saturday-night amateur."

"Perfect," I nod. After all, he just described me! "Now, is it plastic?"

"No, but—" Roger insists, finally pulling the simple apparatus from the case. "That's the *only* thing it's got going for it."

Ignoring his protestations, which dog me all the way to the cash register, I watch Roger ring up the comforting-looking corkscrew and, smiling again at the paltry price, put away the five dollar bill I'd had ready and pull out two singles instead.

Hey, it may not have zig-zags and come in "cheery translucent red, green, or blue," but it certainly wasn't plastic. And, contrary to Roger's opinion, I was taking a giant leap from my old corkscrew. Walking out into the bright sunlight of a glorious day, I feel pretty darn good about my new corkscrew.

Did I mention that it wasn't plastic?

3 THREE

THE BEST WINE IN THE WORLD

We lied. We're not going to tell you the best wine. No book can. It's your choice and the only way to find out is to keep tasting wine until you see grapes in your sleep. Then start tasting again. This isn't a game for lightweights. Geographic hype, the secrets of the wine making art, or the inspiring story about how a wine or winery got its name (Liebfraumilch means what?) may add to your interest in drinking a wine, but the essence of wine drinking is purely sensual. Does it give you a thrill, or leave you with a nasty lip squinch?

That's why so much of the wine business takes place with a bottle open. Wine is a hand-sell. It often takes a sample to close a deal, and there are a lot of sampling opportunities.

TASTING BEGINS WHEREVER

In-store tastings: Many wine and liquor stores hold tastings one afternoon or evening a week, sometimes to showcase the wines of a single producer, or to sample a category, say Chilean reds or summer whites. Prices run from $5 to $20. They can be casual, stand-up jumbles, or sit-down affairs where you can concentrate and take notes.

Winemaker dinners: When winery owners and winemakers aren't working in the vineyards or cellars, they're on the road touting their wines. A favorite way to do this is at a restaurant where the chef puts together a menu of four or five courses to match the winery's products. Prices run between $50 and $100 but may still be a bargain. They can be fun and interesting, or combine the deadly duo of boring commentary and bad food. The most interesting are vertical tastings, which provide a chance to taste older vintages as well as the newest of the same wine.

> *The indentation at the bottom of some wine bottles is called a "kick" or a "punt."*

Grand tastings: Charities, which benefit from these events, and cheapskates alike love wine festivals, where dozens of wineries pour their latest products. In theory, a $30 to $50 ticket allows you to taste 100 or more wines in two or three hours. Do go, but resist the temptation to get the most for your money. Set a limited goal for the evening, to find a chardonnay you really like, or find a different red that suits you better than a cabernet or a merlot

There's no compelling need to venture out among the kind of people who might call themselves "oenophiles." God knows what they do behind closed doors. Let's start at home among friends. We'll make it your first assignment.

YOU'LL NEED

Six bottles of wine, three red and three white, that you can buy for less than $100. You could probably do it for close to $50, but at around $15 a bottle you'll get some good representatives of each. Besides, it'll make a good first impression at the wine store. You can also spread the financial burden among your guests.

We'll split the wines into two tasting sessions, two wine-tasting dinners. Nothing fancy, roast chicken or grilled fish for you and a few friends the night you try the whites; steaks or eggplant for the reds, apples and crackers for appetizers. And lots of wine glasses. Have your friends bring their own, so there are three plain wine glasses for each person, and when they break them it's their problem.

For the tastings, you'll need the following bottles of wines, with their New World name (by grape) and Old World name (by place). Don't jump to conclusions about what you like. Try each one and then see where you go from there.

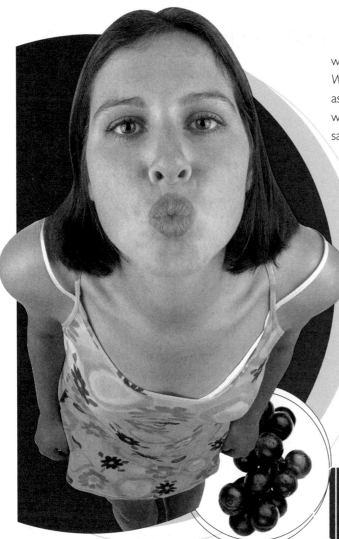

Set out three wine glasses at each place, preferably with a white towel if you have one, but a good *Star Wars* towel is always in vogue. When your guests have assembled, put out apples and crackers, and glasses of water. Once everyone's seated, pour the wines in the same order. Just for fun, wrap the bottles in towels or brown paper bags. Have your guests look at each wine, smell it, and then taste it. Discuss the wines if you want, or bring on the food. Then unwrap the bottles so every one can see the labels. Whatever anyone says, the most telling verdict is which glass is empty first.

Are we oversimplifying ? Of course. We left out sparkling wine, ports, and blush or rosé. But how else to cut that mass of confusion down to size?

We're not the first to do it. The wine industry already does it in a way by bottle shape. Look at the three bottles on the table, and remember those shapes. Most of the world's wine is bottled in these shapes, although they originated in the specific regions of Bordeaux, Burgundy, and Germany. Which wines did you like? We'll use them as a

LET'S START WITH THE WHITES

◼ **CRISP AND DRY.**
Look for a sauvignon blanc from California, or a white Graves from Bordeaux.

◼ **FULL BODIED.**
Buy a chardonnay from California or Australia, or a modest white Burgundy.

◼ **SWEET AND AROMATIC.**
Get a gewürztraminer or riesling from California, or a Rhine wine of kabinett quality from Germany.

SCRUMPTIOUS SONGS FOR A WINE TASTING

KISS "Spit"	**NAKED CITY** "Gob of Spit"
CONCRETE BLONDE "It'll Chew You up and Spit You Out"	**RAINBOW BUTT MONKEYS** "As Far As I Can Spit"
DOOMSDAY PRODUCTIONS "All I Spit"	**SONIC YOUTH** "Orange Rolls, Angel's Spit"
HELLOWEEN "Don't Spit On My Mind"	**STATE OF THE UNION** "American Spit Poems"
HUMAN REMAINS "Chewed up and Spit Out"	**SUKPATCH** "Blew Spitoonias"

What do all the wine tasting words mean?

Here's a list of commonly used tasting terms, in contemporary language:

Aftertaste The flavors or taste that lingers in your mouth after the wine is tasted.

Aroma The smell of the wine in the glass.

Astringent A rough, harsh, "puckery" feel in the mouth.

Balance The harmony of all of the wine's components, fruitiness, sweetness, acidity, tannin, and alcohol.

Body The weight of the wine on the palate (light-bodied to full-bodied).

Bouquet The smell that develops after the wine has been bottled and aged.

Buttery The smell and taste of melted butter or toasty oak.

Corky The smell and flavor of musty, moldy, old newspaper caused by tainted cork.

Crisp Refreshing taste due to sound acidity.

Earthy The characteristics related to the aroma and flavor: positive = pleasant & clean; negative = dirtiness.

Finish The final taste left after the wine is swallowed.

Fruity The aromas and flavors related to fruit.

Hot The noticeably high alcoholic taste.

Jammy The slightly cooked flavors of jam rather than fresh fruit.

Lean The lack of fruit and body.

Nose The aroma or bouquet of a wine.

Oaky The smell or taste of oak.

Oxidized The stale taste caused by over exposure to air.

Sharp The unpleasant bitter and hard-edged taste, often high in tannins.

Soft The opposite of "hard"; describes wines low in acid or tannin.

Steely The almost metallic taste associated with wines high in acidity from mineral-rich soil.

Supple The round and smooth texture.

Sweet The characteristic of richness or ripeness.

Tannins The mouth-puckering substance derived from grape skins, seeds, and stems that acts as a preservative.

Tart The noticeably acidic sharp taste.

Volatile The excessive or undesirable amount of acidity, which gives a slightly sour, vinegary edge.

---

guide to others you might enjoy. Caution: You might like them all, but the differences you noticed will give you a clue to understanding other wines.

If you like the crispness and tartness of the first wine, you should try other versions of the same grape, such as fumé blanc. You might like pinot grigio and other Italian whites that can be crisp but have a delicate, sometimes neutral flavor. For a contrast, try sémillon, a favorite blending partner of sauvignon blanc, which is also mildly flavored but has a very rich, soft texture. To see that these wines can be something completely different, save up for a dessert wine from Sauternes.

If you like the rich feel of the second wine in your mouth, you should explore the wild range of styles chardonnay can have. They run from very buttery and tropical in expensive barrel-aged Californians, to the tart freshness of Italian chardonnays, and the nutty perfection of the white Burgundies, the gold standard of chardonnay. For a change of pace in flavor, but with similar body, try a chenin blanc, white wine from the Loire or the Rhône valleys of France.

Did you like a little sweetness in the third wine or overlook it because the wine was so crisp and the bouquet full of flowers and spices? Don't be ashamed, far more people like German-style whites than they admit to or try to pronounce the names. You can find the same heady bouquet with less sugar in drier and more expensive wines from Alsace. And if you do like a touch of sugar, you should sample muscats, more rich German wines, and the whole world of dessert wines. In a sparkling wine, try a moscato or demi sec.

NOW FOR THE REDS

Now lets get the reds together for the next session, and once again we'll squeeze them into three styles.

■ RICH AND DRY.

Buy a cabernet sauvignon from California of decent quality, or a modest Bordeaux; either one should be at least three years old.

■ POLISHED AND ELEGANT.

Look for a pinot noir from California or Oregon, or a village wine from Burgundy. This could cost $15 or more.

■ EARTHY AND SPICY.

Get a California syrah or zinfandel, or a red Rhône such as a Côtes-du-Rhône or Châteauneuf-du-Pape.

The deep color, strong flavor, and smoothness of the first wine should represent the great tradition of French Bordeaux. It is the most widely imitated of red wines and made largely from cabernet sauvignon; it is considered the "ruling" monarch of noble grapes. These wines do start out dry, sometimes bitter to the tongue, but get better and smoother as they age. In it you can pick out violets and cedar, green peppers or cherries. If you like a softer version, you've probably already discovered merlot or cabernet's other blending partners, cabernet franc and malbec. For the best, try a great château from Bordeaux that's made them for centuries, or an old vintage of a reserve cabernet from California. You might also try the Spanish reds of the Rioja, or the Super Tuscans and better Chiantis of Italy.

The delicacy and finesse of the second wine suggests the opposite pole of red wines, the pinot noir of Burgundy. Its fans are as devout as cabernet partisans, but the grape and the wine are more difficult to grow and make. Still, the best are heavenly. If you like its bright flavor of berries and lighter texture, look for other pinot noirs from Oregon, Carneros, and the Central Coast of California. And save your pennies to sample the top French Burgundies. In the meantime, you might also enjoy the reds of Beaujolais, and the Mâcon.

If you like the earth, spice, and fire of the last wine, adventure awaits you. Although they can be rustic or sophisticated, these are gutsy ripe wines from hot sunny climates. They usually have a mouthful and nose-ful of flavors, from black pepper to raspberry jam. Their homeland in France is the Rhône, where Châteauneuf-du-Pape and Hermitage are the most famous. The south of France makes many less expensive versions using mourvèdre, carignane, and grenache grapes. Australians have the next best, which they call shiraz. American wineries are making a new generation of Rhône inspired wines, in addition to the two gutsy reds that have been in U.S. vineyards for some time, zinfandel and petite sirah. You may also like the big flavors of barbera and other rustic reds from Italy and Spain.

This is just a start, but you've now tasted six of the noble grapes used to make wine around the world, and also had a sensual workout with wine. All you have to do is enjoy more wine. What's next depends on what you think you like.

BOTTLE SHAPES

There are generally two basic bottle styles: the Bordeaux bottle with its sharp shoulders, and the Burgundian with its gradually tapered neck. The Bordeaux bottle was designed to catch the sediment that sometimes builds up in old red wines; the Burgundians didn't need that. (White wines in each region borrowed the same shape.) A third group of spicy wines can show up in either bottle shape depending on style or whimsy.

The fourth group can be almost any thing: shaped like a grape or even a fish. These wines rely more on style than substance to attract buyers.

BORDEAUX

BURGUNDIANS

WINE DIARIES

THE ANNIVERSARY

"This is it," you murmur to yourself as you slide into your car in the employee garage before easing into mild rush hour traffic. "The big night."

After all, you and your girlfriend had officially been dating for one full year. Tonight! Could it have really been 365 days full of passion, fun, and bliss? Already? Why, it seems like just yesterday that you'd gone on that blind date both of you had been dreading and ended up thanking your lucky stars. Not to mention your mutual friend from work!

And now, one whole year later, thanks to a recent episode of *Oprah* and a paperback copy of the book *650 Ways to Stage the Perfect Anniversary Date*, you had actually set the stage for, well, the perfect anniversary date. Although, it hadn't been easy.

First, since you'd planned on working late in order to prolong the excitement, your girlfriend of one year (exactly) would arrive at your cozy apartment almost a full hour before you. There, upon opening your front door with the key you'd finally given her (it really *was*

true love), she would find the culmination of a week's worth of passionate planning.

A path of fresh (this morning anyway), red rose petals would lead her straight to your rarely used, yet spacious guest bathroom. There, clever notes written lovingly on heart-shaped stationary would instruct her to "light up your life the way you do mine" with a row of passion fruit scented candles and an erotic lighter. Another note, placed just so on a box of dark chocolates, advised her to "enjoy this box of sweets for my sweet."

A slinky, pink bathrobe hung from the wall next to a note that read, "Slip into something more comfortable." A collection of erotic poetry rested near the sink with a homemade bookmark that said, "Get some ideas!"

There were soulful CDs stacked next to a boom box temporarily resting on the vanity. A simple note beside them read, "mood music." And, in keeping with the "celebration" theme, a container of expensive bubble bath shaped just like a champagne bottle, complete with a realistic-looking, plastic cork and fancy, faux French writing on the label rested prominently on the lip of the bathtub. Next to it was a note that read, "uncork your desire." Another note instructed her to enjoy a long "soak" and, the *pièce de résistance*, there was an imported bottle of wine resting patiently next to a corkscrew, and a new wine glass resting atop a heart-shaped stem. Naturally, the wine had set you back quite a few green backs and days of research: What was the best year? What was a good vineyard? What would go best with the meal you were planning?

Eventually, after combing the Internet and several stacks of outdated *Wine Spectators* down at the public library, you had settled on a bottle of 1993 Henschke Mount Edelstone Shiraz.

Brick red and delicately perfumed with cassis and vanilla aromas, it had a gorgeous "nose" with some volatile notes, alcohol, and new oak. It was destined to be full bodied, spicy, warm, peppery, and alcoholic with a lovely soft texture, tart acidity, and strong oak flavors. The salesman at the gourmet wine cellar had assured you that this particular bottle would be much fresher and lighter than most of its counterparts, but amazing, with a long tobacco and herb finish.

"Outstanding," he had crowed as you handed over your poor, old credit card, "truly … a five star wine!" Not to mention the price to match.

Still, there was nothing better than a fine glass of wine for a fine occasion such as this. And, could you really put a price tag, even a tremendously overrated, humongously huge, towering, fear-and-sweat-and-

SELECTION SUGGESTIONS

When your Aunt Chloe shows up for dinner at the basement studio you said was a penthouse?

—Whether you serve roasted chicken or a stir-fry shrimp and peppers, pour gewürztraminer. Great aroma and bright taste pleases everyone in the family, and they'll all be impressed you can pronounce it.

tremor evoking price tag … on something as precious as … love?

Gulp!

Rushing home as fast as the traffic will allow, you breath a sigh of relief as you pull into your parking spot right next to your girlfriend's flashy red sports car. So far, so good. After all, you were right on time. Giving her 60 uninterrupted minutes to unwind with soul music, chocolate, aromatherapy, and champagne scented bubble bath in your recently aquired antique bathtub. Who knows, she might even invite you in! Button down Oxford, necktie, loafers and all.

Slipping quietly inside, you hear the soulful renderings of Barry White and the sloshing of a beautiful woman bathing in your bathtub. From the foyer, you can see the faint flickering of strategically placed candles and one whiff fills your nostrils with the heady aroma of passion fruit and expensive wine. And, were those the volatile notes of vanilla and oak you'd heard so much about?

Good. Your only concern had been whether she would figure out the state-of-art wine opener, complete with leather carrying case, hydraulic pump, and reinforced thumb pads. But judging from the overpowering scent of tobacco and herbs, she'd not only opened it, but poured herself a huge glass full. Or two.

Fill ev'ry glass, for wine inspires us,
And fires us
With courage, love and joy
Women and wine should life employ.
Is there ought else on earth desirous?

—John Gay,
The Beggar's Opera, 1728

SELECTION SUGGESTIONS

When the soundtrack jumps from Sarah McLachlan to NWA and back to k.d. lang and you like it all?

—Pinot noir is the wine for the best kind of omnivores, people with tastes that are eclectic and still distinctive. When he wants salmon with mango salsa, she's having the filet with horseradish mash, your date's having a stir-fry, and you've got a wild mushroom risotto, the one bottle for everyone is pinot noir. It's a red wine that has the guts and the whimsy to like both fish and beef—and not lose its own spice.

"Darling," comes her velvety smooth voice, mellowed by passion fruit, chocolate, and vino.

"Is that you?
I can't believe you did all this for me. You must really love me.
Honey, what's wrong?"

What is wrong, indeed. There, standing at the threshold to the bathroom, your mouth agape, you stare at your girlfriend's supple body surrounded by bath water and bunches and bunches of bodaciously wasted bucks! A "brick red" tinge suffuses the bubbles in the professionally refinished antique clawfoot bathtub as your girlfriend basks in a $300 bottle of ... bubble bath?

"Honey," you exclaim. "What happened to the bubble bath?"

"Oh, I just love it," she replies. "Of course, the bubbles didn't last very long. Actually, I don't recall any bubbles at all, come to think of it. But red's my favorite color and I can already tell it's going to leave my skin silky smooth."

You stare at the fancy wine opener, the expensive green bottle completely emptied of its oaky, herby, pricey contents, and then focus on the pristine bottle of $5 champagne-scented bubble bath resting nearby ... completely untouched.

Admiring the ecstatic look on your girlfriend's face, you lighten up and realize that wine is meant to be enjoyed, after all. Okay, usually it's enjoyed by drinking and not bathing, but hey, whatever floats your boat. Or girlfriend.

Silently, you wonder what goes best with champagne-scented bubble bath: fish or red meat?

4

MONEY IN A BOTTLE

W ine costs money.
There it is. True fact. As bare as a starlet's thigh at the Oscars. Yet the price of wine is a topic people are baffled by, embarrassed to mention, or forced to ignore, simply assuming wine costs a lot of money—and just ordering a beer instead.

It's not illegal to talk about money or the best deal. Pay attention to price in stores, supermarkets, and restaurants, even when you're not buying; knowing relative prices will help you in restaurants later.

Money matters quite a bit to the people who make wine, whether it's a co-op in Bulgaria, an ancient wine-making family in Tuscany, or an oral surgeon who just bought a vineyard in Santa Barbara. There are good reasons why one wine costs $25 and another costs $6, reasons that you can often taste.

Money matters to wine drinkers too. Don't let the showoffs fool you. Everybody likes a deal, including connoisseurs, and they look for great values as well as great vintages. Some $10 wines are better than other $10 wines, and some $50 bottles are worth the price; others don't come close. Ask the folks in the middle, the merchants who sell wine, if high price always reflects high value. A few will demur, but most will shake their heads no.

These people know the economics and quality of wine, and service is their business. You know what you want and your budget, so tell them: "I want an Italian red wine, something that's smooth, and not too dry. What's the best for around $10?" Any good clerk knows the stock includes a half-dozen bottles in that category, and can pick a favorite. Some may try to bump you up a couple of dollars, but nobody will try to steer you to a $50 Barolo. This is wine, not cars, and they want you to come back soon and often.

RESTAURANT
STRATEGIES

Start with two tenets. One is immutable: a 750 ml. bottle holds approximately five five-ounce glasses. Got that? Five glasses to a bottle. For a party of two, that's two glasses each and one to split; for a foursome, one a piece and leftovers for the lucky ones.

The other is fuzzier, but you may have already figured it out. Restaurant prices are a *lot* higher than retail, usually a 200 percent mark-up from retail. That means a wine you might buy for $10 at the store can be $30 in the restaurant. The formula varies widely and is often a sliding scale, so that a $15 wine may be only $35 instead of $45. Some mark-up is justified and high prices are sometimes merited at restaurants that take special care with their wine, pay premiums for rare bottles, and keep vintages for a long time. More often it's just an extension of the restaurateurs' rule of thumb that the food costs are 30 percent of the cost of a dish.

It can be even worse. The mark-up on big-name labels at high-end restaurants can be limitless, according to a study of New York City wine lists a few years ago by the Zagat Survey. A 1982 Pétrus could cost $1,000 or $5,000; 1994 Mondavi reserve cabernet ranged from $60 to $160. Everyday diners know that by-the-glass prices often offer little relief. House wines may be $4 per glass for wines that cost $4 a jug at the liquor store; a glass of modestly good cabernet might be $7. If you plan to have more than two glasses, a bottle is almost always a better deal.

Smart restaurants know that they sell more wine when it's fairly priced, and also know you're smart enough to know when it isn't. If there is drinkable wine for $12, you're more likely to buy a bottle on a weeknight, or a fine wine for $25 for a big night. Another welcome innovation is a new way of writing wine lists to give more information than just color, region, or grape variety. Some divide wines colorfully into "cool breezes" and "fire breathers" to hint at their flavors. A "progressive" wine list devised by Beringer arranges wines in easy-to-understand categories from mild to strong, and offers different price choices in each. Consumer-friendly wine lists are increasing, but too often you get the worst of three worlds: high prices, minimal selection, and clueless service.

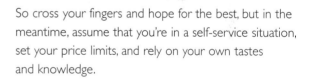

So cross your fingers and hope for the best, but in the meantime, assume that you're in a self-service situation, set your price limits, and rely on your own tastes and knowledge.

SELECTION SUGGESTIONS

When the deal goes through and everybody in the office shows up at the sushi bar?

—Champagne is a good idea, but you're already spending a fortune on sea urchin, so look for a riesling from Alsace, Germany, or California; it's crisp enough to go with the silky feel, and sweet enough to stand up to a little wasabi. Works with take-out futomaki too.

CALCULATE THE MARK-UP

Look for a couple of bottles for which you know the going retail price, which should give you a clue. The lower the mark-up, the safer it is to take risks or even splurge. Otherwise save the fancy stuff for home. Unless you're dining on other people's money, drink a $50 bottle of wine at home, not when you have to pay $150 or $200 for it.

DON'T LOWBALL

The cheapest wines on a wine list are often there simply to offer a cheap wine. Unless you know and like the cheap wine, find the starting point of the wine list, move up at least $5 to $10, and you'll do much better.

NARROW YOUR FOCUS

Wine lists can be as big and confusing as a liquor store, with too many cabernets and chardonnays, or a long list of Bordeaux châteaux. Look for smaller categories, such as Spain, Italy, or smaller French ones, such as Loire or Rhône.

Check out Other Reds and Other Whites. This miscellany often contains wines that are less common but more food-and-people friendly: chenin blanc, Beaujolais, pinot noir, riesling, sémillon, syrah/shiraz and viognier.

ORDER YOUR FAVORITE

Look for wineries you know and trust or areas you know, whether France, Italy, or California. Beware of unknown brands, especially at low and middle price points. Some are produced strictly for restaurants. Don't sweat food and wine matches. If you like white zinfandel, chardonnay, or merlot, go ahead and enjoy.

TOP-5 WAYS TO TELL YOU'RE DRINKING CHEAP WINE

5 Your host's finger is still bleeding from his recent "twist-off" accident.

4 You can't read the label through the paper bag.

3 That importunate wino outside your host's window shouting, "Thief! Thief!"

2 Funny, your taste buds have never sizzled before.

1 Your host serves next to an old oil drum with a fire inside.

ASK FOR HELP

This is not futile or desperate. When you spend $50 or so on a purchase, you're entitled to a sales pitch at least, so ask. Your server or someone in the restaurant should be able to tell you something. Don't fake sophistication about wines or brands you don't know; focus your questions on your tastes and needs: "Is this chardonnay soft?" or "What do you recommend in merlot for $30 to $35?" Their answer will be filtered through their taste, but it's a start.

TIME TRAVEL

A restaurant with a truly good wine list should have a choice of older vintages that are no longer on the market. You can take advantage of it without breaking the bank on first-growths from Bordeaux and Burgundy, or the trendiest California names. You may be able to travel back fifteen to twenty years and show off your wine smarts for less than $100, sometimes under $50. Look for Chiantis, Rhônes, and Rioja reds, or German whites. From California, look for zinfandels, petite sirah, and charbono, reds that age well and inexpensively. When you look at the cabernet sauvignon, take off your modern blinders and remember that brands like Inglenook were grand old names in the 1960s and 1970s.

TAKE YOUR OWN

When you make your reservation, ask if you can bring your own. Many restaurants charge a modest corkage fee of $5 to $15 per bottle, enough to discourage you from bringing in cheap stuff, but low enough that it may be worth bringing a bottle you like from home.

BY THE GLASS

Best use of the by-the-glass system is before or after a meal. Try sherry for an aperitif, or a dessert wine or Port afterward. You still pay the mark-up, but you'd never buy it by the bottle in a restaurant.

PLEASE THE CROWD

Not everyone likes strong flavors, so avoid tart and bitter wines in a table of varied tastes. Beaujolais, Mosel, and Italian whites are safe bets that can be winners. Buttery chardonnays, chenin blanc, pinot noir, and merlot please a wide variety of palates, too. Australians have a particular knack for putting everyone at ease.

WINE DIARIES

CORKSCREW YOU
(TAKE TWO)

This isn't the first time this has happened to you. Not at all. In fact, in the annals of your disastrous dating hall of fame, this is what's known as a "common occurrence":

The pretty girl. The stuffy restaurant. The candlelit table. The romantic strains of a violin and piano competing in the background. The linen napkin caressing your thigh. The promise of a romantic evening stretched out before you like a long, lazy sunset when, suddenly, from out of the blue, a huge meteor comes crashing from the sky. Landing smack dab in front of you, it rocks the table and nearly cuts off the circulation in your legs with its massive weight before …

Whoops! Hold up. That's not a heaven-sent meteor.

It's only the 400-page wine list.

You've decided it was finally time to crack down and learn a little something about wine. Which is why you'd been spending most evenings after work in the local Wine Cellar, strolling the musty aisles of endless bottles with a handy wine guide in tow, and trying not to yawn.

And, after all that hard work, you could finally tell the difference between a Merlot and a Mosel. A Pouilly-Fuissé and a Port. A chardonnay and a cabernet. A sherry and a rosé.

You've picked up on the fact that while France is a great place to get your wine, think twice about those Detroit vineyards. You knew that a nice, dry red went well with a finely aged prime rib, while a pleasant white complemented the Hawaiian chicken quite nicely, thank you.

Surprisingly, however, the favored wine coolers of your youth no longer seemed to go with … anything.

You've given over your twist-off for a corkscrew, learned that "merlot" does not rhyme with "snot," and, finally, have discovered that, in girlspeak anyway, "zinfandel" and "loser" have roughly the same meaning.

And so, on this lovely evening, at this candlelit table, in this oppressive restaurant, barely able to breathe beneath the confines of this two-ton wine list, you are actually prepared to wow your comely companion with a decisive dinner decision.

"I believe," you start out slowly, "that the lady is in the mood for a nutty, balsam aroma with just the faintest lilt of sandalwood, and would therefore enjoy a nice Lafite-Rothschild. Conversely, since I am in the frisky, one might say, frolicsome mood for a fragrant, yet not piquant bouquet, I will judge your finest bottle of Château Haut-Brion."

And you're just getting started:

SELECTION SUGGESTIONS

When the choreographer called and Alexander got the part he's been practicing on for weeks?

—Break out the capital-C—Champagne from France, the $30 stuff with a yellowish-orange label. It's just like him, made with extreme care, yet elegant and a little wicked any time of day. Besides, the Russians like it almost as much as ballet.

"Could you tell me, dear sir, are you familiar with the aroma wheel developed at the University of California at Davis? No, what a shame. In the future, please be prepared to converse when holding your nose up at such an extreme angle. Thank you, that will be all."

Your date, fairly gushing over your performance in the snotty waiter's absence, says, "How impressive. I've never heard anyone order wine like that before."

You nod, buttering your roll and basking in her praise. "Nothing to it," you murmur with just the right amount of humility as you excuse yourself to go to the restroom, leaving your date to reconsider her plans for the rest of the evening, and, no doubt, the next morning as well.

"Thanks a lot," you announce appreciatively to the sulking sommelier when you find him in the kitchen a moment later. His duties over, the whining wine steward simply relieves you of the twenty-dollar bill trembling in your outstretched hand.

"The twenty was for the wine tips on the phone before you got here," the snooty spit-smith sneers. "I'll expect a tip for that 'California at Davis' crap at the end there."

Frowning, you hand him a ten and return to the table just in time to find him delivering your wine.

And, suddenly relieved of thirty dollars, not to mention whatever these bowl-sized glasses of wine would soon cost, you take your first sip to discover approximately the same taste of that cup of glorified grape juice you'd sampled at the local theme restaurant earlier in the week.

"Oh well," you think, as your date sniffs, snorts, and then swallows most of her glass before quickly asking for another. "I wasn't very hungry anyway."

STREET SMARTS

You can buy wine in all kinds of places depending on state laws; check them all out and you'll find they're like wine labels: Judge by what's inside, not appearance. Fancy wine stores are happy to sell plenty of wine for $10; they may want to look exclusive, but they are eager for new customers. Don't avoid seemingly old-fashioned liquor stores either: They can have great wine selections and knowledgeable help hiding behind those big sale prices on bourbon in 1.5 liter bottles, plus their liquor sales can give them clout getting good deals and rare wines from distributors.

Then there are the supermarkets, discount warehouses, and price clubs, but that does not reduce wine buying to a choice between price and service. You can get bargains and bad deals at either; the real alternative is service or self-service. Get the first where you can and for the second, that's up to you.

SELF-SERVICE SURVIVAL

With the promise of lower prices, many liquor stores and discount operations offer larger selections and no help, which can be terrifying. You're on your own here, and it calls for survival skills. Do take advantage of the selection; you're likely to find more wines from smaller vineyards in California and the Pacific Northwest and all of Europe. Plus you'll get a larger choice of varietals made from Rhône and Italian grapes, more expensive reserve vintages, single-vineyard, and dessert wines.

TARGET A COUNTRY

Most big stores are arranged by nationality. Aim for a country you know, and you'll cut the store down to a more manageable size. If you're in a hurry, pick a country with limited distribution here, like Spain for reds. With France or Italy you can narrow it further by region; with the United States and Australia, wines will usually be categorized by varietal. Knowing that you want a California chardonnay, an Oregon pinot noir, or a Mosel riesling gives you a head start. Then focus on your price range and brands you know.

DON'T FORGET THE "OTHERS"

In some corner or lower shelf at the back of the store is a collection of wine from miscellaneous countries. Look here for Greek, Hungarian, Swiss, and Argentine wines. Likewise, within each country there's usually a tail end devoted to lesser known regions and hard-to-characterize wines.

REMEMBER BOTTLE SHAPE

If you see a wine made from a place or grape you don't know, the glass may be a clue to the wine's self image. Bottles with soft curved necks shape the pinot noirs and chardonnay of Burgundy, sharp shouldered bottles have reds somewhat like cabernet sauvignon or merlot, and whites as dry and crisp as sauvignon blanc. Long necked bottles are often German-inspired. And odd shaped bottles are, well, odd; usually a sign of special local pride.

COMPARE VINTAGES

Say you find a number of wines that appeal to you, same price range, but different producers and vintages. You want to make a decision on vintages, which can be important in Burgundy and Germany, but you don't know '92 from '93. Look in the high end of the section for the country where you'll find a selection of vintages from the same producer and vineyard; check which year commands the higher price.

CHECK SHELF TAGS

Announcements of medals and high-flown praise are better than nothing if you trust the source. If you follow ratings by Robert Parker, the *Wine Spectator,* or anyone else, check them out if they are posted. But read their words carefully. They may recommend it for people who like strong flavors, or for sticking in the cellar for five years. And remember, *your* opinion will be the one that counts when you open the bottle.

BE CAREFUL

Ask how and where the wines are stored, and check the bottle to make sure the cork hasn't pushed up against the foil.

LOOK FOR LOSS LEADERS

You're sacrificing service, so look for bargains, especially in sparkling wines and mid- to upper-priced wines.

WINE SPECIALISTS

When you come across a store with selection and service, whether it's a wine store or a liquor store with a savvy owner or staff, take advantage of it. This is your chance to explore the greatest variety of wines, get knowledgeable advice, and treat yourself to a vanishing thing called personal service. Prices and mark-ups will vary, but don't fear that it'll cost you big. Stay within your budget, and you'll get the most for your money, as well as hard-to-find bargains, and solid advice when you want to spend big bucks. Find a store with people and prices you like, and make it a weekly or monthly stop on your shopping rounds, not a special occasion. It's as valuable to improving your everyday life as a good baker or roadside tomato vendor.

SPEAK UP

Don't be afraid to tell someone your price range and your preferences, or feel you're the ignorant student; you're the customer and they should sell you what you want. You don't need fancy wine jargon to state your preferences and interests. Say "I don't like wine that's too dry," or "I've heard some German wines aren't sweet." "We had a great zinfandel last week, it was real peppery," or "I want to try a good Burgundy." The more clues you can give—"I like the Morgan chardonnay"—the more help they can be.

PICK THEIR BRAINS

If you're trying to sort through the châteaux of Bordeaux, find the chardonnay you like best, get to know new grape varieties or Chilean

vineyards, this is the time and place to ask away.

Buy by the case: It's not that extravagant, a dozen $8 bottles is around $100 and you can buy in any price range you want. Many stores often give 10 percent discounts even on mixed cases. Good merchants will help you select a case, and once they know your preferences, they can set wines aside for you, or even make deliveries. Even if your wine source is a little out of the way, having a dozen bottles at home is more convenient than making a last-minute stop at the liquor store.

BECOME A REGULAR

Introduce yourself and get on the mailing list. Most wine specialists have newsletters to promote special buys and announce wine tastings, classes, and dinners where you can meet visiting winemakers. Some also rent space in their storage areas for customers who want to buy in quantity.

May I help you?

SUPERMARKET SAVVY

When you get no help, you supposedly get better prices. So if you have to do all the thinking, reap the rewards. In most supermarkets, selections are usually limited to the biggest brands, which can supply a huge number of customers. That doesn't mean just $4 and $5 stuff; so know your brands. Although wineries can win placement and preferential treatment in chains with big promotions and sheer market muscle, post-Prohibition laws in many states forbid the payment of slotting fees for shelf space, as cereal makers and other vendors sometimes do.

Selection is limited to the most popular varieties, cabernet sauvignon, merlot, chardonnay, and sauvignon blanc. It's usually heavily American, with more Italian than German, some Australian and French, and an ocean of wine from Latin America, eastern Europe, and other new sources of bulk wine. You don't need to dawdle here, but pay attention to price. You may see some of the same wines on restaurant wine lists.

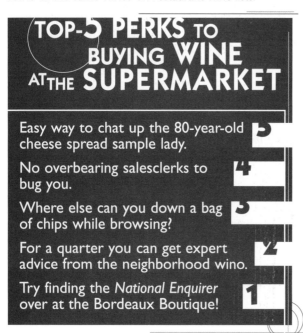

TOP-5 PERKS TO BUYING WINE AT THE SUPERMARKET

5 Easy way to chat up the 80-year-old cheese spread sample lady.

4 No overbearing salesclerks to bug you.

3 Where else can you down a bag of chips while browsing?

2 For a quarter you can get expert advice from the neighborhood wino.

1 Try finding the *National Enquirer* over at the Bordeaux Boutique!

GO FOR BRANDS AND NAMES YOU KNOW

If you're a fan of Napa Ridge, Mondavi, Columbia Crest, or Barton & Guestier, look for them, find them, and be on your way.

BE CAUTIOUS OF NEW NAMES AND LABELS

They're usually massive new lines imported from new vineyard areas, or cheaper lines spun off by old names with an eye toward winning new customers, either up market or down. Still the industry is changing and cranking out good new labels, like Forest Glen and Rabbit Ridge. Others have better marketing techniques than wine-making. Try them at someone else's house first.

SELECTION SUGGESTIONS

When he's late, leaving you sitting in the bar at Helios but you don't want to look like you're cruising.

—Dry sherry is a drink of early evening elegance, crisp enough to refresh, nutty enough to reward the lingering you're in for and strong enough to fortify you for the telling off. Goes well with peanuts, cheese, and other bar food.

DON'T OVERLOOK THE HIGH END

At the opposite end of the aisle from the jugs, there's usually a small collection of better wines and sparklers from $8 to $20, and there can be good values here: Many of the oldest and best U.S. wineries and some European firms sell small quantities of better wines as well as basic lines to supermarkets too. Look for Sterling, Geyser Peak, Simi, Ruffino, Benziger, BV Buena Vista, and Chateau Ste. Michelle. Rely on a good name, look for single vineyard or reserve wines, and put some trust in price. Grocers and their customers are minutely price-sensitive; an $18 wine in a supermarket is generally fairly priced.

LEARN THE JUG WINES

There are decent wines in 1.5 liter bottles. You'll need them for parties or to keep in the fridge, so find a favorite.

WINE DIARIES

PRICE CHECK!

Well, it's Wednesday night and there's nothing in the fridge but two eggs, a bottle of ketchup, and that cough syrup from last month's spring fever. Naturally, your freezer is stocked with good intentions, but if you eat one more serving of Lean Cuisine Beef Portabello you'll scream, and, besides, you've had a hard week. Okay, a hard half-a-week, but still, in all, you're entitled to a little treat now and then.

Of course, since you're in between boyfriends (as in, several years in between) and don't feel like dishing dirt with colleagues in marketing, you grab your check card and head out to the local grocery store. (Hey, it's better than eating alone in some snobby restaurant while the happy couples at the other tables interrupt their adoring gazes to send you pity stares.) There, armed with a metal shopping cart and enough fluorescent light to blind Godzilla, you stalk down aisle after aisle full of Lucky Charms, Cheez Whiz, and Vaseline before locating anything even remotely resembling real food.

After cruising up and down the meat aisle and wavering between the overpriced rock shrimp and an entire canned ham, you finally settle on a nice Porterhouse, a box of mashed potatoes, and a can of asparagus before hitting the Little Debbie display.

Hmmm, Nutty Bars or Swiss Cake rolls? Star Crunches or Oatmeal pies? Okay, okay … Swiss Cake rolls it is. Now, off to the measly wine shelf to pick up a quick bottle of red, preferably with a cork, and … whoa, what's *this*?

There's not just one "shelf" full of Almaden's finest and Boone's Farm's best, but an entire row of shelves, wait, scratch that, you've spoken too soon. For, upon turning around, you realize that there are actually *two* whole rows full of wine to choose from. Why, in supermarket-speak, that constitutes a whole *aisle*! Of nothing but wine!

Sure, it's been a while since you've picked out a bottle here, but … not that long. Or has it? Certainly you would have remembered such a superior selection.

Setting your basket down on the floor, you gaze in wide wonder at the limitless possibilities facing you. From floor to ceiling, it would seem, is nothing but wine. Red and white, foreign and domestic, twist-off and cork. There's saké. There's sangria. There's Port. There's sherry. There's champagne. There's MD 20/20. What to do, what to do?

If only they'd hired a sommelier to go along with their Ernest & Julio expansion! How are you supposed to choose from so much? Back in the old days, you'd run in for a T-bone, grab the most expensive bottle of cabernet, and hit the express aisle. Of course, that was when one shelf had been red, the other white, and they'd still had room leftover for those handy sleeves of plastic champagne glasses!

Now there were dangling vines bearing dusty rubber grapes tethered around each shelf divider. There was a stand for corkscrews and another for those clever, tuxedo-themed wine bibs and matching cocktail napkins. And the wine aisle itself was divided into regions: California. France. Spain. Germany. Chile. Argentina. Even Australia.

This was nuts. You'd never choose a wine with this much selection! Hold on.

"Excuse me?" you shout to a passing stock boy. "Sir?" Although it's hard to refer to a freckle-faced teenager in hi-tops and low-riders with such a mature moniker, it nonetheless grabs his attention and he saunters over to "assist" you.

"Yes, ma'am?" He grins as you try and reassure yourself that his unnecessary "ma'am" is just an automatic response to your complimentary "sir." (It better be, anyway.)

"Uh, yes, listen …" you stammer, not sure where to begin. "I'm just here pacing up and down your wondrous aisle of wine, and I'm wondering if you can help me."

"Did you spill something, ma'am?" he asks good-naturedly, searching for broken glass.

"Well, no," you admit.

"Can't reach something?" he continues, standing on his toes.

"No," you add, shaking your head.

"Need a price check?" he inquires.

"Not exactly," you interject. "I just don't know whether to go with this '94 Shiraz or the '96 Merlot. Or perhaps the '97 Chianti—I'm just not sure."

"Shazam?" he asks, perplexed. "The cereal aisle's two over, ma'am. I lave a Kash Grocerama day."

Abandoned, you fight back tears and approach the next human being you see, a little old lady stooped low from osteoporosis. Either that, or she'd just come from scouring the generic tea bags arranged at floor level.

"Oh, sure," she offers to help your dining dilemma. "I always go with the quart jug of Vinorama. Its heady aroma and tart sweetness are the perfect all-day drink (with ice). And it's so big, it lasts me most of an afternoon." Undaunted, you continue to flag down unwary wine shoppers. Like the businessman who claims he "… only knows whites."

Or the trashy teen who offers you three bucks to buy her a pint of Thunderbird. And the frazzled mother of three who insists, "Oh, I don't drink the stuff, it's strictly for cooking. Honestly. Really. It is."

Eventually, you grab a mid-priced, mid-decade, middling bottle of cabernet sauvignon and put it in your cart before finally heading off to the express aisle. Exhausted, you don't even have the energy to flip through the *National Enquirer* as you sag against the candy bar rack.

"Phew," you think to yourself as the old man in front of you buys 200 cans of cat food, "Next time I'll just race into Circle K for a burrito and a Budweiser."

LINING UP OTHER SOURCES

You can also buy wine via mail-order from wineries or wine merchants in other cities and states, in person at wineries, at home parties, and over the Internet. Be aware, however, that none of these methods provide a safe way to beat taxes. Tax collectors around the country are getting tougher, and some businesses no longer ship to all states.

So it's best to weigh these options on the service, selection, and price they offer. Buying direct from a favorite winery gives you a chance at special wines that might not be sold at retail. Mail-order wine clubs and direct sales may be more convenient and less intimidating, but you'll get a larger and more consistent selection at a local retailer.

WINE FOR OTHER PEOPLE

Wine is convenient and easy to buy, wrap, and give. What makes it hard is trying to please, let alone impress, someone else's taste.

GO BY THEIR PREFERENCES

If you know they like old California zins, always drink chardonnay, or had a great time in Italy, follow their lead in picking a wine.

GO BY YOUR TASTE

Give a bottle of wine you like. "This is our favorite pinot noir; we have it with everything, and it's great with salmon" is far more personal than "The guy at the wine store said this is really good."

BUY A TREAT

Don't try to second guess someone's favorite wine. Try a good sherry, Port, or dessert wine (many come in half-bottles).

BIRTHDAY AND ANNIVERSARY YEARS

Want to buy a bottle of wine to commemorate the year someone was born or for just-married friends to open 20 years from now? Don't. Not right now. First, not all years are great years, and only red wines and sweet white wines will last that long (most Champagne and chardonnay won't). Second, most old vintages are expensive and can be found only at auction, and wines from the current year aren't ready yet.

Still, it's a charming idea and there is a way if you can wait or work backwards. Wait four or five years after the special year when you will know when and where there were promising vintages, and buy it to tuck away. A more immediate solution is vintage Port, the one wine for which 10-, 20-, and 30-year-old vintages are still kept and sold (for $50 to $100). Since the Portuguese don't declare a vintage every year, there may not be an exact match. You have to peg it to the year you broke your leg, your daughter entered kindergarten, or your friends moved into their first house.

WINE STORAGE

Keeping wine at home for a short time is easy. Stick the cork back in the bottle and put it in the fridge. The wine will do fine for 48 hours. What about long term, especially after you've bought a whole case of wine? You may be proud of your wine, but it wasn't designed for decoration or use as furniture. It won't hurt to keep the bottles out that you plan to drink in the next few weeks or so. Wine you want to save to drink months or years from now is different.

Your goal is to let the wine age gradually. Oxidation will speed up in high temperatures or if the cork dries out and lets in too much air. So lay wine on its side someplace that's cool, dark, quiet, out of the way, and not too dry. A cave would be perfect.

> "You don't need a $50,000 cellar. You just need someplace that doesn't change temperature too much. It can be 65 degrees, a little cooler than room temperature. And just as long as the temperature doesn't fluctuate, which is what really kills the wine, then it's fine. And then lay it on its side and it will last you three years, easily."
> —Trey Jenkins, winemaker

Failing that, look in your basement and your closets for a place where the temperature doesn't vary wildly from winter to summer. The ideal goal is to keep temperatures close to 60 degrees and humidity at 50 to 70 percent, but you and your wines can survive if the place never gets over 70.

If you do decide to stock up on wine, there are two ways to protect your investment at home. Free-standing wine cellars are like refrigerators except they keep the humidity high (a refrigerator does the opposite). They come in various sizes and styles starting between $600 and $1,000 for a small 50-bottle unit. To give yourself more room, dedicate a closet or unused room to your wines; special temperature-humidity coolers cost $1,000 and up depending on the space. Maybe what you pay in higher utility bills will be offset by the money you save by buying by the case.

> *Ideally, a wine should be stored on its side at a temperature of 55 degrees, but most wines will keep perfectly well at up to 70 degrees (a cellar or interior closet works well). A wine's worst enemies are heat and fluctuations in temperature.*

WHY THE PRICE?

Laws of supply and demand apply to wine and affect both price and quality.

They start with the main ingredient. Some varieties of grapes command higher prices. One ton of noble cabernet sauvignon may cost three times what carignane does. Grapes that are hard to grow and may produce poorly (such as pinot noir, nebbiolo, or riesling), or are in sudden demand, such as merlot, will cost even more. So even a cheap cabernet is likely to cost more than a plain red.

Whether bought from a grower or grown by a winery, grape prices also reflect the underlying cost of vineyard land. Land on Napa's Rutherford Bench, in the Chianti Classico District, or St. Julien is extremely expensive compared to acreage in the Central Valley, Apulia, or a non-AOC area of the south of France. Those with specific track records for particularly good grapes, such as Martha's Vineyard in Napa Valley, can command more. A small treasured vineyard in California may make only 500 cases of wine; perhaps only 50 will be shipped to your state, and only a few dozen bottles to your city.

Wherever grapes grow, the yield is crucial to price and to taste. When a vineyard contains old vines or is pruned and managed so that it produces two tons per acre instead of the ten tons it might produce, the vines focus their energy into fewer grapes. Flavors are more concentrated and grapes

more costly. On a larger scale, bad weather can cut the yield of an entire region and that can push prices up, but it doesn't necessarily mean higher quality. Too much rain and too big a harvest, however, can mean the grapes are heavy with water, not sugar or flavor.

The actual winemaking costs, too. Assembling and maintaining all the stainless steel tanks, oak barrels, and refrigeration equipment costs money and this hardware can play a big part in the flavor, delicacy, or smoothness of a wine. Many underdeveloped wine regions can make only rough, very cheap wine until they can invest in modern equipment. Aging of any wine more than two years will also usually cost more as the consumer pays for the time the wine went unsold.

Wine requires labor, sometimes a lot of it. Picking grapes on steep hillsides of Germany and Portugal, or sorting through individual grapes in a late harvest take the most work in the field; the sparkling wines require the most in the winery. Differences in national pay rates in eastern Europe, South Africa, and Latin America figure in their low prices too.

DEMAND

Since wine shows up sporadically on the pages of slick magazines and still appears only occasionally on television and radio, advertising budgets are not huge expenses. But wineries have been savvy to the value of the buzz and prestige for centuries. They just used quieter ways to promote their reputations. It could be through handing out free samples, making personal contact with the

THE PRODUCERS & PRICE: A PRIMER

Matching the name of the winery and the wine is not so simple. Many wine operations produce more than one brand or line of wines. They are usually created to reach a different group of customers, either up or down the price scale. Sometimes they will be made of grapes of different quality and price, or from different vineyards or areas, or completely different wineries. Even first-growth châteaux in Bordeaux have second-label wines, but even those still cost $50 and up.

Given California's usual abundance of grapes and American marketing strategies, many California companies have numerous lines. Stag's Leap Wine Cellars and Markham, for instance, have less expensive labels in Hawk's Crest and Glass Mountain, while Napa-based Franciscan Estates produces Estancia, Mount Veeder, and Quintessa, as well as the famous Franciscan Oakville.

In recent years the biggest companies have raised the biggest "families" of lines and brands. Robert Mondavi's first crush was in Oakville in 1967; in 1978 he opened the huge Woodbridge winery in the Central Valley and started the Opus One project with Mouton-Rothschild. Today the lines include Napa Valley Reserve, individual Napa districts (such as Carneros pinot noir), Napa Valley, La Famiglia di Robert Mondavi (Italian varietals), Robert Mondavi Coastal (from North and Central), Woodbridge (from the valley and the coastal regions), and Byron (a Burgundian specialist in Santa Barbara with regional estate and reserve wines). From

royal court, or getting the inside track in governmental rankings like the Bordeaux classification of 1855. In a crowded market they've always sought endorsements.

Reputation, particularly one that goes back 300 years, may cost the winery very little today, but you will pay for it—$100 and up for the great crus of Bordeaux and Burgundy. It's like buying stocks: If you don't want to pay blue-chip prices, you're going to have to look at less appreciated properties to find a wine that's been undervalued. Or go boldly into Italy where the wines are many and unranked.

That often holds true for modern ratings by the wine magazines and critics, who reduce wines to statistically manageable two-digit numbers. They can be handy guides, but even if you doubt them, enough people believe in them to push up the price. Almost as soon as any wine gets an 85 or better from anyone, the news will be hanging from a shelf tag. Most of the raters do list average retail price, so check the numbers as well as the words.

Packaging can be costly if you go for the fancy glassware of prestige Champagne cuvées. Lately label design has started to catch up with modern graphic design and even post-modern styles. A wine aisle today can be a gallery of floral illustrations, native American artwork, WPA woodcuts, clever cutouts, sight gags, and specially commissioned art. The name on the label and the wine in the bottle is still most important.

SELECTION SUGGESTIONS

When you've bought your first sports car, but it's a Miata not a Ferrari?

—Take some of the money you saved, and buy a Burgundy from a good vineyard and a good year. If you get a good one, it's just as red, sleek, and racy.

Jess Jackson,
Proprietor, Kendall-Jackson

Family owned Kendall-Jackson, headquartered in Sonoma County, California, had its first success blending grapes from all over California into smooth inexpensive wines, a basic Vintner's Reserve and the better Grand Reserve. Today, it has thirteen more labels, from Calina (Chile) and Tapiz (Argentina) to small estate wines with distinct regional character and over-$50 pricetags, including Lokoya and Cardinale in Napa and Stonestreet and Legacy in Sonoma.

You can bet the future holds more labels, not fewer. So pick your favorites now, and make your choice on what's inside the bottle.

overseas and in joint ventures, Mondavi has Opus One (Oakville), Vichon Mediterranean (southern France), CaliTerra (with Errazuriz of Chile), and Luce and Lucente (with Frescobaldi in Italy).

The massive winery of Ernest & Julio Gallo has also gone through a *risorgimento* (resurgence) to show off diversity and style that brings new respect to the brand. Although headquartered in Modesto, California, Gallo has long had land and contracts with growers in the best parts of the state as well. The newest generation is trying to reserve the family name on its best wines and to establish new brands for other regions and price points.

At the top are the new Gallo of Sonoma Estate wines from Gallo-owned vineyards in northern Sonoma. A bottle can sell for $50. A less expensive label with fruit from the estate and local growers is called Gallo of Sonoma, available by single vineyards and by counties. Gallo has also introduced labels for grapes bought in four other regions: Marcellina (Napa), Indigo Hills (Mendocino and Coastal), Anapamu (Monterey and Central), and Rancho Zabaco (Sonoma). Below them, a host of less expensive lines made with grapes from all over the state: Turning Leaf, Gossamer Bay, E&J brandy, Livingston cellars, plus Andre, Eden Roc, Tott's, and Ballatore sparkling wines.

MIDDLE MAN

Another feature about the wine business customers should know is that there's someone in the middle. It doesn't necessarily change the price, but it may affect your selection.

Like all alcoholic beverages in the U.S., wine is sold through a three-tier system set up after Prohibition to prevent the breweries and other makers of alcohol from taking advantage of the small business on the retail end. The top tier of producers, both U.S. wineries and companies that import wine, are not supposed to sell directly to the retail level, and instead ship their wines to a middle or wholesale level of businesses called distributors. Three or four major distributors exist in most markets and each handles hundreds of lines of wine, liquors, and beers. These distributors then deliver wine (as well as beer and alcohol) to the retail stores, bars, restaurants, and grocery stores.

5
WINE & FOOD

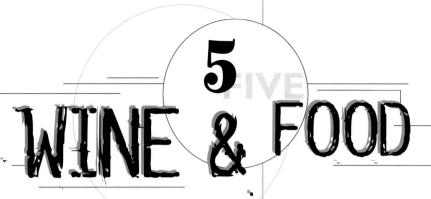

On the eighth circle of hell, where Dante put hypocrites and others of evil counsel, are the snobs who pretend that only they can appreciate good wine. Even lower, in the ninth circle with the greatest frauds, are the people who think they are the only ones who can enjoy good wine and food at the same time.

If you dare retreat to "white wine with fish; red wine with meat," they snicker that simplistic rules no longer apply. They then proceed instead to establish an elaborate theoretical construct to explain why only a Côte de Nuits of the best vintage, which you can't afford, is appropriate for pheasant, which you can't even find except running around in some corn field in South Dakota.

MIX AND MATCH

Yikes! This whole business of matching food and wine is unnecessary and irrelevant. Maybe it made sense for the gilded few at grand feasts that started with oysters and went through endless courses of soup, game, poultry, fish, and roasts with different wines for each. That way of dining went down with the *Titanic*.

While some mourn the passing of Edwardian excess, even the very rich rarely eat like that today. Now we take wine in moderation, and enjoy our food in unrestrained diversity. Our plates are filled with phad Thai, couscous, blackened salmon, risotto, and goat cheese pizza. Rarely are two plates the same, especially in restaurants where the pretension of food-and-wine matches is most enshrined. Even with only two diners, there are likely to be two wildly different entrees, say pork loin with Thai spices and pasta and seafood in a light cream sauce, and one wine. Consider the possibilities with four diners—and still only one bottle.

What to do? Well, sauvignon blanc, dry riesling, or Beaujolais would taste great, or you could go for wine by the glass, but the first answer is to stop worrying. Have merlot or chardonnay if that's what you want. Do try the

wine by itself, and then with your meal, and you'll see how they affect each other. This isn't a test, by the way. It's your dinner.

Even if you were cowed into giving some waiter the authority to grade your paper, most of your wine and food will be consumed at home at work night suppers, dinner parties, and holiday feasts. That's one time when everyone will be eating the same course—and you have your pick of wine (at better prices).

"Wine is meant to go with the meal. It's not something you drink between meals. It's something that belongs on the table like a napkin and a fork."

—Faith Willinger,
Italian food expert

THE PERFECT PAIRING

So the place to start in pairing food and wine is with your tastes. The best match will be food you like with wine you like. They may unite in a pleasure beyond your dreams. If they don't, there's always next time. That's not just dumbed-down, anything-goes advice. In much of the world and for most of history, people paired the food they had with the wine they had. They made do quite well most of the time. Maybe the lovers of the great hams and cheeses of Parma had to go to Tuscany for fine wine, but on the coast of France they washed down oysters with lowly muscadet, and it worked. Trout and riesling from the Rhine matched; so did Neapolitan tomato sauces and red ordinario.

You're probably still not comfortable because we New Worlders lack the centuries of tradition

and have an unprecedented array of choices in food and wine. That's not a bad thing, says Miami chef Norman van Aken, a founder of the Florida fusion of Southern, Caribbean, and Spanish cooking that calls itself New World cuisine. "Our food didn't grow up with wine," says Van Aken. He feels free to look through all the varietal wines, not just cabernet and chardonnay. There's no prescribed wine for a veal chop with Cuban adobo seasoning, so why not a cherry-red barbera, one of those forgotten Italian varieties?

"Drinking good wine with good food in good company is one of life's most civilized pleasures."

—Michael Broadbent

Serving Wine

You may enjoy much of the fussiness about serving wine at home or in a restaurant, but you don't have to worry about it. The important elements are simple: Use clean glasses (watch out for soap scum) and serve at the right temperature. That affects the aroma and the taste of the wine.

Warm reds and cool whites generally hold true too, but too often the reds are too warm and the whites too cool. The right temperature ranges are in the 60s, a little below room temperature. Adjust for quality as well as color. Big or rough red wines need a little more warmth to soften them. Cheap white should be colder than a good chardonnay.

Unless you have an old expensive red wine or Port, you won't need to decant. If you do, set the bottle right side up the day before opening to let the sediment collect in the bottom. After you open the bottle, place a candle or flashlight behind the bottle so you can make sure the sediment does not slip out as you transfer the wine to the decanter.

Don't worry about smelling the cork (just make sure it's wet) or letting the opened bottle "breathe." Pour the wine into the glass and let it aerate there. One old wine custom worth keeping alive, however, is making a toast. Do it regularly, to friends and everyday blessings. You won't feel silly; you'll feel good.

"IT AIN'T ROCKET SCIENCE."

When it comes to eating and drinking, remember what John Ash, the resident food expert at Fetzer says: "It ain't rocket science."

Surely you trust your taste in food. You know and like—or don't—foods from Louisiana, Latin America, and Asia that may be peppery. Turkey breast is "lighter" than prime rib, white sauce is richer than red, barbecue tastes smoky, lemons are more tart than melon, and so on. And you know that some fish have more fat and flavor than others.

The problem was that you didn't have the same confidence when you thought wines were either red or white.

Now you know wines of all colors differ in body, flavor, intensity, and complexity. And one of the most important features of wine is acidity. The crispness may cleanse and whet the palate so many foods taste better. Sauvignon blanc and rieslings have good acidity; sémillon doesn't.

Beaujolais and Bardolino and pinot noir can be light in texture just as pinot grigio and sauvignon blanc are. Some chardonnays and rosé Champagnes are relatively full-bodied; cabernet sauvignon and nebbiolo much more so. Gewürztraminer and riesling can be as spicy in their way as Rhône reds and zinfandels. You can find as much sweetness in Port and Madeira as in a Sauternes, muscat, or German auslese. Alcoholic strength can be light in a Beaujolais or a riesling, and much stronger in a Rhône red or a chardonnay.

Sauvignon blanc and many Italian whites are crisp and dry, while chenin blanc, pinot blanc, and sémillon can be fatter. Many chardonnays are round and soft in the mouth. White wines can be sweet (Sauternes), and spicy (gewürztraminer), or dry (muscadet). There's woodiness in oaky chardonnays and big Italian reds.

Once you realize the character of wines as well as foods, combining the two is a matter of common sense and personal style. It's as simple as the clothes you wear, or the way you decorate your home. Harmony can be beautiful or boring, sometimes contrast is delicious; sometimes one overpowers the other.

Wines of similar weight, texture, and richness usually go together, like a heavy red wine and a thick steak, or Sauternes and *foie gras*; and lighter wines with picnic fare. Yet the lively tingle of Champagne is a great counterpoint to creamy soups and slippery sushi.

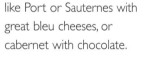

A salad or fish with a lot of lemon and a high acid wine can make for too many sour tastes, yet spicy red wines go great with pizza. And rieslings and gewürztraminer are perfect with Asian dishes probably because they too are spicy, and their sweetness and crispness contrast with hot peppery foods. While the sweetness of dessert wines sometimes show up a dessert, or vice-versa, they make some of the great contrasts, like Port or Sauternes with great bleu cheeses, or cabernet with chocolate.

Food, or just a sauce, can also change the taste of a wine. An ancient maxim in the wine trade advised tasters to "Buy on apples, sell on cheese." The premise was that the apples keep the palate critical, while the fat in the cheese makes any wine taste softer.

Beringer's Tim Hanni shows how food and wine interact with a piece of salmon. With the salmon and a sweet teriyaki

sauce, the acidity of the wine was obvious. When the salmon had a squeeze of lemon giving it some acid of its own, the tartness of the wine faded by contrast. Which is better? Up to you again.

Hanni, a former chef as well as a wine expert, has carried his research to an iconoclastic conclusion. Have any wine you like with food; he says. If the wine tastes jagged, too sharp or too bitter, it's the food's fault and easily fixed. Within the magical chemistry of taste, Hanni has isolated salt and acid, not fat content, as the elements of food that affect its taste with wine. Like chardonnay with steak but it's too tart? Add a little salt to the meat. Have a problem with Chinese food, adjust it with soy sauce and rice vinegar. It's worth a try.

"When a wine has high acidity, it just blends beautifully with food."

-Mary Ewing-Mulligan, Master of Wine

WHAT GOES WITH WHAT?

If you're still worried, let's look at these supposed problems:

Vegetarian entrees: Even if there's no meat, the meal can still be light or hearty. Spicy reds and full-bodied whites are great with bean, mushroom, and cheese-and-egg dishes. Go lighter with pastas and salads (dress them with olive oil and bring vinegar to the table for individual seasoning).

Take-out: Get over it. Put the pizza, pasta, or Chinese on regular plates and pour some wine anyhow, whether it's Chilean cabernet or refrigerator white.

Great wines: When you do have a special bottle, a fine reserve chardonnay, a first-growth Bordeaux, or Burgundy at home or in a restaurant, let the wine be the focus and keep the food simple. Salmon, lamb, a thick steak, or roast chicken is all you need.

Cigars: No easy answer here. Yes, some wine-loving Europeans may smoke cigarettes while eating and drinking, but it doesn't work when you're trying to enjoy wine fully, and the bitterness of cigars can desensitize your taste even more. Save 'em for later with something very strong like brandy.

Holiday dinners: Turkey, the classic American feast, is wonderfully democratic. The meat is juicy, the dressing full of spice, and the table full of every other flavor. Almost anything works. Gewürztraminer, a Beaujolais, or a light zinfandel are especially accommodating for the big bird.

Barbecue: Grilling or smoking food does add a strong flavor. You can match it with a spicy red or tart white, or lighten up and have a glass of white zin or merlot. It's a picnic, really, isn't it?

Cutting out alcohol (Egad!)

Several brands of wine, such as St. Regis and Sutter Home Fre, are de-alcoholised. They are made by fermenting grapes into wine and then removing the alcohol by various methods; they contain less than one half of one percent alcohol. Other products such as Meier's grape juice have not been fermented and do not contain alcohol.

People who abstain from alcohol may find these acceptable alternatives to traditional wine, but others may prefer bottled water, coffee, tea, soft drinks, or fruit juices.

less than half of 1% alcohol

Organic wine

Several wineries cater to customers seeking "organic" wines, which generally means grapes grown without chemical fertilizers or pesticides, and vinified with natural ingredients. Fetzer's, Bonterra, and Frey are the primary California producers. Chapoutier, Beaucastel, and a few other Rhône and German wineries practice organic or biodynamic agriculture. Few critics cite any improvement in taste, but that may not be important to the target audience. Wine has always been a very "natural" product, since grapes come with the needed yeast. Also because grapes don't demand rich soil, many vineyards get little or no fertilization. Although chemicals are sometimes used to control fungus, disease, and other pests in humid areas, that can be avoided in hotter, drier climate zones.

CREATIVE
SOLUTIONS

Some other therapies for the next time you have wine and food anxiety.

Be different: Wine for food isn't just red or white. Rosés can be great for more food than just picnics. Dry sherries are made for nutty, salty flavors. If you've never had Champagne with dinner, try it sometime.

Try two: If you have a small crowd at home or a restaurant and plan to drink two bottles, open both at the beginning of the meal. Compare them.

Think fast: There are two ideas that require no thought. Match any wine that's in the food, whether it's coq au vin or a white wine sauce on shrimp. Stay within ethnic borders; rieslings with German food, light French reds with Provençal dishes, sherry with tapas, or a Barolo with osso buco. If it doesn't work, blame the chef—or the entire country.

Go easy: Some wines seem to be crowd pleasers. They go with lots of foods and lots of people. Mosels, pinot blanc, pinot grigio, and sémillon are good universal soldiers. Beaujolais, cabernet franc, merlot, and pinot noir can be handy reds; so can most modest zinfandels, Chiantis, and other Italian reds.

WINE DIARIES

THIS WAS A MISTAKE . . .

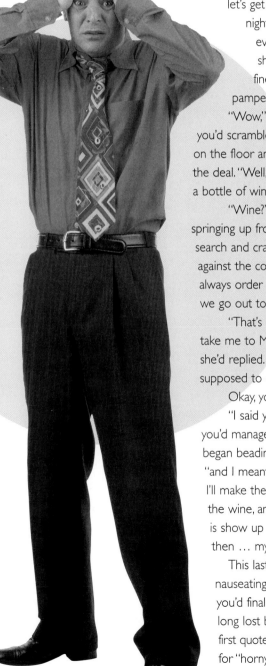

She'd mentioned it casually, really. In conversation. In passing. It was nothing. Just another four-letter word tossed off in between smaller words in front of it and bigger words behind. The word: cook.

"So how about you come over for dinner this Saturday?" you'd asked on the phone earlier that week. An innocent enough question, you'd assumed. Naturally, your recently purchased copy of *1001 Ways to Woo a Woman* was perched conveniently in front of your face. It was cracked open to a chapter called, "Recipe for Love: Aphrodisiac Appetizers, Horny Hors d'oeuvres, Missionary Meals, and Desirous Desserts," and you were following it verbatim.

After several minutes of laughter, disbelief, and throat clearing, your girlfriend of three months had said, "You? *Cook*? For *me*?"

"Sure," you'd answered, following closely the detailed script in your book. "My mom taught me how to cook. I'm very close to my mother, you know."

"Really?" she'd countered awkwardly. "I thought you said you hated your mother."

Whoops. Of course you had. You *did* hate your mother. Stupid book!

"No," you somehow managed to recover nicely. "I love my mother. It's my *brother* that I hate! That bastard!"

"The one in the wheelchair?" she'd asked, obviously shocked.

"No, no," you'd shouted, somehow dropping the book in your momentary panic attack. "My other brother, the one in the state pen. Now, listen, let's get back to Saturday night. I'll take care of everything, you just show up with your fine self and let me pamper you for a change."

"Wow," she'd whistled as you'd scrambled to find your book on the floor and somehow close the deal. "Well, can I at least bring a bottle of wine?" she'd asked.

"Wine?" you'd shrieked, springing up from your floor-bound search and cracking your skull against the coffee table. "But you always order a margarita when we go out to eat!"

"That's because you always take me to Mexican restaurants," she'd replied. "So what else am I supposed to order?"

Okay, you'd thought.

"I said you bring nothing," you'd managed to croak as sweat began beading on your forehead, "and I meant you'll bring nothing. I'll make the menu, I'll pick out the wine, and all you have to do is show up and enjoy it. Until then … my sweet."

This last line was mega nauseating, to be certain, but you'd finally recovered your long lost book and it was the first quote you found. So much for "horny hors d'oeuvres!"

"Uh, sure," she'd managed to utter in between giggling. "See you Saturday."

Naturally, you'd thought of nothing else since that catastrophic call except the worst 4-letter word of them all: W-I-N-E!

You'd slept it. Chablis? Dreamt it. Zinfandel? Sweated it. Merlot? Oh, no, Bordeaux!

You'd searched the Internet, consulting everything from the Cyber Sommelier to the vineyard vixens at Champagne.com. You'd browsed through the local liquor store, a tattered copy of *Wine Spectator* in hand and a dogged saleswoman whispering sweet nothings full of tannins, malolactic fermentation, and oaks in your eager ear. You'd suffered through trips to the library, the gourmet supermarket, the Wine Cellar and, more important, the bank.

After all, who knew how much this bottle of wine was going to cost when you finally got around to choosing it!

Naturally, you were still clueless at this point. Despite the research. The bulging wallet. The strained eyes. The nightmares. The sweats.

A lifelong "suds swallower," with the 1,000 beer can collection to prove it, your only experience with wine was the time you helped your mom cater a hoity toity party downtown when you were sixteen, and you ended up drinking what was leftover in everyone's glasses at the end of the night. (Hey, that's variety!)

Since then, you'd been a beer man and proud of it. After all, none of your other girlfriends had ever made you pick out the wine.

They knew what they wanted when the waiter came to the table, ordered it, and you paid for it at the end of the night. That's what guys *did*.

Of course, it wasn't entirely her fault. After all, you had insisted on picking out the wine. Although, that was when you were still following the advice of that stupid book.

And now it was suddenly Saturday afternoon and, not only had you not picked out the wine, but you hadn't even decided on the dinner that you still hadn't picked the wine to not go with. Why were things so complicated? Why was life so hard? Why wine? Why couldn't everyone dig beer with their dinner? Why were there so many Chinese restaurants crowding downtown? Why were you so hungry?

Why … hadn't you thought of this before?

"Hello?" your girlfriend announces after knocking on the door three hours later.

"Come on in," you shout from the kitchen, where you're busy re-heating take-out lo mein and stir-fry on top of the oven with one hand while shoving the telltale dragon-and-calligraphy-covered boxes to the bottom of the trash. "I'm in the kitchen!"

"Wow," she says, shocked at the sight of soy sauce steaming and litchi nuts sizzling in your brand new wok. "What's that you're wearing?"

"Oh," you shrug, tugging at the neck of your recently purchased ji-fu, or semi-formal court coat. "This old thing? I thought, since I was cooking Asian, I should dress appropriately. When in Rome, er China, that is."

She smiles and sniffs admiringly at your "home cooking."

"What a great idea," she says around a mouthful of fried noodles. "But isn't it hard to cook Chinese food?"

"No," you shake your head, going straight for the sympathy vote. "Not when you've been practicing all week!"

When you receive the obligatory "sympathy smooch," you instruct her to take a seat at the table and, several minutes later, present her with a spread worthy of Chairman Mao.

She gushes over the moo goo gai pan. Blushes over the bonsai tree centerpiece. Caresses the chopsticks. Winks at the wontons. And then, just like clockwork, the microwave dings, signaling the final dish of the evening.

"More food?" she asks, her eyes already bulging over the sagging dinner table.

"Not at all," you bow before entering the kitchen.

"It's your wine," you announce upon your return, bearing the brand new ceramic pitcher and two miniature cups. "Ji-fu. Chopsticks. Chinese. What other wine could suit your palette tonight but … saké?"

FOOD & WINE ACCESSORIES

Parmesan cheese knife

Lobster and nut cracker

Cheese slicer

Self-cleaning garlic press

Crumb scraper

Pepper mill

Olive oil mister

Cheese shaver

Battery powered frother

Truffle tongs

Caviar spoon

Herb grinder

Cork retriever

Cheese dome with board

Olive fork

Grapefruit spoon

She smiles: "Saké is Japanese, silly."
Whoops!
You pour, anyway. She sips. You sigh. Mission accomplished.
It may not have been pressed beneath the feet of beautiful, naked French girls in the vineyards of France. It may not have come with a cork. It may have been made from rice in Japan.
But rice wine or not, she'd asked for wine. And, rice wine or not, she'd gotten it.

6

I'M OVER THE EDGE
AND MUST KNOW ALL

You've done everything in the first five chapters twice.
You want to know more? Here it is:

"**Y**ou must come out during crush. It's really crazy then." If you get to know anyone from wine country, you may eventually get this invitation. Accept it immediately.

"Crush" is that month or two every fall when grapes make that first leap into wine. Any wine region anywhere in the world—from the Douro River Valley in Portugal to Santa Cruz, California—roars to life. Hundreds of people flood the fields to pick the grapes. Huge trucks piled with grapes clog tiny country roads and force traffic jams in one-stop towns. Eventually they queue up outside wineries that become round-the-clock factories, run by winemakers and crews who haven't slept in days. Winery foremen yell at truck drivers, the drivers yell at each other, and everyone's hot and tired. It's performance art with you in the middle.

That's one way to go. Less hectic is a trip in January when the vines are dormant, or even in July when they are full of big fat clusters of grapes. About 10 months out of the year, the places look like they're hibernating. The quiet little château, the hilltop castle, or the sprawling hacienda look very much like their labels. It feels like farmland … cropland, row after endless row.

You can still drink wine, however. The tasting rooms are open and often there are good restaurants nearby. And behind that beautiful historic building house at the end of the long drive is the real winery. To be honest, it's a warehouse, where wine merely sits in storage, though sometimes it's below ground in cool caves and cellars. Still, most of the time it just sits in huge stainless steel vats, oak barrels, dusty bottles, or it's packed into freshly minted cardboard boxes. The only excitement is watching workers charge around the warehouses on a forklift or wrangle big hoses like firefighters or crank up the bottling line.

IT ALL ENDS UP IN A BOTTLE

Two groups of people are most responsible for wine up to the drinking point: the growers who tend the vineyards, and the winemakers who work in the wineries and cellars.

The farmers and workers who grow and pick the grapes sometimes work for a winery that owns the vineyards, which gives the winery the greatest control over the grapes. Wineries, which use only their own grapes, proclaim their ownership by labeling the wine as estate-grown or bottled.

"I wonder what the vintners buy one half so precious as the stuff they sell."

—Omar Khayyam

Other growers are independent farmers who own their own vineyards and sell grapes, juice, or already fermented wine to wineries, co-operatives, or merchants, who bottle and sell the wine. Independent growers exist throughout the wine world, sometimes growing huge crops for bulk wines, and sometimes tending the most prized vineyards. They may sell on the open market, or under contract to a specific winery. Wineries that buy most or all of their grapes say it gives them greater freedom and flexibility to search out the best grapes to make wine each year. A few buy from other growers in other countries, routinely, or when crops fall short.

WINE ACCESSORIES

- Vino Plate Clip
- Rapid-Ice® Wine Chiller Sleeve
- Tastevin with Ribbon Set
- Plat Wine Bottle Coasters
- Tuxedo Wine Bottle Drip Collar
- Wine Thermometer with Wood Handle
- Friar Bottle Robes
- Cork Retriever
- Bota Bag
- Thermal Wine Cooler
- Vacu-Vin® Vacuum Wine Saver
- Drip-Not® Wine Pourers
- Hologram Wine Bottle Gift Bag Assortment
- Tuscan Bottle Cooler
- Santa Fe Carafe
- Double Vino Bottle Cooler
- Black Marble Wine Cooler
- Black Marble Champagne Cooler

GROWTH
CYCLE

Given their slow start and the agonizing passing of the vintages, grape vines become strong, tough survivors, wiry, and gnarled. At sixty or even one hundred years of age they can produce their best wine, in small quantities, but with intense flavor. That's why many wine drinkers seek out and pay more for wines that claim to be made from old vines (vielles vignes in French).

Like most deciduous plants, grapevines become dormant each winter. Their fruit plucked, their leaves dried up and fallen away, they look like crude fence posts with a crown of dried up canes around them, better for making wreaths than drink.

When the sun returns to chase away the late winter chill and warms the soil, sap rises and the ends of the old canes "weep" with milky white bubbles. By March, tiny buds form on the branches, and in a few weeks leaves and shoots with tiny clusters of bright green berries burst out. This "berry-set" will be the grape cluster at the end of the year.

But first the berries must flower in May. Once pollinated, the berries will drop their blossoms and begin a long summer of growth. The fields become thick with foliage, and the berries slowly grow to grape size.

The final month can be miraculous. Those grapes

we consider red or black will turn from green to those darker shades. The sugar content of all the grapes will increase until the individual grape is bursting with 20 percent sugar or more.

Much could have gone wrong: a late frost, spring hail, bugs, or a blisteringly hot summer. Vineyard workers must train the young canes, trim the leafy canopy, and prune away bunches so that the vine can put its energy into the best grapes possible. Some vines will produce only six bunches a year.

In August (January in the southern hemisphere) the crop and the vintage are largely what nature dealt. Growers and vintners are in the vineyards armed with their judgment and handy devices called refractometers. They pick a grape and look at its raw juice through the refractometer and hold it to the light to measure sugar content.

Then they make the all-important decision to pick now or give them more time to ripen—and risk rain, hail, or frost.

Then it's time to pick the grapes. Sometimes by hand with a small curved knife in a back-breaking day in the sun. Or the grapes can be muscled out by huge mechanical harvesters.

Some wineries pick in the cool of the evening or at night under searchlights, especially to preserve the delicacy of white wine grapes. "If you bite into a wine grape, you notice there are two astringent portions, one is the seeds, and the other one is the skin," says Ted Bennett of Navarro in Mendocino. Picking at night keeps the "must" (the juice, skins, and seeds of the grape) cool so it picks up less astringency from broken seeds and skin.

"Compromises are for relationships, not wine."

—Sir Robert Scott Caywood

HOLD THE GRAPES!
THE *OTHER* FRESH FRUIT WINES

Blueberry	Plum
Apple	Kiwifruit
Raspberry	Boysenberry
Peach	Lemon
Pear	Passionfruit
Rhubarb	Mulberry
Marionberry	Crabapple
Dandelion	Nectarine
Apricots	Strawberry
Elderberry	Peanut
Cherry	Chili Pepper!
Cranberry	
Apple	

IN THE
● WINERY

Now the steady stream of trucks brings the winery to life. Virtually every step—how, when, and at what temperature to crush, ferment, blend, and bottle—will be a calculated choice by winemakers. Where the growers' challenge was to cultivate the grape into making sugar, the winemaker works on the second equation of turning sugar into alcohol, and making grape juice into wine.

Color is another challenge. Grape juice is naturally neutral, somewhere between cloudy white and watery green. Forget the jelly-colored juice that stained your teeth as a child. The color lies in the skins. Remember that, for it dictates the formula for making wines their color.

Winemakers start by identifying every truckload as it comes in, noting the variety, time, date, sugar content, and precise block of the vineyard where it grew.

White grapes usually arrive first and are the most fragile. They must be protected from the heat, which

To preserve their crispness and protect their delicate flavors from delicate aromas, white wines are fermented at colder temperatures in glass, metal, or stainless steel tanks (and a few in wooden barrels). Within a week or two all the sugar has turned to alcohol and the wines are stored until spring when another bit of natural magic happens. Called malolactic fermentation, it will change the wine's tart malic acid into the kind of mild-mannered lactic acid in milk, creating a softer and rounder texture. Although it's a natural process in both white wines and red, wineries can accelerate it or retard it as they wish.

When red or black grapes arrive, the winemakers' goal is to get as much color, tannin, and flavor as possible to give the wine character and longevity. So they go slower. Red grapes are usually de-stalked and sometimes de-stemmed, but the rest of the fruit and juice will stay together longer. For a prized wine like its Rutherford Reserve, Cakebread Cellars may let the grapes and juice remain on the skins for as long as two weeks before they are pressed.

decreases their aroma. They go immediately into the hopper of a de-stemmer and crusher that separates the woody stems and stalks from the grapes. Most often the crushed grapes go straight to a press, where they are squeezed into the "must" (the juice, skins, and seeds of the grape), which will ferment into wine. Occasionally the first flow of juice from the grapes, called free run, is saved to be fermented separately or used as juice. (Some winemakers do leave the juice of white grapes in contact with the crushed skins of grapes for up to a day to pick up extra aroma and flavor.)

Since the white grapes were separated so quickly from their skins, they often lose much of their wild yeast. Winemakers will add cultured yeast to begin the fermentation process. In many wineries, particularly in cooler regions and in years when grapes do not ripen fully, wineries also add sugar to the must, a process called chaptalization (sometimes used for red wines in Burgundy).

For red wines, the must of both juice and crushed grapes, skin and all, may be kept together throughout fermentation. Sometimes cultured yeast is added, sometimes the wild yeast is enough. Fermentation of red wines is often done in open vats, made of wood, steel, or cement (even the great Château Pétrus of Bordeaux uses cement). It usually takes place at warmer temperatures, as high as 85 degrees, to produce the most color and flavor, although it can be cooled down and prolonged into months if a winemaker wishes.

(To make rosés, winemakers simply give the wine shorter time in contact with the skins of red grapes, maybe only a day. That's how the same zinfandel grapes can make a white zin with only a peach blush of color, or a rich hearty red.)

The bubbling of carbon dioxide released during fermentation is so powerful that it pushes a "cap" of grape skins and sediment to the top. Years ago workers had to push the cap down to keep the skins and juice together. Today most wineries simply draw the fermenting juice from the bottom of the tank and pump it back over the top.

An alternative used in some wineries to make wines like Beaujolais is a "hands off" method that lets the grapes crush themselves. In this carbonic maceration process, whole red grapes are placed in a sealed fermenting tank. The sheer weight of the grapes crushes the bottom-most grapes into juice. It begins fermenting and bubbling its way up through the correspondingly sinking mass until many of the grapes are fermenting inside their skins. The fermented juice is then drawn off, and the remaining grape matter is crushed to produce the most intensely colored and flavored liquid.

With any wine, stopping the fermentation process is tricky and depends again on how ripe the grapes were and how much sugar they contain. In cooler climates, such as Germany's, there may be only enough sugar to make a wine of 9 percent alcohol. In the heat of California, Australia, or southern Europe, the natural sugar content could create a strong wine with as much as 14 percent alcohol.

If winemakers let all the sugar turn to alcohol, the wine will be bone dry; if they halt the process, some sugar will remain and give a touch of sweetness to the wine.

Once fermentation has stopped, however, all the yeast cells are still in there as well as other solids. Pull a sample out of the cask and you'll see a murky substance, not the brilliant clarity wine drinkers want.

There are a number of ways to achieve that clarity. The wine can be fined, a chemical version of filtering, where winemakers add eggwhite or other substances to cause the yeast cells to collect and drift to the bottom. They can also whirl the wine in a centrifuge or filter it physically. Again some winemakers reject both processes, saying they remove too much flavor. They label their wines proudly as un-fined and un-filtered.

The simplest method used for centuries is to pump the wine into new tanks every few weeks during the winter leaving the sediment behind, which is called racking.

When the young wines have been stored after fermentation, winemakers begin experimenting with blends. How much chardonnay from vineyard A should be mixed with that from vineyard B, or with chardonnay C, which was fermented in oak barrels? Or should they sweeten the wine by adding some unfermented chardonnay grape juice, as some mass-market makers have done?

Winemakers are the chefs of the winery and may try one hundred combinations before making a decision on the proportions of the final blend of a wine. And that's for a pure varietal that contains only one kind of wine. A Bordeaux red could have five different grapes, a Chianti even more.

IN THE CELLAR

While a few nouveaux or novello wines are released in November, most wines will stay at the winery all winter before bottling. The simplest wines—white wines from the 2000 vintage, will be ready to sell and drink in the spring of 2001, and light inexpensive red wines a few months later.

Most fine wines will stay at the winery longer either in barrels or bottles. Since Biblical times, wine drinkers have valued "old wine;" today chemical analysis shows why. Over time various compounds in wine slowly break down and reform, moderating the tannins and acids, changing the color, and creating new flavors and aromas.

How and how long a wine ages depends on the wine as well as chemistry. Most white wines are shorter lived and rarely held more than two years before release. Long-lived red wines with strong tannins and high alcohol are often held much longer in the winery.

The length of time is a matter of tradition and law. French châteaux generally release their red wines after two years. Many U.S. and Australian wineries keep their best wines three years or more; and Spanish wineries may wait ten years before they feel the wine should be released.

Aging is a costly process for the wineries although the consumer will eventually pay for it.

First, the longer the wine sits in the cellar in barrels or bottles, the longer the winery waits to collect its profit on the vintage. Second, the barrels to store the wines are not cheap.

Barrel-making is a dying art, and oak forests are shrinking, so much so that truly picky vintners go to oak auctions to secure adequate supplies.

Many people do like the toasty softness oak gives to chardonnay, but the way wine connoisseurs go on about new oak, small oak, French oak, etc., seems laughably arcane. Yet the distinctions can be important and subtle.

Oak barrels differ from glass or metal containers in ways you can taste. The porous nature of the wood allows air in to oxidize the wine and allows wine to evaporate, which concentrates the flavor. The inside of the barrel, often made from charred wooden staves, gives its own tannins and toasty vanilla flavors to the wine. But not too much, since "very oaky" is not often meant as a compliment.

To figure out what kind of barrel is best takes only a little physics and botany. Put wine in a 55-gallon *barrique* (barrel) and more wine will touch the oak sides of the barrel than in a 500-gallon oak barrel. A new barrel will have a stronger smell, rougher wood, and more freshly

cut pores that will interact with the wine than an old barrel that's been used for 20 vintages.

American versus French or Slovenian oak? You're forgiven for not knowing that European trees have closer grain with smaller pores, or that American trees have bigger pores and are milled in a way that releases their flavor more easily. The difference between oak from the Argonne forest and Nevers, you don't need to know. Suffice it to say that large old European barrels would impart the least oak flavor; new small barrels of American oak the most.

After bottling, the best wines continue to evolve at a slower pace and many wineries cellar wine in bottles for several more years. Eventually, however, merchants, restaurateurs, and consumers take over the aging. A few white wines with high sugar and acidity like the great rieslings of Germany can be cellared for decades.

Most red wines live longer than whites. Big tannic cabernet sauvignons and zinfandels can keep for decades. Only a few white wines with high sugar and acidity, like the aforementioned rieslings, will live as long.

SPECIAL WINES

The magic winemakers conjure with grapes could stop here, and we would have a wide world of beautiful still table wines.

Thank goodness it doesn't, for we would be missing something very special—like the sparkle discovered in the wines made around Champagne in the 17th century. They had a pesky habit of fermenting again in the spring. A nuisance until winemakers discovered that people liked the bubbles and found a way to control this second fermentation and make bottles thick enough so they wouldn't explode.

Winemakers from Portugal to Sicily tinkered with very ordinary local wines, fortifying them for the sake of shipping to export. By adding brandy during fermenation, they created the lusciously sweet ports; by adding brandy afterwards and aging wine in the salt air, the Spanish gave us sherry.

"There are two reasons for drinking wine. When you are thirsty, to cure it; the other, when you are not thirsty, to prevent it. Prevention is better than cure."

—Thomas Love Peacock

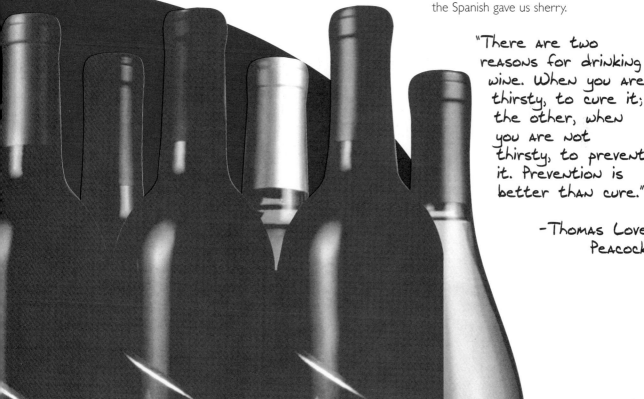

WINE DIARIES

VINO VISIONS

You don't know how it happened, really. This Merlot Madness you've been experiencing of late. How about your recent Piesporter Psychosis? Not to mention your Zinfandel Zaniness or your Syrah Schizophrenia. But either way, you just can't help it. You've gone over the edge, looked into the abyss, and realized that the meaning of life can only *really* be found inside a six-year-old bottle of Garofoli Rosso Conero Grosso Agontano!

With its purplish red, its mysterious, lurking nose of black fruit and leather. Its full, ripe, and rich flavors of mulberries and toasted oak. Voluptuous and mouth-filling with its ripe, crisp acidity, and good, firm tannins. So sweetly fruitish throughout with spicy oak on the finish and a bouquet not unlike … oh, sorry.

See? The bottle, the vino, the grape juice, the … wine has taken hold of your life and won't let go. And you don't know how it happened. After all, in school you'd strictly been a beer man. All the way. Nothing but Budweiser and Miller's High Life for you and your fornicating frat buddies. Back then, splurging meant some import in a green bottle and a cap you'd have to haul out the rusty bottle opener for!

Even in your post-college life, you'd never ventured too far off the beaten beer path. Sure, there were the occasional New Year's Eve cork poppers and birthday toasts, but never in your life had you stooped to picking out a bottle of wine for yourself. Why, you'd sooner be caught in an adult bookstore! Oops!

Yet, gradually, over time, as your early twenties slowly gave way to your mid-twenties, you'd found a moldy maturity somehow forming over you. Your tattered jeans gave way to Dockers. Your belt buckles grew lighter and your collars tighter and, before you knew it, you found yourself covertly studying the wine lists at restaurants and bars.

Well, why not? Everything else about you had changed. Why not your drink of choice? After all, now that most of those sissy, sassy, sweetie wine coolers had gone the way of 8-tracks and black velvet Elvis portraits, wine had become much more acceptable for guys to drink. Besides, your collars weren't the only thing getting tighter these days. If your size-32 Dockers got any more "claustrophobic," you might have to move up to the dreaded 34.

And didn't all those health reports you were always hearing on the news every night go on and on about the positive affects of wine, such as lower cholesterol levels in all those wine-drenched Frenchies. And they'd all been drinking it since they were, what, eleven?

Inevitably, you found yourself wondering what took you so long to hop on the Bordeaux bandwagon in the first place. And that was when it all started—your long, steep decline into Dom Pérignon dementia.

First came the books: *Larousse Encyclopedia of Wine. Loire Valley & Its Wines. Parker's Wine Buyer's Guide. The Oxford Companion to Wine.*

Then came the magazine subscriptions: *Wine Enthusiast. Wine Spectator. Food & Wine.* Even *Wine Business Monthly,* for heaven's sake! Your living room coffee table looked like something out of the Ernest & Julio Gallo corporate office!

Naturally, in the grand tradition of those famous wine drinkers Aristotle and Sophocles, more wisdom only led to more questions: When should I drink 1997 Chianti Classico? Is it time to rethink the 1855 Bordeaux Classification? Will wine survive a few hours journey in a hot car? If all my wine glasses are dirty, can I use a juice glass? Coffee mug? Gulp … paper cup?

Then came all those stifling, snobbish wine terms: acetic acid, ampelography, botrytis cinera, carbonic maceration, enology and, your all-time favorite, malolactic fermentation! (You'd impressed quite a few potential girlfriends with that one, hadn't you?)

And, finally, armed with all of this noxious knowledge, you'd ventured out on your own to make your first few, tentative purchases. Some had been misses, some had been bonafide hits. You'd learned the art of fine wine shopping, noticing which stores were kept cool to avoid those wine killers, "sunshine and heat." You'd examined fill levels for proper liquor levels and corks to see if any oxidation had occurred. You'd even schooled a few clueless cork clerks in on your superior shopping wisdom.

From there you'd joined a local tasting club, where each of you brought one expensive bottle, say a Château Lafite Rothschild, a Romanée-Conti Gaja, or a Château d'Yquem, and spread them around in order to defray the high cost of pursuing such an expensive hobby. Unfortunately, despite your wealth of recent knowledge, you'd found yourself a little out of place with the sémillon snobs and Bordeaux bores constantly in attendance. After all, wine was meant to be enjoyed, not dissected and overanalyzed like some corpse at a coroner's convention.

"Fresh, upfront citrus nose with some oak and orange peel. Full bodied and ripe with lots of alcohol, lemony fruit, and crisp acidity. Rounded and fleshy but fresh. Muted/dumb nose with hints of floury apples, wet fur, and oak.

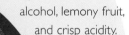

TOP-5 SIGNS YOU MAY BE OBSESSED WITH WINE

5.) You ask for the "wine list" at McDonald's.

4.) Your pool is shaped like a wine bottle. (And filled with wine.)

3.) During the Superbowl, you shop for the oldest six-pack of beer you can find.

2.) Your wine cellar/humidor/cask/bedroom.

1.) Your cork house.

Rich, rounded, mouthfilling palate with spicy, apple fruit, sweet alcohol, and oak. Good spicy finish. Appealing drinking now but a bit one dimensional."

Good gracious! Were all of you tasting the same wines? Your brief comments had been, simply: good, better, and best. In the end, while group tasting was a more economical way to sample several vineyard's finest without shelling out for all of them from your own pocket, you'd opted out of your local wine tasting group. After all, it was worth an extra Pouilly-Fuissé purchase a month to be rid of those Dom Pérignon dorks.

Eventually, your purple passion had resulted in the ultimate for wine aficionados: buying wine futures. In this way, young, unbottled wines are sold at discounted prices through retailers or wineries. Once the wine is bottled and ready for sale, it is delivered to the consumer, i.e., you. Most of the time, consumers, such as your savvy self, pay less for futures, and futures can be a good way to obtain hard-to-get wines.

Naturally, this left you with little left to do in the way of wine wisdom except to twiddle your fingers and wait for them to be delivered. And wait and wait and wait.

Now, where was that latest copy of *Wine Business Monthly*?

7

OLD WORLD, FRANCE

Old World wine is old. Go figure.
Grapes were grown and turned into wine somewhere in Asia Minor five thousand years ago. Virtually every ancient civilization from Persia to Egypt made the stuff. By 1000 B.C., the Greeks turned wine grapes into a major cash crop and perfected many of the techniques used today in modern vineyards. In the following centuries the Romans carried viticulture, not to mention vivisection, farther north and west. Although their civilizations crumbled and the rise of Islam (teetotalers) erased the vineyards of North Africa and the Middle East, the vines planted in Western Europe flourished. By the end of the Middle Ages, the great vineyard regions of France, Germany, Italy, and Spain were established.

Over the centuries, grapes, wines, and tastes matured. The French liked theirs dry, the Germans prized a touch of sweetness, the Italians preferred a hint of bitterness, and the Spanish liked theirs old and mellow. While the English had few vineyards of their own, they made Bordeaux their claret and sought out sweet strong spirits wherever they could find them, from Marsala to Oporto and Cognac.

THANK HEAVEN

If the first glass of wine was not poured in France, Frenchmen believe it should have been. Certainly enough glasses have been filled with the pride of France or lifted in her honor that it is rightly considered the home of modern wine. From the châteaux of Bordeaux and the cellars of Champagne to the bistros of Paris and the cafés of the Riviera, wine is an integral part of French life. Ponder these: France without wine? Wine without France? No France? Just kidding. Also: No Château Pétrus, no Romanée-Conti, not even Beaujolais nouveau. No cabernet sauvignon of any kind, no merlot, no chardonnay, nor dozens of other grapes. No one would know how to make Champagne. No barrels made from the great oak forests of France, no sommeliers (this is a loss?), and not even a system for naming wines.

With only a few exceptions, the great noble grapes made into fine wines in Australia, Chile, the U.S., and elsewhere came from France. They are known by their French names. From Bordeaux: cabernet sauvignon and sauvignon blanc. From Burgundy: chardonnay and pinot noir. From the Loire: chenin blanc. Even the characteristic bottles, shaped centuries ago in these regions, are still used around the world.

There is something else of the French character—a preference for precision and fussy organization—in another contribution to wine: the appellation system. The French model of regulation and geographic identification from broad regions down with increasing specificity to the smallest village and commune has been widely imitated. It is the French penchant for candid, unforgiving

> **"When we started at the very beginning of the '80s to produce French varietals in the south of France, many traditional winemakers called us the American producer in France. It's a compliment, but fifteen years ago, it was not a compliment."**
>
> **—Robert Skalli, Fortant, Sete**

ratings of quality, from not-good-enough to great, that sets the standard.

Does that make French wines the best in the world? Few still argue that is true, but where is the cabernet that does not aspire to be a first-growth Bordeaux, the sparkler that does not wish to be equal to Veuve Clicquot, or the dessert wine that does not dream of Château d'Yquem? Wine has been an important part of French life and France's relations with the world before there was a France. While the first vines may have come from the Greeks, Phoenicians, and Romans, the French had made wine part of their international trade by the year 1000 A.D. Charlemagne had vineyards himself. Trade flourished in the Middle Ages with merchant fleets from England and the Netherlands.

With wine as a significant part of the economy, authorities from medieval burghers to tax collectors to royalty moved early to regulate and codify the wines. Most of the wine-growing areas, their grapes, and their methods were established by the 1500s, so they have had five hundred years to perfect their method. Or, in some cases, to let them fall into neglect and disrepair, or at least complacency. That happened while the New World wineries were expanding and reaching new levels of sophistication. The competition produced the "shocking" Paris tasting of 1976 when red Bordeaux and white Burgundies were upstaged by Napa's Stag's Leap and Château Montelena.

Since then a revitalized French wine industry has refined its techniques, increased its research, and shamelessly borrowed new ideas, grapes, and styles from the U.S. and Australia. More recently they have imitated the Italians and Chileans by producing large quantities of inexpensive varietals by creating new vineyards for noble grapes in older, rustic corners of southern France. As a result, by 2000, France was once again the largest wine producer/shipper in the world.

THE GRAPES

Although French grape varieties are rarely mentioned on the label, their names are familiar from their prominent use in U.S. wines: chardonnay, cabernet sauvignon, sauvignon blanc, pinot noir, chenin blanc. Many others are also a crucial part of the nation's wine lineup: cinsault, sémillon, grenache, pinot blanc, mourvèdre.

THE LABELS

The appellation system devised by the French divides wine into grades of quality: The lowest grade is vin de table, which can come from anywhere in France and is rarely seen in the U.S. Next up is vin de pays, wine made from a wide but specific region, with the region named; it's of better quality and should show some regional character. The highest category is appellation controlée wines, which must be made within a

region known for distinct wines and according to certain regulations. These geographic AC (also known as AOC) wines can be subdivided in increasing degrees of specificity and quality. Given the importance of terroir (French for soil), the narrower the source of grapes, the greater the distinction. Thus you might buy a wine from the broadest region such as Bordeaux AOC, more narrowly a Médoc AOC, a wine from the village of St. Estèphe, or most specifically from the vineyards of Château Phélan-Ségur.

In prestigious regions like Bordeaux and Burgundy, the government set up a system to rank each individual château or property or cru (growth). The best are usually grand crus, ranked from premier down to fifth, and then cru bourgeois beneath those. The exact structure of naming and ranking can differ from region to region, but the same principles generally apply.

THE PRICES

For French wines, you can pay the highest prices in the world for the rarest vintages of the most famous labels. You can also buy an ocean of wine for $10 a bottle or less, from exceptional to dismal. You can also have a good selection of Beaujolais, petits châteaux Bordeaux, Rhônes, and simple Burgundies for $20. If you pop for another $20 you should be able to buy most current vintages of minor châteaux in Bordeaux and most Champagnes. Older vintages, prestige cuvées, and first growths will cost you $100 or more. Do remember that French prices should be sensitive to the exchange rate. During periods that the dollar is strong, importers should have been able to buy at a good price and your $20 bill should buy you a better bottle of wine.

THE VINTAGES

No one prizes vintages like the French. The weather does change dramatically year to year and from region to region: too wet in Bordeaux, too cold in Burgundy, or too hot along the Rhône. These changes will affect both the quality and the quantity of that year's harvest—and the price.

Great vintages are often over-inflated in reputation and price, and conversely, good wines can be undervalued in vintages officially deemed "poor." Although even bad producers can make good wine in good years, the good producer can usually make pretty good wine in a bad year, as well as great wine in a good year. Most fine French wines are released while still young, two or three years old at most. Most vintages show their greatness much later in life, but they will have to wait in your cellar until that happy day. As a rule, remember the 1980s plus 1990 and '95. It was a great string of vintages with the closest to a dud being 1984 (Orwell was right) and 1987; 1985 and the 1988, '89, and '90 were especially good. Nothing in the '90s compares; 1995 is the best.

If you want to show off for the rest of your life, commit one of these years to memory: 1961, 1966, and 1976. A cabernet from one of those great years could still be good many years later.

FINDING **YOUR** WAY

An extended drinking tour of all the wine country of France would later require an extensive stay in alcohol rehab. Your mind would whirl from the endless streams of names and rivers of wine. Somewhere around the Loire Valley, you honestly would believe you could speak French. Why else would they always be filling your glass?

If you actually go to France, you in fact will learn the great wines of the world. Better still, if you don't go, you can buy really good wines on the cheap because you (1) bought this book and (2) kept a couple of rules in mind.

Only 35 percent of the wines produced in France are AOC. (For a label-reading refresher, see Chapter 2, "Basic Training.") The names can vary in how they are phrased on the label: Appellation Mâcon-Villages Contrôlée or Appellation Vouvray Contrôlée; all mean the wines have a solid chance of being good. And because the foreign exchange rate favors the dollar, the wines can cost less than $8 a bottle.

This has the obvious reward: you save money. But you also have the satisfaction of enjoying the hard work of the French without having to pay much for it.

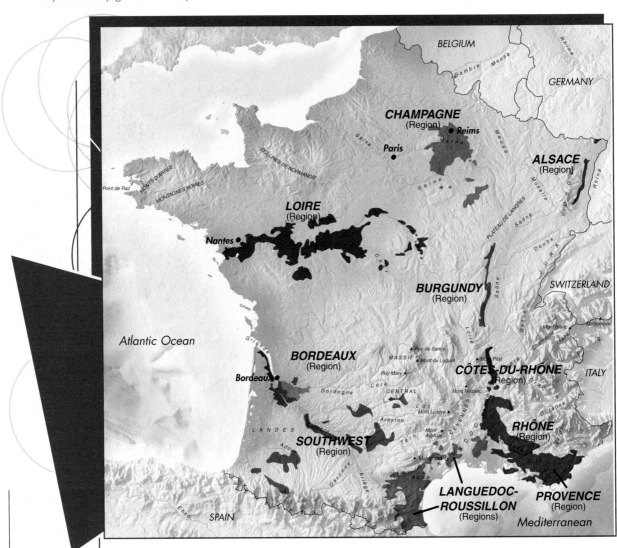

BORDEAUX:
COME TO THE CABERNET

The fame and dominance of French wine probably starts here, in this ancient port city in the southwest corner of France, almost to Spain, and about as far from Paris as you can get. You'll know why before you visit a single famous château, for the destiny of geography is obvious. It is warm here, blissfully mild almost any time of year. The summer days are long and nightfall almost always means a sweater or jacket. The central role of the rivers that define the land and its history is inescapable.

Here on the banks of the Garonne, sixty miles inland from the Atlantic, the city of Bordeaux is a terrific harbor and has been since the Middle Ages. Walk among the cafes

That was almost one thousand years ago, and it involves a love story, or what passed for one. Remember Eleanor of Aquitaine? The dowry of French territory she brought to King Henry included Bordeaux, as well as Aquitaine and most of western France. Along came the wines, and at bargain prices.

By the time the English were expelled three hundred years later, England's favorite wine was claret and Bordeaux had a new industry established. Many vineyard areas of Bordeaux were already prestigious by the 1500s. They built a tradition of reds, distinctively

Words for wine:

Cru means growth or property in French. Grand and Premier are supposed to be best, but bourgeois and exceptional can be good buys.

Cru listings:
Burgundy
Bordeaux
Alsace

and wine cellars that still line the quays here, and you are standing where much of the world got its first taste of the marvelously mild blends of Bordeaux. Certainly the British did.

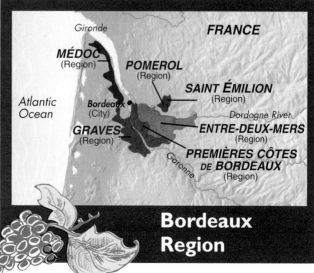

Gironde

FRANCE

MÉDOC
(Region)

POMEROL
(Region)

SAINT ÉMILION
(Region)

Atlantic
Ocean

Bordeaux
(City)

Dordogne River

ENTRE-DEUX-MERS
(Region)

GRAVES
(Region)

Garonne

PREMIÈRES CÔTES
DE BORDEAUX
(Region)

**Bordeaux
Region**

mild, rich, and velvety, and unlike some French wines, they are the product of a blend of up to five grape varieties. The most famous are cabernet sauvignon and merlot, but petit verdot, cabernet franc, and malbec are grown as well. The mixture varies within the region and at each château. Because the wine is a blend, each property produces only one red (although a few make a cheaper version from lesser grapes).

In theory each grape contributes something to the Bordeaux: red-softness from the merlot, perfume from the petit verdot, black color from the malbec. Yet because each grape matures differently—cabernet franc and merlot are harvested earlier than cabernet sauvignon—the mix also provides insurance if bad weather cripples one of the varieties. Some vintages may see the proportions shift, others may be perfect balances, or happy accidents.

They are exceptionally long-lived, and because sediment accumulates, they have long been sold in bottles with sharply defined shoulders, which ideally catches the dregs while the pure wine is poured out the neck. This Bordeaux bottle is used around the world for cabernet and other wines that aspire to the Bordeaux style.

The whites of Bordeaux are two. The most common is a crisp white, made of sauvignon blanc and usually some sémillon. The most exquisite (and expensive) is an opulent dessert wine made of the same grapes, but only in years when vineyard conditions are just right. While Bordeaux's basic wine types are few, there are hundreds of châteaux and other wine-producing properties. The myriad choices have been organized extensively by geography and quality rankings.

The geography is fairly simple thanks to the rivers that form a "Y" dividing the area into basic wine regions: the Garonne, on which Bordeaux sits, and the Dordogne, a little to the north. A few miles below the city of Bordeaux, they join together into the Gironde, a long estuary that broadens as it flows into the Atlantic Ocean. This area is largely flat and enjoys a mild climate warmed by the Gulf Stream.

To make a clockwise tour of the area, head north from Bordeaux and stay on the "left bank" of the Gironde. You are in the Médoc, largest and best known of the red wine regions. Cross the Gironde, and on the "right bank" there is more luscious red wine in St. Émilion and Pomerol. The area that lies in the fork of the "Y" is named with some exaggeration, Entre-Deux-Mers (between two seas), and is the home of ordinary white wine.

Cross back over to approach the city from the southeast side and you are in the best country (Graves and Sauternes) for white wine, both sweet and dry. It's also one of the few places that produces both reds and whites. All of this is rigorously classified by appellations, from broad Bordeaux AC to smaller regions such as Médoc AC, down to individual villages or communes.

Remember: Look to Pauillac and the rest of the Médoc for more cabernet sauvignon; turn to St. Emilion and Pomerol for merlot, and Graves for dry whites.

What distinguishes Bordeaux further is the cru ranking, which was born here in 1855. As part of a grand exposition promoting French food and wine, Bordeaux merchants designated 61 red wines of the Médoc as grand crus or great growths and ranked them in five categories. The rest they classed as grand cru exceptional or cru bourgeois. Those designations are on the bottles today.

Before you protest that much has changed since 1855, including the lands owned by some of the vineyards, remember that one hundred fifty years is not so long a time in a wine trade that dates back seven or eight centuries. The four châteaux ranked at the top in 1855 were already old favorites: Lafite-Rothschild, Latour, Margaux, and Haut-Brion. They had been singled out for praise by connoisseurs since Samuel Pepys and Thomas Jefferson. And the Bordeaux merchants based their rankings on the prices these wines commanded in the marketplace.

Price still fascinates wine fans today: They love to insist that a first growth is no longer worth top price or that a third growth is a better buy. Yet most are thankful to have the 1855 rankings as a starting point. Combine the rankings with the geography and Bordeaux begins to make sense.

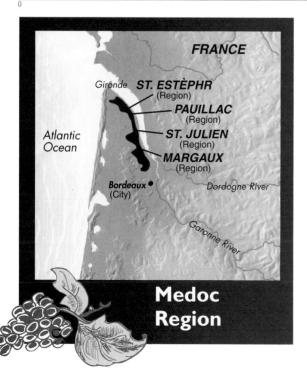

Medoc Region

FRANCE

Gironde **ST. ESTÈPHR**
(Region)

PAUILLAC
(Region)

Atlantic Ocean

ST. JULIEN
(Region)

MARGAUX
(Region)

Bordeaux •
(City)

Dordogne River

Garonne River

CABERNET TO THE LEFT

The Médoc region on the left bank is the largest collection of red wine vineyards, and they stretch from the city along the Gironde practically to the Atlantic. The land here is so low that it was marsh and cornfield until Dutch merchants devised a way to drain it. Here the wines are made largely with cabernet, which grows well in the stony gravelly soil, holding the heat it needs for slower ripening. Running north from here is the chain of small villages filled with grand cru vineyards. The first village you come to is the one to remember—Margaux. It is home to the first growth of the château of the same name and more grand cru vineyards of all ranks than any other village. Also, look for unranked châteaux from here and neighboring Cantenac-Margaux for good buys.

The other name to memorize (and look for on less expensive bottles) is the appellation of Pauillac. This is the address of Lafite-Rothschild, Latour, as well as Mouton-Rothschild (a former second-growth elevated to first in 1973, the only change in the classification since 1855). Other names you may have heard of come from here too, such as Lynch-Bages and Pichon-Longueville.

In between are two other villages with famous residents. St. Estèphe is the home of Cos d'Estournel,

Montrose, and Calon-Segur. St. Julien is the site of Léoville, Beychevelle, and a number of other well-ranked properties that are less well known.

Wines made from grapes picked from unranked vineyards throughout the area are sold as Médoc AOC. A better grade and better buy are wines from the southern half of the area, near the most prestigious châteaux. Wines from this section are labeled Haut-Médoc AOC.

MERLOT ON THE RIGHT

On the far side of the Gironde, the Bordeaux blend is made soft and rich with merlot. Here the soil has more clay, which is colder and wetter, but the merlot vines don't mind and grow well in the two regions on this side, Pomerol and St. Emilion.

St. Emilion is the prettiest wine village in Bordeaux, a small collection of tiled roof buildings on low hills in the middle of what is the largest appellation in the region. Since the 1855 classification covered only the west bank, St. Emilion created its own ranking in 1955, rating the top vineyards as premier grand crus classes and a slightly lesser group as grand cru classes. Most famous of the first growths here are Cheval Blanc, Bel-Air, Canon, and Figeac.

Neighboring Pomerol, however, is the smallest appellation in Bordeaux. Pomerol has no official classification system and doesn't really need one; its wines are few and expensive. There is little doubt which is the top ranked. The wines from the twenty acres or so of Pétrus managed by the Moueix family are the most expensive in Bordeaux. It is also one of the safest of show-off purchases, a luxuriously soft wine, almost all merlot blended with a little cabernet franc. Pomerol's other wines, however, are worth searching out.

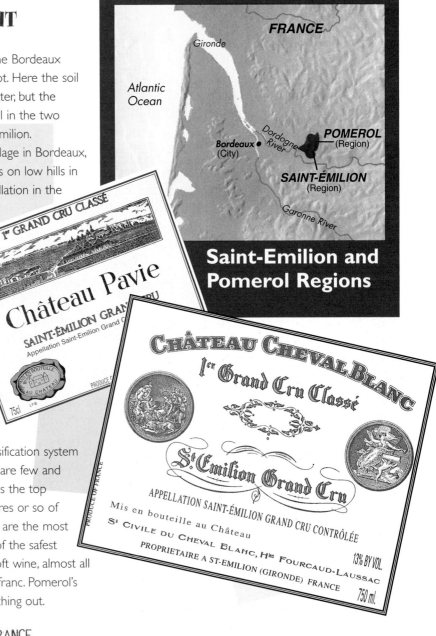

Saint-Emilion and Pomerol Regions

BORDEAUX WHITES

Skipping over Entre-Deux-Mers—and there is little reason to dawdle—you are back on the west side of the Garonne. South of the city is the one region that produces the essence of all three of Bordeaux's great wines.

The name Graves is most often heard describing Bordeaux's crisp, austere white wines that are the best example of sauvignon blanc. But the gravelly soil here probably produced the original Bordeaux wines, mostly cabernet sauvignon, as stony to the taste as the Graves whites. The vineyards here are among the oldest and most prestigious in Bordeaux, including Haut-Brion, which makes first growth white as well as red.

Not far away is another treasure, Sauternes, where the same white grapes work a special magic in the fall of most years. Mists rising off the rivers hang in the morning air and encourage a fungul growth, botrytis cinerea "noble rot" on the grapes. The fungus pierces

SHOPPING 101

There is generic Bordeaux AOC, both red and white, under $10 but the region's lowest shelf lacks the quality to compete with other inexpensive varietals.

Step up a grade to AOC wines from the Haut Médoc region, surrounding districts like the Libourne, or individual communes such as St. Estèphe, and you can get good reds in the $15 range. If you're lucky, you can find a few petits châteaux for not much more. Stick to Pomerol and St. Emilion if you like merlot; switch to Pauillac and other west bank communes for more cabernet blends. Current vintages from '94 on are good value and worth keeping, but '95 is the one that gets the hype and the money.

You can get a good taste of the crisp whites of Graves for $15, and a half-bottle of modest Sauternes or Barsac for not much more.

When buying Bordeaux in a restaurant, pick a less expensive château from Haut-Médoc, Lalande-Pomerol, or St. Emilion. Look for the oldest good vintage they have—anything in the '80s, except '87 or '84, will do.

the skin and lets out water, which increases the ratio of sugar to water. The rich golden wine that results has been a delight for centuries and makes d'Yquem among the most sought after today.

In the meantime you should seek out other Sauternes and half-bottles–or look for less expensive wines from neighboring Barsac as well.

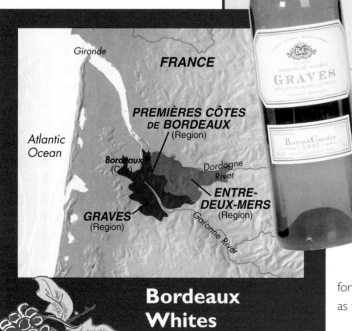

Bordeaux Whites

BURGUNDY: SEARCHING FOR TREASURE

To appreciate the glory of Burgundy you need only look at the grand old Hospices de Beaune in the middle of the narrow medieval streets. At this point you are already halfway through the Côte d'Or, the long, skinny valley that is the prestigious heart of Burgundy.

Here, looking up at the gables of what was once a hospital in the 15th century, the tradition of wine making is inescapable. The building's half-timbered construction may seem English Tudor or even German; surely the weather here must be colder than Bordeaux. It is, and that coolness is a critical factor in Burgundy's greatness—and its weakness. The wonderful intricacy of colored tiles on the roof brings to mind the same complexity you will find in the fields of pinot noir and chardonnay vines.

To call Burgundy France's second wine region would be to join the longest-running debate in wine. The only agreement is that it is different, very different, from Bordeaux, in size, climate, and organization. If Bordeaux's wines are velvet, Burgundy's are like silk, lighter and sleeker. Who is to say which is more beautiful?

You can only say that the fine wines of Burgundy are more rare, which enhances the pleasure of finding one. The vineyards and production here are far smaller than in Bordeaux. There are no grand châteaux, only domaines, small *clos* (a walled vineyard) and parcels so small a grower may own only five or ten rows in a given vineyard. Growers, whether small holders or larger domaines, can make and bottle their own wine or sell to a négociant or larger winery. Treacherous weather cuts the number of good vintages dramatically.

Accordingly the price of basic wine can be high, $25, and of great wines astronomical, $1,000.

The grape varieties are limited too, again unlike Bordeaux. Reds are made from pinot noir and whites from chardonnay. What distinguishes one Burgundy from another is whatever genius the winemaker brings to the terroir, the taste of the land that seems to reach up through these vines.

Burgundians revere terroir and guard it jealously, a tradition that dates back centuries and is reflected in the ancient names and complicated ownership of the vineyards.

> "The only way to understand Burgundy is to come to Burgundy, and ... not only to come to Burgundy with a jacket and tie. It's to come with boots on and definitely to have the boots dirty."
>
> -Pierre Henri Gagey, Winemaker

Burgundy Region

FRANCE • Beaune

Saône River Doubs River

SWITZERLAND

Saône River

Rhône River

• Lyon

The wines made of grapes from throughout the region are sold as Bourgogne AOC, or a better grade, Bourgogne Passe-tout-grains. Then there are wines of various villages, and of individual vineyards. In Burgundy the best vineyards of white and red grapes fall into two categories, grand cru classe, for the best, and premier cru classes for the others (in other words, first is second here).

In case you think you understand the system, beware that villages containing a famous grand cru vineyard may have unilaterally added the grand cru name to their own, such as Gevrey-Chambertin. It gets even more complex. After the French Revolution, the vast lands owned by the church in Burgundy, including its most famous vineyards, were redistributed to the peasants. Over the years they have been further divided among each generation of heirs, or simply bought and sold. As many as thirty different growers may own grape vines in a five acre vineyard and are entitled to make wines under the same name. Granted, they may only be able to make a barrel of that famous name.

Enter the négoçiants, and especially Burgundy's négoçiant-éleveurs. They buy the grapes, juice, and wine of hundreds of growers and "elevate" them into wine of passable quantity and sometimes much better than that. While many wine drinkers prefer to buy from a grower or domaine, which owns its own vineyards, others see the négoçiant as someone who can make sense and dependable wine out of Burgundy's chaos. For most, however, the real guide is American wine writer Robert Parker's *Wine Advocate*. Bordeaux was Parker's first love, but his homework on the latest from Burgundy alone is cheaper than a couple of mistakes. There are other Burgundy fanatics to help you, from *Wine Spectator's* Per-Henrik Mansson to Israeli Internet critic Yak Shaya.

CÔTE, CÔTES, & CÔTEAUX

CAN REFER TO HILLSIDES, COASTS, OR FRINGE AREAS.

CÔTE D'OR:
TREASURES RED AND WHITE

The best of Burgundy is in the north, first in Chablis, ninety miles south of Paris, and then on the golden slopes of the Côte d'Or along the auto-route.

Chablis is the place that was dishonored by American winemakers who used its name for cheap white wine until consumers learned to say, "I'll have a chardonnay, please." Taste a glass of true Chablis and you'll dismiss those ideas of radiator fluid in a hurry. Grapes grown in the limey hills of Chablis produce a pure, austere white wine. It is one of the great parts of Burgundy: Its grand crus are among the great white wines; its premier crus among the best buys.

The Côte d'Or is larger than Chablis, but you can get a basic grasp of it heading south along the A6 auto-route in an afternoon's drive from Dijon, the mustard town, down to Santenay.

On your right is an almost endless line of small hills, covered with vineyards all the way down the slope to the flatlands, facing southeast to catch as much sun as possible. Yet in this modest countryside, million dollar names pop up every kilometer or two.

In the first twenty miles of the Côte d'Or, the hills are called the Côte de Nuits, and the vineyards are full of pinot noir. The great wines here are red, indeed virtually all the grand cru red wines of Burgundy come from the northern half of the valley. First you drive through Gevrey-Chambertin, Morey-Saint-Denis. Chambolle-Musigny, Vougeot, and Vosne-Romanée. Stop in any and you will see signs pointing to the individual vineyards such as Le Chambertin or La Tache. Examine the vineyard more closely, and you'll see the rows of each grower.

You'll also pass through Fixin, a name worth remembering for premier cru reds and good village wine, and Nuits-St. Georges, which lacks a grand cru designation but not grand wines.

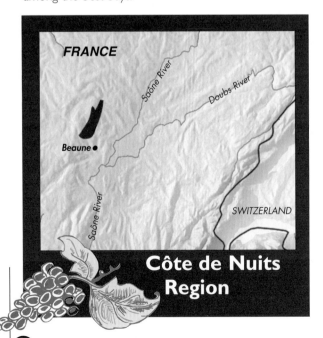

FRANCE

Saône River

Doubs River

Beaune •

Saône River

SWITZERLAND

Côte de Nuits Region

CÔTE DE BEAUNE:
CHARDONNAY'S FIRST HOME

Farther south is the Côte de Beaune. The white limestone exposed on the hillside signals that you have reached the vineyards that produce great white Burgundies.

There are reds, but only one grand cru, and it is in the first town we come to, Aloxe-Corton, a picturesque village at the base of the hill where Charlemagne once owned vineyards. It is then roughly at the dividing line of great reds and great whites we arrive in Beaune. The names treasured by chardonnay drinkers are here—the villages of Savigny-les-Beaune, Volnay, Meursault, and Santenay, and most famous of all, Le Montrachet.

The sunny hillside vineyard is so renowned for its richness that four other grand cru vineyards include Montrachet in their names, among them the communes of Puligny and Chassagne. There also are superb reds to be had here, without grand cru status, especially Volnay in the south.

The prestige and fashion may fade as we leave, but Burgundy does not end with the Côte d'Or, which is good news for most wallets.

For more affordable pinot noir, keep on going to the Côte Chalonnais, which sits back a little farther

Côte de Beaune Region

west from the river. Here the best names are Mercurey and Rully, which make wines both as villages and from premier cru vineyards.

Chardonnay drinkers get their shot again in the Mâcon. Most of the Mâcon's whites are best sold as village wines, but the vineyards in Pouilly-Fuissé are the stuff of grand crus and St. Véran is a good source for bargains.

BEAUJOLAIS: MORE THAN A ONE-NIGHT STAND

Still farther down the river, and debatably within Burgundy, are the vineyards of Beaujolais. Technically it's Burgundy, but it's more like the region's outback. This is where an early duke of Burgundy banished the gamay grape hundreds of years ago. You can forgive the Beaujolais for smiling: They've done quite well in the briar patch with that gamay grape.

So what about Beaujolais nouveau, is it a joke? No, not for the people of Lyon and the surrounding area. They have long enjoyed getting light, bright wine by the barrel for their basements and bistros as soon as the fermenting wine stopped bubbling. And not for the winemakers of Beaujolais who cooked up the race to Paris with the first "nouveau" wine more than fifty years ago.

But the laugh is on many consumers: the cost of promotion and airfare pushes very simple wine to $10 or

> **Words for wine:**
>
> When "Villages" is appended to the name of a region, such as Mâcon or Beaujolais, it means the wine comes from a small group of select villages in the region.

SHOPPING 101

The price of real Burgundy, red or white, will always be high: $200 a bottle and up for grand cru at retail is the going rate. So never pass up a chance to drink Burgundy at a tasting—or if someone else is paying.

At the other end of the scale, the broad Bourgogne AOC may cost $15 retail for generic pinot noir or chardonnay. Better to spend that money on cru Beaujolais or Chalonnais reds or a chardonnay from the Mâcon. For another $10, you can find some village wines and premier cru, but always look for a good producer and a good year. Best recent years were 1995 and 1996 and before that the string from 1988 through 1990.

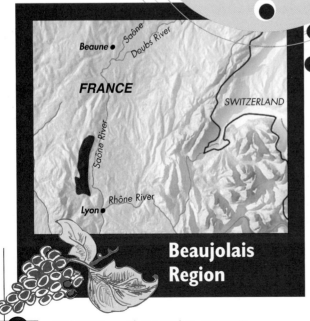

Beaujolais Region

more a bottle. That's not a high price for a day to celebrate wine, but it shouldn't distract consumers from Beaujolais' real wines. They cost only a little more and are twice as good.

True Beaujolais is gamay at its elegant best, and like most reds, is released in the first year after harvest. The best grades are Beaujolais-Villages, from the better growing areas, and the cru Beaujolais, from the eleven top growing areas, which vary from cheery strawberry flavors to surprisingly forceful reds. When good, they are the Burgundy for everyone.

THE RHÔNE: RIVER TO THE SUN

From Lyon, keep heading south toward the Riviera but switch auto-routes to the A7, and you are on another of France's great wine rivers, the Rhône. It's lined with fabled names like Hermitage and

Rhône Region

Châteauneuf-du-Pape, and awash in ancient history from the early Romans to the popes of Avignon. You are, indeed, closer to Italy.

For many wine drinkers it is a new adventure: After Bordeaux and Burgundy, the Rhône feels warmer and livelier, and so do its wines. Rhône wines are proudly different with the bolder tastes and stronger fragrances of the south; the reds can be spicy, the whites rich, and the rosés stunning. But the taste is not simple or crude; it is a careful blend.

Centuries of winemakers here took France's less well-known grapes and gave them great sophistication and finesse. If you wish to see the models for Australia's shiraz or America's Rhône rangers, here they are.

The Rhône vineyards divide conveniently in two, each with claims to fame and value. The landmark in the north is Hermitage, named for a hermit, not a palace; in the south it is Châteauneuf-du-Pape, named for the home of those curious French popes of the 1300s.

In the northern Rhône, syrah is strong, so strong and rich, in fact, that it is often blended with a touch of viognier or other white grapes. The best is red Hermitage, a wine that is elegant, powerful, and highly regarded since Roman times. More affordable and easier to drink syrah blends come from Côte Rôtie, St. Joseph, and Crozes-Hermitage; the sturdiest straight syrahs come from Cornas.

The whites of Hermitage and Côte Rôtie can be just as distinct, with bouquets full of fruit, flowers, and honey. Condrieu is the finest of the Northern Rhône whites and available with a touch of sweetness or completely dry.

Farther south, the vineyards are a carnival of grape varieties. The stern syrah here has been displaced by grenache, a light-hearted but gutsy grape and a host of others—mourvèdre, cinsault, and carignane. They mingle easily with white counterparts like muscat and viognier.

Nonetheless they come together, as many as thirty different grapes, to make Châteauneuf-du-Pape, the southern Rhône's most famous red. As is the Rhône custom there is a white, also blended, that has considerable body and aroma. The other big name here is Gigondas, which is made largely of grenache and is usually softer. The best of the less expensive wines here are Côtes du Ventoux and Côtes-du-Rhône-Villages (from the best villages in the Côtes-du-Rhône).

Given the hot summers and the abundance of red grapes (and blendable whites) this is good rosé country. The famous one is Tavel, one of the most expensive rosés in the world, but the others are better values. Try them if you see them. When shopping, look for wines from '88-'90 and '95 throughout the region. Latest great vintages in the making are 1996 from the north and 1998 from the south.

LOIRE:
MORE THAN JUST A PRETTY PLACE

If you can visit one region in France, even for a day trip, make it the Loire for the wine and food, as well as the châteaux. The châteaux are not the nice little mansions of Bordeaux, but grand châteaux of Chinonceaux, Chinon, with real crenellated castles sitting atop Rabelaisian medieval towns. They dot a beautiful countryside of richfarmland, trout-rich rivers, and

SHOPPING 101

Except for Sancerre, Loire wines are relatively inexpensive although not widely available, so try them when you get a chance. They make fine everyday wines, soft enough for a family gathering where everyone can enjoy a glass. In some French restaurants, Vouvray chenin blanc and reds from the region may be the best value, if the restaurateur knows the region.

Atlantic Ocean

FRANCE

Nantes

Orléans

Loire River

Char River

Loire Region

royal game preserves. There is good wine hunting here for value, especially for lovers of white wine. The wines of the Loire lack prestige, but they are almost always good.

You can while away a day or two along the course of the river, follow it all the way to the Atlantic, and taste a surprising range of wines.

The Loire's vineyards begin not too far from Burgundy. The white grape of preference is sauvignon blanc, which excels here. Although the weather is cooler than Bordeaux, it makes a crisp, almost smoky wine, in Sancerre and Pouilly-Fumé. (Perhaps Robert Mondavi got the name fumé blanc here; don't confuse it with Pouilly Fuissé, a chardonnay from Burgundy.)

As the Loire heads west into Touraine, the châteaux seem to embrace every bend in the river, and the wines begin to change. The whites are made of chenin blanc, a neglected grape that's at its best and most diverse here, producing wines of significant aging potential.

In Vouvray, the vineyards sit above the river on chalky cliffs, in which the winemakers have dug caves to store their bottles. The wines are just as ingenious: Vouvray chenin can be dry, sweet, or sparkling, and sometimes in between.

Touraine reds are not so well known or available, but make for easy drinking. They are made from cabernet franc and gamay, between Bordeaux and

Beaujolais in style, and are good food wines. The best are from Chinon or Bourgeuil, and if you're there during the game season, try to stay for dinner. Farther west in Anjou the red wines made with cabernet franc get darker and richer. They also get a little pink, for Anjou is the major source of French rosé. It also makes some of the best chenin blancs in Savennières.

Last, just before the Loire reaches the Atlantic salt flats, it provides still another distinct white wine, muscadet, dry as a fishbone and the world's best match for oysters. Muscadets should be inexpensive; the best are from Sèvre-et-Maine and look for any others that say they were made "sur lie," meaning the wine remained with skins and yeast for extra flavor.

THE SOUTH OF FRANCE

What could be more exciting, or less exact, than the south of France? Whether you mean the romantic fantasies of life in Provence, or the entire Midi, along the Mediterranean coast all the way to

Catalonia, or up into the rustic mountains that reach almost to Bordeaux, it is another world from northern France, so foreign it once had a distinct language; the natives said "oc" for yes instead of "oui," hence Languedoc and Pays d'Oc.

FRANCE

● *Montpellier*

● *Beziers*

Aude River

Mediterranean

Spain

Languedoc-Roussillon Region

Although grapes have grown here for thousands of years, they were cultivated more for bulk than style. The South was for fun, not serious wine drinking. The local wine might be acceptable on holiday; its rustic grapes would show up in the north only in supermarket jugs as vin de table or vin de pays.

In the last twenty years, however, it has become the nouvelle California franchise, especially Languedoc-Roussillon, which literally threw out the past. They tore out old fashioned grapes and replanted with France's better known grapes. Creaky musty old wineries were replaced with shining stainless steel. Australian winemakers flew in to show how to cater to the global palate, and the sun in the south of France arose on a new day.

Now, even American wineries facing shortages come here to buy wine. The region is ripe with wines of good fruity flavor, smooth drinkability, and affordable prices, old as well as new. The best and most distinct local wines remain, while the new wave replaces the worst of the old vin de table. These are the vineyards where Fortant de France, Michel Picard, and Val d'Orbieu do their thing.

In the vast expanse of Languedoc stretching from the Rhône to the Spanish border and the Pyrennees, there are a number of enclaves with proud long-standing blends of carignane and grenache. Minervois and St.-Chinion make the best and smoothest. But Fitou and Corbières can produce very good wines too. Dessert wine lovers who explore Languedoc-Roussillon will find luscious and affordable vin doux, from apricoty muscats to the red Banyuls that turn the southern grapes into a near port.

Leave the Mediterranean and make your way slowly up into the rugged southwest and you will find yourself not in the Midi but on the frontier of Bordeaux. Indeed many Bordeaux grapes were planted here long before any new wave, perhaps even before the Médoc. The wines of Bergerac, for instance, are as Gascon as Cyrano's nose and as proud as his wit; merlots and even dessert wines are styled after Sauternes. Nearby Cahors won fame for its wine making with malbec, so intense in flavor and color they called it black, not red, wine.

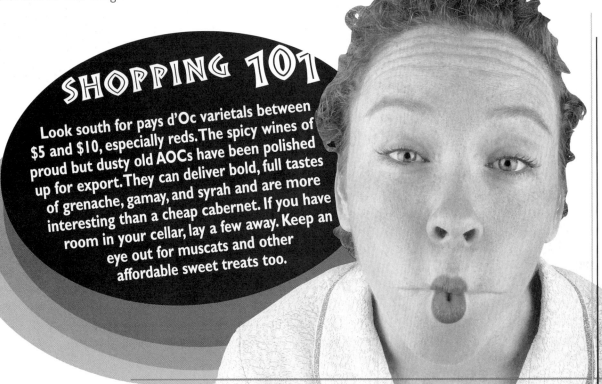

SHOPPING 101

Look south for pays d'Oc varietals between $5 and $10, especially reds. The spicy wines of proud but dusty old AOCs have been polished up for export. They can deliver bold, full tastes of grenache, gamay, and syrah and are more interesting than a cheap cabernet. If you have room in your cellar, lay a few away. Keep an eye out for muscats and other affordable sweet treats too.

ALSACE: GERMAN GRAPES, FRENCH ACCENT

If you're a white wine drinker who's getting bored with chardonnay, even the chardonnay of white Burgundy, head east toward Germany. Not all the way, but cross the mountains and stop just short of the border, and you will be in a ten-mile plain, the Rhine valley, and still in France.

If Alsatian wine could talk, its French-German accent would be a charmer. Certainly its taste and smell are striking products of an unusual intermarriage, the crisp dry tartness of French wine making offset by the familiar floral bouquet of riesling and gewürztraminer. Alsatian wines are such good food wines, they not only go with sauerkraut, they elevate choucroute to a gourmet meal.

In the last ten years Alsatian wines have become the rage with U.S. wine drinkers, who get a thrill out of the perfume of German grapes but insist they don't like German wines or a hint of sweetness.

This international character is so imprinted on the geography and history that Strasbourg is not only the Alsatian capital of the province, but the seat of the European Union.

On a wine map, the similarities to Germany are inescapable. This is cool country, farther north than any French vineyards except Champagne. Physically it has the same sun-embracing western hillsides as the Rheinpfalz to the north.

Alsace Region

LA!

Although Alsace was only a part of Germany briefly, the grapes and traditions of German wine linger. These are the only fine French wines sold in tall, swan-necked bottles and identified by the varietal name of the grape and with no real fuss about vineyard geography. About fifty vineyards wear the designation of "grand crus" on their labels (granted twenty some years ago); otherwise they say simply Alsace.

There's no mistaking them. The gewürztraminer and riesling have all the aroma of peaches, honey, and flowers you would expect with the same crisp acidity of German or American versions. Yet they are fermented much drier. Alsace also makes pinot gris, sometimes called tokay, which is pinot grigio but spicier and far more interesting than the Italian version. Similarly, pinot blanc has more character than it does elsewhere in France. Usually, pinot blanc, sylvaner, and lesser grapes are better in a unique Alsatian blend called Edelzwicker.

Alsace does indulge in a little sweetness, but not to the rigorous degree of German winemakers. The late harvest Alsatian wine is labeled Vendange Tardive; richer wines made from individual grapes are sold as Sélection de Grains.

CHAMPAGNE:
SPARKLING IN THE CHILL

The gaiety and vitality that bubble up from a glass of Champagne rise from what might be the least likely corner of France. It's a chilly land that lies between Paris and Belgium, well north of the fragile vineyards of Burgundy or Alsace. Were it not for Champagne, the region around Reims and its massive cathedral might be best known as an important site during World War I.

Champagne Region

But the Great War is but a brief episode in the five glorious centuries of Champagne.

Despite the cold, wet, unpromising terrain, or maybe because of its difficulties, Champagne is the perfect place to make wine with this verve.

Winemakers around the world can put bubbles into bottles to make wines sparkle, but nowhere are they as hard to make as in Champagne. Its only real asset is the chalky soil, much like Burgundy's, for the vines of chardonnay, pinot noir, and pinot meunier. These three grapes, two red and one white, make the wine.

These are France's northernmost vineyards, and the weather is terrible for the grape growers here. It is so cold frost can last into spring and return in the fall; rain comes at the worst times, knocking off the first blossoms in spring and hampering the harvest with mold and mud. The grapes must be picked by hand and crushed very carefully.

Despite these difficulties the vineyards allowed to produce grapes for Champagne are limited and tightly controlled. Only sparkling wine from this small area may be called Champagne; bubbly from others parts of France is called Crémant or Mousseux. (Champagne houses themselves have vineyards around the world making similar wines, but they do not call them Champagne either.)

Where Burgundy may have good vintages and bad, Champagne blends most years' crops into an undated, non-vintage wine. At best, only one year in four should be good enough to wear a vintage date. Thus the most valued talent of winemakers in the great Champagne houses is in blending, to take each year's widely varying crops, ferment them, and blend the wines to match an ongoing house style.

Giving Champagne its distinction and sparkle is the laborious process in the cellars known as the *methodè traditionelle*. Winemakers pour the wine and a mixture of wine sugar and yeast into bottles and cap them tightly so that the wine and yeast will ferment again. When the yeast turns the sugar into alcohol, two byproducts are captured in the bottle: the carbon dioxide that will form the bubbles and the unsightly debris of dead yeast cells that settle out as sediment. Although the yeast cells add flavor, winemakers eventually want to remove them while keeping the fizz.

This crucial step is the job of a corps of workers called *rémuers*, or riddlers, who perform a tedious art that is nonetheless the most impressive thing you'll ever see in a wine cellar. As the second fermentation begins, the necks of the bottles are stuck in slanted holes in wooden racks. At first, the bottles are parallel to the floor. For the next two months, the riddler will rotate each bottle by hand to loosen the sediment and encourage it to collect in the neck. At each turn the angle will change and at the end of two months, the bottle will be inverted. It will age upside down for a year with all the sediment piled up in the neck.

Removing the sediment is explosively exciting. Workers remove the bottles and stick the necks into a

> "Nothing is easy for the vines here. Vines struggle to survive many foes, many enemies and the result is an extraordinary white wine."
>
> —Claude Taittinger, Champagne.

freezing solution. Then the wine is disgorged: When the cap is removed, the carbon dioxide that has been bottled up inside blows the frozen sediment out of the bottle. At that moment workers move quickly to reseal the bottle with a permanent cork, while replacing any lost wine and adding the final ingredient. It is a syrup that will set

"When you drink Champagne, you don't drink only the wine. In fact you enjoy the region. You have the region in your nostrils. You have the region in your glass."
-Andre Enders, Champagne

dispatching her yellow labels to the czar's court. Hype and history are not the only distinctions between houses. The significant difference you can taste is called the house style. Champagnes range from light and floral to full-bodied and almost toasty. (If you have the courage to admit you don't like Champagne, you may not have found the one for you—or you could be right: skip the bubbly.) Each Champagne house or brand has a style that is evident in their non-vintage year after year, and should be reflected in their premium wines as well.

For all the magic winemakers add in the cellars, grapes still determine the character of Champagnes. Tart chardonnay gives structure, pinot noir provides body, and pinot meunier delivers immediate aroma. Houses with a full-bodied style generally use more pinot noir.

the sugar level that determines the dryness of the Champagne. (On French bottles, sweetness ranges from crémant or demi-sec down to brut or extra brut for bone-dry.)

Whew. Small wonder that many wine regions have sought cheaper ways to make bubbly in bulk—or why true Champagne is a luxury product.

It has nonetheless been profitable and the foundation of the fortunes of dozens of famous houses or grand marques that dominate the trade. While the houses do little of their own grape growing, they realized the value of good marketing centuries ago, when Champagne Charlie Heidsieck was peddling bubbly around the U.S. and the widow Clicquot was

• **Vintage Champagne:**
This is made only in years when grapes ripen fully and each house makes that decision individually. The best grapes are held out to make a separate cuvée, or lot, rather than the house blend, and are usually aged longer. Vintages were widely declared in 1988 and 1990 and again in 1995 and 1996.

• **Rosé:**
Most are made with pinot juice left in contact with the skins long enough to pick up some color, although some is made pink by adding a still red wine to the bubbly white.

• **Blanc de noirs:**
In French, literally "white from black." A white wine made from black grapes, which usually gives it more body. The blanc de blancs is, as you might guess, more white grapes, in this case, chardonnay.

• **Tête de cuvée:**
The absolutely best grapes are saved for the house's best wine, which will get the fancy bottle and the $100 price tag. This may be vintage dated as with Moet & Chandon's Dom Perignon or non vintage such as Krug's Grande Cuvée. You may have bought one or been given one once in your life. That should be souvenir enough.

WINE DIARIES

"POUR" DE FRANCE

You should have known better than to book your "exclusive" tour of the best French vineyards over the Internet. But that's what you get for being lazy, not to mention getting sucked in by all that e-commerce hype you've seen so much of on the evening news lately. And, while you certainly had no trouble ordering the *Frommer's Guide to French Vineyards* off of Amazon.com, or even those nifty Andrea Bocelli CDs off of CDnow.com, booking a (very) expensive vineyard visit over the net was slightly more involved. Still, you keyed in your credit card number, packed your bags, and thought that just because your transcontinental tickets arrived overnight via FedEx, things would run just as smoothly once on foreign soil. Yeah, right.

But then, why would you have worried? The well-written brochure on the Virtual Vineyards Web site promised "An in-depth journey through the real French wine country." There were "captivating landscapes" to savor, "historical châteaux" to explore, and "boutique winemakers" to meet and greet. You were booked in a "cozy" villa and already drooling over the "authentic" meals and historical ambience you were sure to encounter for your whirlwind, six-day romp through the fertile French fields.

There was the stop in Champagne at Champillon, followed by a tour of the Trimbach vineyard in Ribeauville. Of course, you'd opted for the obligatory swing through the Burgundy region, followed by a dip into the Rhône Valley and a lingering stay in Provence, famous for its hilltop villages and the nearby Fontaine-de-Vaucluse, a spectacular resurgence of underground alpine water which inspired the term "vauclusian spring."

Think of the history, think of the culture, think of the food. And, of course, there was the wine. But you already knew all about that. You'd popped all the corks, read the labels, and enjoyed the fruity bouquets and heady aromas of the best France had to offer, in bottles anyway. Now you were ready for the real thing.

And so, arriving in Paris three hours late and being whisked away by a crusty old man with a penchant for speaking in a foreign language, you found yourself standing in a cramped hotel lobby surrounded by fellow tourists from all over the country, *your* country, all clutching the same, albeit misleading, Virtual Vineyards brochure.

There was no "personal tour guide with an approximate four guests to one guide ratio," as promised. No "friendly, congenial" interpreter, no complimentary wine and cheese "blow-out" in the cramped and humid hotel lobby. Only the usual list of customer complaints lobbed at a largely uncomprehending front desk clerk who looked to be not over the legal drinking age herself:

"But I was promised a non-smoking room."

"S'il vous plaît, mademoiselle, but why does the TV only get 3 channels? Don't you have HBO?"

"Let me get this straight? You're telling me that there's one bathroom, at the end of the hall, for all of us? But what about my sensitive bladder?"

You eventually check in, exchange misunderstood pleasantries and an obviously too-small tip with the bellhop and, thanks to numerous hours spent crammed into an economy seat on a transcontinental flight from hell, collapse onto a coffin-wide slab of a bed and promptly sleep through the very first vineyard tour of the morning.

Apparently, however, you weren't the only one. Half the "tour"-ists are still milling around the lobby when you finally emerge at noon, only to hear more grumbling about not enough room on the tour bus and grunted, misguided meanderings by a downtrodden young native in a Virtual Vineyards T-shirt whose sole English vocabulary seems to be the single word: overbooked.

Accordingly, you spend the rest of the afternoon watching *Green Acres* re-runs on the 8-inch TV in your room and thanking the good Lord that you remembered to pack granola bars, "just in case."

Eventually, however, after numerous hours spent trying to get an open line back to the Americas, you push past the same disgruntled customers in the lobby and, armed with enough francs to choke a horse, or at least grab a croissant or two, you forge forward on your misguided and now tardy "tour."

Fortunately, there is a quaint little café just down the street that looks dimly lit, approachable, clean, safe, friendly, and, most important, open. You walk inside to the surprised looks of what are obviously regular customers unaccustomed to seeing visitors. So much for the Virtual Vineyards claim to having been in business for over twenty-five years!

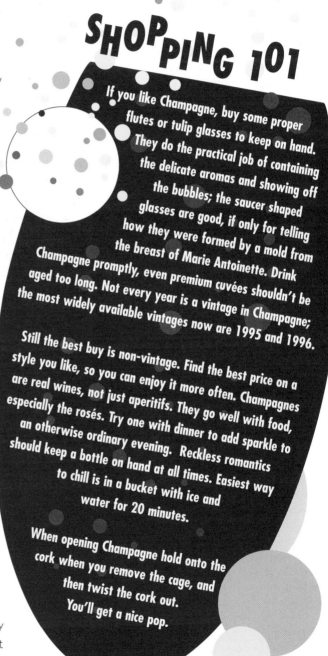

SHOPPING 101

If you like Champagne, buy some proper flutes or tulip glasses to keep on hand. They do the practical job of containing the delicate aromas and showing off the bubbles; the saucer shaped glasses are good, if only for telling how they were formed by a mold from the breast of Marie Antoinette. Drink Champagne promptly, even premium cuvées shouldn't be aged too long. Not every year is a vintage in Champagne; the most widely available vintages now are 1995 and 1996.

Still the best buy is non-vintage. Find the best price on a style you like, so you can enjoy it more often. Champagnes are real wines, not just aperitifs. They go well with food, especially the rosés. Try one with dinner to add sparkle to an otherwise ordinary evening. Reckless romantics should keep a bottle on hand at all times. Easiest way to chill is in a bucket with ice and water for 20 minutes.

When opening Champagne hold onto the cork when you remove the cage, and then twist the cork out. You'll get a nice pop.

You take a seat near the window, watching chubby tourists in their free T-shirts complain their way from souvenir shop to souvenir shop outside, and examine a menu written entirely in French. Where was your "personal 4:1 interpreter" when you needed him?

"Madame?" inquires a deep male voice somewhere well inside your personal space, surprising you as you try to decipher what sounded the least like fried calf's brains on the frustratingly French menu. "Comment allez-vous?"

Fortunately, you *did* take French in high school. Unfortunately, this is the only phrase you remember.

"Très bien, merci," you gush gleefully, surprising your young (not to mention handsome) waiter with a gush of fractured French. "Et vous?"

"Très bien," he smiles, before launching into a stupefying soliloquy of which you can understand nothing at all. Naturally, you don't let your waiter know any of this. You simply nod, smile, and do your best to order a medium priced glass of wine off the extensive and mostly unintelligible wine list.

Apparently, your background research pays off in at least this one respect, since your handsome waiter smiles and heads off to the bar to retrieve the first stop on your very own, personal Virtual Vineyard tour, sans complaining tourists, crowded buses, and "vauclusian springs."

Now, if only you could get your hands on an English-to-French dictionary. But then, you did have five whole days to find one. Surely, by then, you could learn how to proposition one very handsome waiter in his native tongue, er, language.

TOP 5-SIGNS YOU'RE ON A BAD FRENCH VINEYARD TOUR

5 BRAZIERS HAVE CHARCOAL BRIQUETTES STAMPED WITH AMERICAN FLAGS.

4 THE "RESTROOM" IS A COUPLE OF EMPTY WINE BOTTLES IN THE BROOM CLOSET.

3 OLD WINE BARRELS WORN AS EMPLOYEE UNIFORMS.

2 YOU'RE PRETTY SURE YOUR INTERPRETER'S LYING WHEN HE TELLS YOU ALL PARISIANS POINT WITH THEIR MIDDLE FINGER.

1 DAILY WINE TASTING INVOLVES PASSING A BOTTLE.

8 EIGHT
GERMANY,
THE MISUNDERSTOOD

Pity the poor winemakers of Germany. They labor in the most difficult climate, toughest conditions, strictest regulation, and the heaviest burden of misconception: Their country makes only beer, and its only wines are white, too sweet, and impossible to understand. (Who prints those labels? Gutenberg?)

We wine drinkers should pity ourselves, for these mistaken ideas deprive us of some of the lightest, most refreshing, perfectly balanced wines in the world.

To prove it, one U.S. importer has spent years touring American restaurants putting German wines up against the chef's choice of U.S. and French chardonnays course-for-course, and daring wine fans to compare the two. It's a winning demonstration. The crispness and fruit of good German riesling excites the palate and complements foods from Pacific Rim fusion to rich, creamy seafood.

Yet American wine drinkers and the German winemakers have been stuck in a bizarre tango. For a time we loved liebfraumilch, Blue Nun, May wine, Black Tower, and other whites of little flavor; then we decided that red wine was better for us. And we were told to never, ever admit that we like a little sweetness. We never bothered to learn about the good stuff. Mistake.

A FEW
CENTURIES
LATER

Germany does make far less wine than France, Italy, or Spain. And much of what it does make for export deserves a mediocre reputation. Yet Germany has made good and great wines treasured by connoisseurs for six or seven centuries. It still makes the world's longest lived white wines from riesling, which some critics argue is a better white wine grape than chardonnay. It makes the most luscious dessert wines of your dreams and refreshingly crisp everyday wines low in alcohol and calories.

To win back their reputation (and sales) the Germans have agonized through thirty years of clumsy changes in wine laws, toyed with new grapes, fallen in love with drier wine styles, and even borrowed a French trick or two. And a few have tried the unthinkable, designing understandable, even attractive labels. (Try harder, please.)

Nonetheless, you can understand German wines with only a little effort and you'll be delighted with the results. They're far better than liebfraumilch, which is pretty darn popular for a bad wine.

Some of the stereotypes may actually help. That mental image of tiny vineyards stretching among castles on staggeringly steep hillsides above the Rhine, for instance, is true. You can see this beautiful winescape in the cool autumn breeze on any tourboat down the river, and the experience is instructive as well as picturesque.

Germany is a cold, steep place to grow grapes. These vineyards high in altitude and latitude are among the world's coolest wine-growing regions. They are too cold for almost all red grapes and for many white ones as well. The grapes that do grow here have difficulty ripening and reaching full sugar content. Thus, German grapes produce wines that are lower in alcohol, rarely more than 9 percent compared to the more common range of 12 percent elsewhere, and 14 percent in the hottest regions. German grapes are often high in acidity, which gives the wines a refreshing tartness and backbone.

Because German summers are short, vineyards delay picking into the fall to get as much warmth and sugar as possible. Sometimes crews pick the ripest grapes individually and even leave some on the vine until they are covered by winter snows. To make up for the missing sugar in some inexpensive wines, winemakers keep some of the grape juice unfermented, and add it back into the wine to raise its residual sugar.

Grapes grow in greatest quantity and quality only in two areas, along the Rhine and Mosel Rivers. Vineyards are almost always planted on hillsides facing south to get the most of the day's sun and bask in the heat reflected by the rivers.

You probably already noticed that German wines come in either brown or green glass. Good observation.

The green bottles are for Mosel-Saar-Ruwer wines, which are faintly greener in color, and more spring-like and floral in flavor. The brown glass of the Rhine wines is an appropriate hint that their color and tastes are more golden and honeyed. German wine glasses have green and brown stems for the two kinds of wine for the same reasons, to magnify the distinctions of the wines.

THE PRICES

The cheapest bulk liebfraumilch starts around $5 but you can get a taste of better stuff, Mosels and Rhines of QbA (Qualitätswein bestimmter Anbaugebiete), quality wines from specified regions, for under $10. You'll find some QmP (Qualitätswein mit Prädikat), or wines with distinction, of kabinett grade (driest and least expensive) around $10 and get a decent selection of better grades and vineyards between $10 and $20. The best and richest wines cost ten times that.

THE GRAPES

There are relatively few grape varieties and the undisputed champion is riesling, the most expensive and delicious of German grapes. In the right vintage and with the right care, the tiny berries show their true magic, a perfect balance of fruit, acid, and sugar. But always they have an inviting aroma, ranging from apples and citrus before turning tropical and eventually to peaches and apricots, and eventually a pure nectar. In the crispiness at its center you can also taste the terroir of the sun and different soils: Some are flinty, others have a hint of slate.

The other white grapes are sylvaner, gewürztraminer (a spicy version of the traminer grape), and a host of hybrid versions of riesling. The most common is Müller-Thurgau, but the best and most riesling-like are kerner and scheurebe. A few parts of the country grow varieties of pinot, including pinot noir, called spätburgunder as Germany's main red grape.

THE LABELS

No wine labels in the world are harder to read than these. They are crowded with information, most of it in the Gothic blackletter typeface like Gutenberg used for his first Bible. Ironically, the labels are intended to be the most helpful, full of information for consumers that go way beyond the producer, geographic location, and vintage. Look close enough and you can even see the batch number used by the winery and government inspectors. It's all too much to the unfamiliar eye.

Most important to first-time buyers is the varietal name of the grape. Most German rieslings will now brag about what they are.

The official German wine geography is, however, not for the faint-hearted. The thirteen large wine regions are called Anbaugebieten and that name is printed on each label. Those broad categories, such as Rheingau or Franken, can give you useful clues.

Get more specific and it gets ugly and fuzzy quick. The next division is still a very large area called a Bereich. Each Bereich contains many Grosslagen, which are groupings of Einzellagen, the smallest vineyards. At one time Germany had 30,000 individually recognized vineyards, but wine reforms reduced the number to less than 3,000. Before you express a sigh of relief, that consolidation infuriated many German wine lovers, who complained that mediocre vineyards were now lumped in with the great ones. Well, they've got a point but you're not likely to sympathize with them much.

The bigger problem is that even at 3,000, none of the vineyards are ranked, and some larger divisions have stolen the names of famous vineyards. Ideally you should see a town name ending in -er, followed by a vineyard name, but the uninitiated can get easily confused. To make matters worse, each vineyard has many owners, just as in Burgundy.

"[Making wine] is like having children; you love them all, but boy, are they different."

—Bunny Finkelstein

On the other hand, the German labels have something very useful—a precise rating of quality, as measured by ripeness and expressed in jaw-breaking terms.

The lowest categories are similar to those in other countries: tafelwein or table wine, and landwein, a country wine from a particular region similar to vin du pays.

Above that is Qualitätswein or quality wine, which is where you should start. To be designated a quality wine, a wine must pass the approval of German laboratories and experts in blind tastings every year. Some critics say the judging is forgiving, but few other countries try anything like it.

Quality wine is divided into two categories. The largest and basic level is QbA or Qualitätswein bestimmter Anbaugebiete, meaning most of the wine comes from within one of those very large regions and has some of its characteristics.

The best category is QmP, Qualitätswein mit Prädikat, or quality wine with special character. The QmP wines are Germany's best and are further ranked, not surprisingly, by sugar and alcohol content. But don't be scared away—remember the acidity keeps them fresh. If you can't understand the German terms, remember these words and that the more complicated the word, the longer its life, and the richer the wine—and the higher the price tag.

TOP-5 SIGNS YOU'RE HAVING GERMAN WINE WITH DINNER

5 The delicate ceramic wine steins on the table.

4 What else goes with bratwurst, sauerkraut, and Black Forest cake?

3 It's a tradition whenever Nick-at-Nite runs a *Hogan's Heroes* Marathon.

2 Two words: Blue Nun.

1 Your boyfriend's dusting off his monocle again.

Kabinett: The lightest and most common category, usually at least 9 percent alcohol, the most common category of good German wine most Americans have with food.

Spätlese: Wine made from a late harvest of grapes, and consequently higher in sugar and alcohol, but also a good food wine.

Auslese: Wine made from a select late picking of the most ripe bunches, some of which may have botrytis cinerea, the noble rot. In some cases it may have 15 percent alcohol.

Beerenauslese: Rare wine made from a late picking of the ripest individual berries, often affected with noble rot, so sweet that the must may be 25 percent sugar and the wine could be 18 percent alcohol. Production varies with the vintages.

Trockenbeerenauslese: Even sweeter, and rarer, from the ripest grapes individually picked only in certain years. Some years there is none at all. This wine can be more than 21 percent alcohol and costs hundreds of dollars.

Eiswein: This wine is made from grapes left on the vine until January or February when they are frozen raisins, so their sugars are especially concentrated. It is not however, the sweetest of German wines; it is often exquisitely flavored, crisp, and clean, more like an auslese.

Got that? Good, now you can be told that Germany's making dry wines—and you can find the best of them in this same sweetness scale. Well, not quite the same. The QmP actually measures ripeness or sugar in the grapes at harvest time, but that sugar could be allowed to ferment into a drier wine.

When a QmP wine is made dry, it is labeled Trocken for dry or Halbtrocken for not quite so dry. The best are actually made from wines of spätlese quality, because it has enough body and flavor to make a fine wine without any sweetness.

Another category is sparkling wine, called Sekt in Germany. Most is made from cheap grapes, or wine imported from other countries and bottled by the bulk tank method. Better stuff is specified as Deutscher Sekt, which means it is made from German-grown grapes, and sometimes fermented in the bottle the way Champagne is.

SHOPPING 101

Skip the cheap stuff and stick with at least a QbA level, preferably one that specifies a varietal, preferably riesling. For a few dollars more you should have a good selection of QmP kabinetts and spätleses. Try one riesling from the Mosel, and another from the Rheingau. If you can find help knowledgeable about German wines, get wines from recommended vineyards, or look for the Charta mark, or the VDP black eagle.

Before you call them too sweet, serve them chilled with dinner, or at least as an aperitif. If you'd like to treat yourself to the ripe taste of Germany's sweetest achievements, expect to pay at least $20 and up for an auslese.

THE **VINTAGES**

Because of its northerly location, the amount of sunlight and rainfall is crucial to German wine, so vintages vary considerably. However, the German vineyards have had a great streak of luck from 1988 through 1990, and good but not great vintages since. If you want to talk great vintages, look back to 1983 and 1976.

Most qualitätswein is made to be drunk within a few years. Good kabinett wines are best after four or five years and QmP wines of auslese level and above can last decades, the best of them 50 years or more.

PRETTY BOTTLES:

Bottle colors and shapes are the first clues to German wines. Long necked green bottles are from the Mosel-Saar-Ruwer; brown ones from the Rhine. Flat round flagons are from Franken.

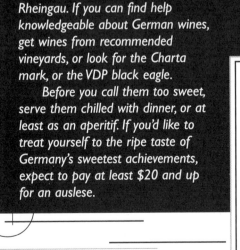

PIESPORTER DISORDER

At last, it's here. The time for your much-anticipated tour of German vineyards is finally at hand. You couldn't believe it when your boyfriend mentioned it, oh-so-casually, just last Saturday during your annual weekend wine tasting at the local country club.

"This time next week," he whispered in your ear after a quick trip to the rapidly filling spittoon, "you and I will be wandering leisurely through the best that Germany has to offer: Liebfraumilch, Spätlese, Riesling, Eiswein, and Mosels. Just you and me and the private tour guide I've hired for the duration of our trip."

Of course, this was really the first you'd heard that Germany was such a major player in the wine world. Unfortunately, you said this out loud.

"What?" he nearly shouted, dragging you away from the "inferior" domestic wines served up by your ritzy country club and setting you straight on the way to the free cheese and crackers. "Why, Germany is one of the hardest places in the world to grow wine, yet they manage to overcome harsh winters, semi-sweet grapes, and narrow vineyards to bottle some of the best whites in the world."

The German inquisition continued, however. You heard more about altitude, latitude, acidity, and backbone than you'd ever imagined could squeeze out past a mouth full of cheese and crackers. By the time he was through, you had a hard time believing anyone would drink anything *but* German wine.

All you could think of were those poor, German grape pickers standing on the side of a hill reaching up, up, and up to pick all those high-altitude grapes!

In the long run, however, the relevance of

Germany in the wacky world of wine was really of little consequence to you. You'd already tasted Blue Nun, after all. Who needed to go all the way to Germany just to taste more of the same?

Still, as soon as you heard the word "trip," you began packing. For an entire week, you checked the weather updates for any region bordering the Rhine and Mosel Rivers on the Internet! Packing accordingly, you were too embarrassed to inquire as to how long a stay you and your cosmopolitan beaux were undertaking. After all, every time you brought the subject up with your boyfriend, he would smile cryptically and simply give you his best Sergeant Schultz impression: "I see *noth*-ing, I know *noth*-ing!"

Of course, while this was cute and always worth a smile or two, it wasn't exactly illuminating. However, a free trip to Germany was a free trip to Germany, and

you weren't about to interrupt his (sort of) cute (sort of not) *Hogan's Heroes* imitation just to get nit-picky about details like travel arrangements, double beds, and ice buckets.

So you did what every other red-blooded American girl worth her salt would do in the same situation: Stuffed an overnight bag with as much as it could hold.

Either way, the day had finally dawned and you waited patiently in your living room surrounded by Internet printouts, German-to-English dictionaries, and colorful maps of the rugged German vineyards. You heard your boyfriend's honk (such a gentleman, but, in this case, you were more than ready to forgive him) and rushed out with your single bag.

Dashing off, you were barely settled before you saw him drive straight past the turn-off for the international airport. When you mentioned it, he assured you that this German vineyard tour was so "exclusive," so "private," that you had to charter transportation from the private airstrip on the edge of town.

Okay. Fine. Whatever. Germany, here we come. Of course, when he passed the tiny airstrip on the border of town, your sixth sense started kicking in. And, by the time you pulled into the potholed Bargain Bordeaux Bin parking lot just past the fabled airstrip, you were well on your way to about your seventh or eighth sense!

"What the—" you shouted as he turned the ignition off. "I thought we were touring the famous vineyards of Germany, fabled for their complex, honeyed, delicate, floral nectar." (Wow, you really *had* done your homework! You even impressed yourself.)

"We are, sweetheart," he said smoothly, grabbing your bag out of the back of his burgundy Yugo. "Inside these hallowed doors is one of the best selections of German wines this side of Frankfurt. Why do you think we had to drive so far out of town? You think the local liquor store has this kind of collection? They've got Liebfraumilch. They've got Auslese, and Beerenauslese, and Trockenbeerenauslese, and

even rare Eiswein. My God, don't you see the possibilities? I'm prepared to open your eyes to the big wine world, and all you can do is complain?

"And," he added slyly, hunching his own overnight bag over his crafty shoulder, "when we've completed our tour and made our selection, I've got us a room at the Motel 6 right next door. Then our 'exploration' can really continue."

Sighing, you toss your dog-eared English-to-German dictionary in the backseat and shake your head. Fine. Great. Whatever. There was bound to be a beer cooler someplace inside the state's biggest liquor store.

So instead of spending the evening staring into the endless black depths of the historic Rhine, you'll cozy up on a double bed with a six-pack of Lowenbrau and a twelve-inch TV.

Who knows, maybe there'll even be a *Hogan's Heroes* marathon on Nick-at-Nite.

FINDING **YOUR** WAY

WINE VALLEYS, GREEN AND BROWN

The Rhine is one of the world's great rivers and one of Germany's great wine rivers. Most of Germany's great vineyards lie along it or its tributaries. At one time, wine lovers needed only to know the Rhine's main districts and the Mosel.

Not enough anymore. Too many people, in all parts of Germany, are trying to improve things, and that has changed the wine map too. Still, all of the nations' vineyards are in the southwest quarter of the country where Germany borders France and Switzerland. But there's a lot of variation from place to place.

That's obvious in the Ahr, the first tributary you encounter heading south from Bonn. The valley is surprisingly warm this

far north and has dedicated itself to growing spätburgunder (pinot noir) and other red wines, most of them rather sweet but some dry. The most significant area of the tributaries is actually the watershed of three rivers, the Mosel, the Saar, and the Ruwer. Here riesling is especially crisp, citrusy, with a clean taste of the rocky terroir and sometimes a little spritzy, bubbling with carbon dioxide. It has an exciting, almost "fast" taste to it.

Many of the best vineyards are concentrated in the middle stretch of the valley, around the famous wine villages of Bernkastel and Piesporter. They may have also been your first inoffensive and disappointing taste of Mosels. They're far better if they come from specific great vineyards such as Bernkasteler Doktor or Piesporter Goldtröpfchen. They can even be exceptional.

The most expensive and prestigious Mosels, however, come from farther down the valley in the Saar region where the soil is gray and black with slate. It is home to Germany's most fashionable winemakers, such as Egon Muller. Although there are promising vineyards in the Nahe valley (more like Mosels than Rhines) and the Mittelrhein stretch of river, it is when the Rhine bends east that you enter the heart of brown bottle country.

RHEINGAU:
RIESLING
TURNS FOR THE BETTER

The most famous and northerly of the great regions is the Rheingau, which centers on the castled town of Johannisberg that many think of as the home of the riesling grape. The region is filled with riesling vines, producing wine full bodied and peachy with aroma. Still the Rheingau's reputation has weakened over the years, enough so that some of its great growers and estates, including Schloss Johannisberg, took matters into their own hands, a little like the super-Tuscan fever of Italy. The 50 members agreed to market their wines as pure, estate-grown riesling with

Upper Rhine Valley Region

at least 12 percent alcohol and made in a dry style. Each winery's wine would wear the Charta name and logo, a Roman arch, on its capsule and label. It combined with the national group of quality-oriented wineries, the VDP, in 1999, which uses a black eagle with a clutch of grapes on its labels.

As the river turns south, it passes through Rheinhessen, which is the largest producer of German wine and the site of the church-side vineyard in Worms that gave birth to liebfraumilch. The "milk of the Holy Mother" was never revered in Germany, but it sold like blazes overseas. It may have once been a decent local riesling, but it was watered down long ago. Rheinhessen still makes more than half of the liebfraumilch dumped on the world, but there's also good wine in the Rheinterrasse section around the town of Nierstein and some experimenting with scheurebe and sylvaner.

PFALZ: SOUTHERN PRIDE

The southernmost and warmest region is Pfalz on the west side of the Rhine and here the sun shines particularly brightly on imagination and creativity. The rieslings taste almost tropical here and there's a greater

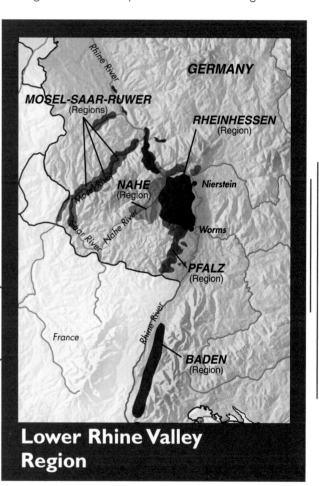

Lower Rhine Valley Region

diversity of grapes, more sylvaner, scheurebe, and various shades of pinot.

Other wines from regions worth exploring are the Nahe valley for rieslings that have the crispness of the Mosel and the honey of the Rhine and Franken for the best sylvaners. In far south Baden, just across the border from French Alsace, you'll find the driest whites and reds from an increasing diversity of grape varieties and oak aging.

WORDS FOR WINES:

German wines are ranked in order of quality:

- Qualitätswein bestimmter Anbaugebiete (QbA)
- Qualitätswein mit Prädikat (QmP)
  - Kabinett
  - Spätlese
  - Auslese
  - Beerenauslese
  - Trockenbeerenauslese

German wine geography has four levels, from largest to smallest:

- Anbaugebieten
- Bereich
- Grosslagen
- Einzellagen

9 NINE
ITALY, THE BAFFLING

All across Europe winemakers brag that the hills and fields of their region have been growing grapes and making wine "since Roman times."

In Italy they started long before that, probably about three thousand years ago. No culture has produced wine in such profusion—and confusion—as the Italians.

Here are the most ancient and traditional wines, made from grapes so primitively crushed you can taste the stems, or they can be the most modern and innovative to come out of stainless steel.

But in the U.S., just try to buy a bottle of Italian wine to go with a pasta dinner. They seem a perfect match, but it's easier to buy wine from virtually anywhere else.

The wines, especially the reds, are as bright and fresh as a picnic of pizza rustica on a sunny day in the hills, and as elegant and complex as a cathedral. Whites never reach such heights, but they can still be as refreshing and fun as a fountain in Rome.

Italy was the largest wine-making country in the world until the late 1990s. Since Italians could not drink all of their production (they did try, with one of the world's highest rates of consumption), they became one of the great exporters of wine.

Therein lies the contradiction that has driven Italian winemaking for the last fifty years: How can a country that has made wine for millennia to satisfy its own tastes sell to the rest of the world?

Meeting the changing demands of international customers, especially Americans, has added extra layers of complexity.

IT STARTS WITH THE LABEL

It starts with the label. Italian labels can be harder to read than German ones (even though the Germans cleverly use an unreadable typeface).

There are all those unfamiliar words on the bottles, and in Italian, no less: Barolo, Barbera, Barbaresco, Bardolino, and Brunello di Montalcino, and we haven't left the "Bs". So if your knowledge of the language stops at ravioli and your mental map shows only Rome and Venice, you can't tell which words refer to where the wine was made, with what, how, or by whom.

The most important designation is geographic. Every wine-growing region, actually every village, has its own favorite grapes, wine, and style, and above all pride. To the knowledgeable, the place will be a clue to the grape, although some wine names specify the grape too.

Italy has hundreds of place names and grape varieties. Sometimes the same word, such as Montepulciano, can be both: It is a village in Tuscany that produces a wine called Vino Nobile, and also a grape used in Abruzzi to make a very different red wine.

Which is why some Italians took the easy way out, first by creating generic but well advertised house brands like Cella, then labeling their wines with the French names of the grapes that Americans already knew. Even simpler, they put "red table wine from Tuscany."

Italy may also have the world's greatest variety of winemaking techniques. Sometimes the wine has been through a special process to make it sparkling, extra sweet, or dry enough to make your tongue roll up like a shade.

Of course, one of those proud Italian words on the label refers to the person or company that made, bottled, or exported it to the U.S., but you don't need to worry on this count. The names you see most commonly in the U.S. are reliable, and so are those you'll only rarely see, like Gaja, on the upper, pricier shelf.

And even in the wine shops with great Italian selections, you'll see only a tiny fraction of the choices available in Italy. In the fifty years since World War II, wine became one of Italy's biggest exports and sank to the lower shelves in American supermarkets. But starting in the mid-1970s Italian winemakers realized there was more lira in quality than quantity, and switched strategies.

neighbors, both France and Germany. Market-savvy Italy did what many other countries did to compete in the world market—they planted more of the well-known French grapes such as cabernet sauvignon and chardonnay, selling them both as varietal wines and blending them with traditional Italian grapes.

As a token of mutual admiration, a number of American wineries now make "Cal-Italian" wines from Italian grapes. Italian grapes are virtually native in California, for Italian immigrants have long grown vines brought from home; and their descendants have now planted the prestigious sangiovese and nebbiolo as well.

THE LABELS

The Italians have passed a number of laws in recent years to establish quality grades and make their wines more understandable, and respectable, to the rest of the world. Although the naming system theoretically follows the French Appellation system, it is more rococo than bureaucratic. After endless revisions, Italy still has too many designations and too few that mean anything. They haven't worked, even for many

THE GRAPES

Of the near countless selection of grapes, only two of Italy's red grapes are considered truly great. The nebbiolo is used in the Piedmont to make the great Barolos and Barbarescos. The sangiovese is at its best in Tuscany, in Chianti and other wines.

Italy's best known white wine grape is the light and crisp pinot grigio, but also noteworthy is the wonderfully floral malvasia.

"God in His goodness sent the grapes,
To cheer both great and small;
Little fools will drink too much,
And great fools not at all."

—Anonymous

There are many, many, many more. Some are native grapes, grown only in Italy, little known to the outside world—or many Italians; others are borrowed from its

Italian winemakers, who would rather make the best wine they can than worry about complying with the rules, which you will see can be as twisted as a Fellini movie:

Vino da Tavola is supposed to be the lowest kind of wine—table wine. However, it can be made from any kind of grapes grown anywhere. So is this the cheap stuff? Hardly. This category also includes Italy's best and most expensive new wines, the Super-Tuscans and other blends.

Denominazione di Origine Controllata (DOC) is wine made with grapes from the district named on the label. Hundreds of areas have been granted DOC status and most simply reflect local boundaries or tradition.

Denominazione di Origine Controllata e Garantita (DOCG) is a more select designation granted to Italy's best-known districts, with somewhat tighter restrictions on production.

What the Italian labels don't include is a true French cru system, which would rank the properties by quality. In a country where reformers claim the rules are already bent or ignored, any expectation of a more meaningful system is a daydream.

THE VINTAGES

Weather and production do vary across Italy and from year to year, but sheer age can matter more than vintages. Most of Italy's white wines should be drunk as young and fresh as possible, preferably within a year of harvest. So too for many light reds, but the biggest and best reds are always better with significant bottle age, say . . . ten years after the harvest, and sometimes twenty years. When in doubt, remember: young whites, old reds.

Primitive techniques dating back to Caesar's day once made Italian wines very vulnerable to nature's whimsy. Dramatic improvements in Italian winemaking techniques in recent years have produced a generation of winemakers, especially in Tuscany, with the talent and modern techniques to make better wines even in bad years. Some relatively recent years, 1996 and 1997, were great.

THE PRICES

Once you get out of the jug wine market—and you should—Italy makes a full range of less expensive varietal wines and local favorites in the $5 to $10 range. Spend another $10 and you can taste better quality Chianti, Super-Tuscans, and the more modest wines of the Piedmont. The best from Tuscany, famous Barolos and prized Amarones, will cost far more and often reach show-off prices in restaurants. Don't buy at your own risk; make your merchant or restaurateurs vouch for them.

FINDING **YOUR** **WAY**

For proof that wine and confusion thrive in Italy, just look at a wine map. In other winemaking countries, the major wine districts stand out. Don't try that here. The entire country, from the Alps to Sicily, is shaded red, for each of twenty zones produces wine. Some of those you don't readily recognize may in fact be the biggest producers. And each will often make both red and white wines, with the reds divided into the rich, the famous, and the everyday. Whites are more modest. Since geography is key to understanding Italy's rainbow of wines and their names, let's work our way across the country and down the boot. The main stops are the Piedmont and Tuscany for reds, and the northeast for whites, plus a few drinking detours along the way.

THE PIEDMONT: GREAT REDS

Cross the French border into the broad north of Italy and here you find the greatest range and selection of wines, from the biggest, most traditional reds, to some of its freshest, newly-minted whites.

The most prestigious zone lies in the Piedmont, the foothills of the Alps. Here in the gentle rolling plains of northwest Italy, the vineyards are full of its most revered red grape, nebbiolo.

Nebbiolo reaches its height in Barolo, where it is aged at length, producing a dark robust wine with a high alcoholic content that peaks twenty-five years later. A more elegant nebbiolo, slightly lighter on the wallet and the palate, is made in Barabesco.

In the surrounding towns of the Piedmont, the everyday grapes and everyday wines are also red: dolcetto, which is easy to drink, and barbera, a gutsier wine ranging from rustic to a poor man's Barolo. Both

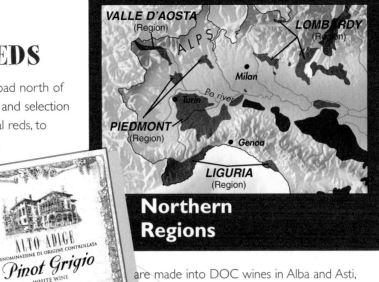

Northern Regions

are made into DOC wines in Alba and Asti, with a lighter red being made from grignolino. You might have heard the name Asti before, but it wasn't in reference to red wines. It is here that Italy's most famous spumante (sparkling wine) is made, using the light moscato with its faint hints of peach. Beyond moscato, Piedmont wine makers have tried to elevate cortese, a local white grape, into chardonnay status. Sometimes sold as Gavi, Gavi di Gavi, or Cortese di Gavi, it can be oaked like a soft, full-bodied white, but rarely achieves the character of a California chard or a white Burgundy.

THE NORTHEAST: CRISP AND CLEAR

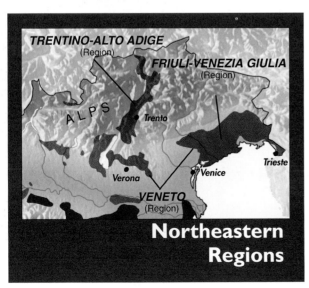

Northeastern Regions

We'll tarry only briefly in Lombardy to try the wines of Franciacorta, classic French-style sparklers, and a clever and unique red blend of nebbiolo and barbera grapes with cabernet franc (imported here two centuries ago).

There is so much to explore at the top of the boot in the three zones that make up the northeastern region, where the hills are planted with the largest varieties of wines. Here are the wines Americans came to know well, like Soave and Valpolicella, and more recently, pinot grigio and merlot.

The northeast is home of Italy's strongest traditions, from musty Venetian favorites that use and then reuse dried-out grapes, to the meticulous diversity of German-speaking growers in the Alto Adige. Altogether, the Northeast winemakers took sharp aim at making crisp, clean varietal wines for the American market.

The Northeast is actually divided into three zones—although they have a total of six names. Hey, it's Italy.

On the west, Trentino-Alto Adige stretches up to the Austrian border. This is Italy's Alsace, where the grapes, names, and wine-making style can be as German as they are Italian. The northern half, Alto Adige, specializes in white wines, from riesling to chardonnay, that are particularly well-balanced and the perfect examples of their grape. If you want to know what pinot grigio should taste like, try it from here. Better yet, try a pinot blanc.

The most common grape grown here is red schiava, most of which is consumed locally, or shipped to neighboring countries. What does come to the U.S. in great numbers are inexpensive Italian versions of the most popular international red varietals, particularly, merlot.

Americans' love affair with merlot may have started here. The second grape of Bordeaux blends, merlot had stood on its own for centuries in Italy. Italian-American winemaker Louis Martini found it growing and produced the wine in Italy, and then brought the wine back to California in the late 1970s.

Another region, Friuli-Venezia Giulia, lies farther east and closest to Slovenia. It produces a wide range of whites, and also a Bordeaux red grape, malbec, difficult to grow elsewhere, but which thrives here. Grape growing is oriented toward mass production and export, but it is done with precision and subtlety.

The traditional heart of the northeast, between the other two zones, is the Veneto, which includes both Venice and Romeo and Juliet's Verona. This is the zone that makes Soave, which, though a commonplace white, can be much better than you might realize; the reds are easy and fun to roll on the tongue, Bardolino and Valpolicella, and to drink.

The wines most Americans come to know are from the local corvina grape. While Bardolino is at best picnic-perfect, the grapes of Valpolicella have the strength, tannins, and acids to become two much more complex wines, recioto and amarone. To make them, grapes are left to dry before crushing, which reduces the water content and increases the sugar content, achieving the same raisin effect as a late harvest.

After crushing, these high-sugar grapes and their juice ferment. If fermentation is stopped while some sugar remains, the result is a rich, full-bodied sweet recioto; if the fermentation continues until all the sugar is converted to alcohol, you have the same lusciousness, but since there's no sugar, it's bone-dry. The Italians call it amarone, but the bitterness is a taste worth acquiring for its texture and aroma. There is also a white recioto made in Soave, but rarely seen here.

TUSCANY: GOING BEYOND CHIANTI

Tuscany Region

Heading southwest on our way to Tuscany, we cross the Po river and stop in the flat plains of Emilia-Romagna. Here it's more tempting to eat the parmesan reggiano and prosciutto di Parma than to drink most of the wines, except in passing. For the local grape and wine is lambrusco, slightly sweet and fizzy, which delights some palates but dismays others. It grows in the same volume as local cattle herds, and with, some say, a similar flavor!

It is on the other side of the Appenine Mountains in Tuscany's hilltowns and the valleys between that we find Italy's other great wine cellar.

This is Chianti country, for better and for worse. Let's go back and start with the grape, and here there is primarily one, sangiovese, a red grape that grows throughout Italy, but reaches its peak in Chianti. Sangiovese, in its various clones, is at the heart of very elegant reds, but also some terrible plonk.

For years, cheap Chianti, light red fizzy stuff, symbolized the sad state of Italian wine and inspired decades of effort to win new respect. And although Chianti was designated as a DOCG, the honor was spread thin with all the wineries in a very wide area south of Florence, including the great, the near-great, and the nowhere-near great.

The best guide is to look for Chianti from the smallest area, called Chianti Classico, in the center of the region. It has the greatest freedom to use the high quality grape varieties. The other clue is to look for Chianti Riserva, which have been aged three years before sale. At their best they can be drunk twenty years later.

A more consistently superb wine is made a few miles to the south from a

special clone of sangiovese, brunello di Montalcino. The wine here is made entirely of sangiovese, and is so thick and tannic, it can age as well as a Barolo, as much as twenty-five years, and may take that long to become drinkable. A lighter, less expensive version that is much easier to drink is called rosso di Montalcino.

Another long-established wine, also made with a sangiovese clone and a blend of other red and white grapes, is vino nobile di Montepulciano. It too has a lighter, cheaper cousin, rosso di Montepulciano.

But Tuscany's best wines play by the fewest rules. Hundreds of them qualify only for the lowest vino da tavola status, but their quality earns them the title of Super-Tuscans, and price tags sometimes well over $50.

The growers have the freedom to plant where they want, use the grapes they want, in the proportion they want, to squeeze, age, and bottle as they wish. The first and most famous was Sassicaia, made entirely of cabernet sauvignon; it was followed by Tigananello, made with much more sangiovese. Others have chosen Bordeaux blends of grapes, or even borrowed shiraz from the Australians to add to the blend. They now come in price ranges from $10 up, but their chief distinction is that, unlike most Italian reds, they are good for both immediate drinking and aging.

After decades of showing up the local traditionalists, the Super-Tuscans may just now be hitting their stride. Look for a more estate-grown Chianti by proud families who want to be regarded as in the same class as Bordeaux. No point in looking for white wine here: The only white of renown is Vernaccia of San Gimignano, a post card pretty place but offering little else.

TO THE SOUTH: LIGHT WHITES AND BARGAIN REDS

In the rest of Italy, there is no shortage of either vineyards or hype. The vineyards started more than two thousand years ago, and the hype goes back to the Middle Ages. The wines have largely been familiar whites. Yet the south also has some of Italy's largest vineyards where there was the greatest room for improvement—and it is fast being made in the 2000s.

The freshest of the whites is frascati, the simple white of Roman cafés, best immediately after harvest. Other whites are similarly plain and crisp at best, and with quirky packaging at worst. You may have seen the fish-shaped bottles of verdicchio from the Marches. Enjoy the distractions. They're better than the wines.

The hot vineyards of the south have always made reds too, but they were coarse, bulk wines until a recent infusion of new ideas and new money. They have, of course, planted some international varieties, but they have also given new polish and sophistication

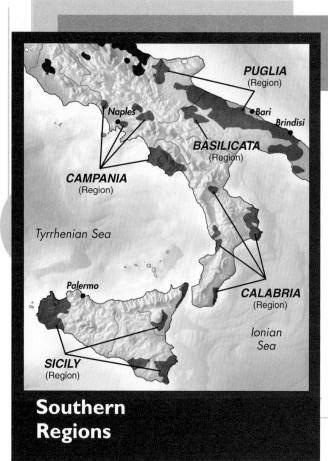

Southern Regions

From Apulia, the actual heel of the boot, where we usually get bulk generics, red and white, now comes an even more polished bargain red made from negroamaro and called Salice Salentino. So what if it is seven syllables? Try it. You'll love the cheery, plummy taste and almost Burgundian texture—and the under-$10 price.

In the Campania region around Naples, the rising star is the old aglianico that has a dark red color, lots of fruit, and a little peppery spice. It makes great reds in Taurasi and Vesuvio.

This revival in the south has even spread to the island of Sardinia. A great export hope is a fruity, slightly earthy red called Cannonau (DOC), which is made mostly from grenache.

Sicily remains the home of all those bottles of Corvo (the red was always better and is now improving) and Marsala, a fortified wine that was invented by an English shipper. Marsala is made in various degrees of sweetness, colors, and aging, and can be drunk as a dry aperitif, a dessert wine, or used in cooking. A more charming treat wine now reaching U.S. markets is a peachy passito made from moscato grapes. The best is from the island of Pantelleria.

to the local wines, including those made from ancient grapes, like aglianico and greco di Tufo that the Greeks passed on to the Romans.

Learn to pronounce a few new words, and eventually they'll slide off the tongue as easily as fettucine Alfredo. They'll repay you with superb inexpensive reds, much easier to drink than the high-tannin biggies of the north.

Cross over the Apennines to Abruzzo, and you'll find Montepulciano d' Abruzzi (DOC), a smooth red made of Montepulciano grapes and sometimes Chianti's sangiovese grapes. New polish and an export push on this old wine is making it the house pour for smart Italian restaurants in the U.S.

10
SPAIN & PORTUGAL, THE FORGOTTEN

Fixation on France as the greatest winemaking country has led wineries from Japan to California to boast that they have similar latitude, soil, or grapes. It's the same product, but without the haute *attitude.*

The French, and other European wine lovers, long ago discovered fine vineyards next door in Spain and Portugal. Indeed, the winemakers and merchants of Bordeaux moved across the Pyrenees en masse *for the last half of the 19th century. Starting in the 1850s as plagues of powdery mildew and infestations of phylloxera destroyed more than two million acres of vineyards, the French slipped into the Rioja Valley of the Ebro River in northeast Spain. Although most returned home by 1900, they left the Rioja as the Bordeaux of Spain.*

Vineyards have been part of the landscape of the Iberian peninsula for three thousand years. Phoenicians, Carthaginians, and Romans all enjoyed the wines made here, and they remain some of the most distinctive fine wines of the world, especially the sherry, which traces its ancient roots to where the very first Spanish grapes were grown.

Yet, except for the fizzy flagons from Portugal or cheapo rosados, many American wine drinkers have missed out on these wines. Or they found them on the bottom shelves in back corners of liquor stores, and feared the wines would be as dusty as the labels. Sometimes they were. If you lucked upon a Gran Reserva, however, you may have gotten a bargain taste of Spain's long-lived reds at their best—smooth and supple, ten to twenty years of age.

Today, the modernizing wine industries of Spain and Portugal, and the smart American wine buyer, are reconnecting in the global marketplace. The rewards are delicious, distinctive table wines, with flavors as diverse as cherries and plums, coffee and cinnamon. It pays to explore them; vintage Ports and the great Spanish names already command high prices, but there is still good value in the red wines, and Spain is certain to provide far more in the future.

SPANISH FLAVOR

Countless vineyards are planted across Spain from the chilly, rain-swept Atlantic coast of Galicia, to the sun-parched south, and up into the mountains. The vines don't climb on trellises but are head-pruned into bushes, as they have been for centuries. Some of the oak barrels in the *bodegas* (wineries) seem almost as old. Though the third largest producer of wine in the world, Spain makes half as much wine as France or Italy.

Spain's labels cover a wide spectrum, from sparkling cavas and rich sherries, to neutral whites and elegant reds. It is the reds that have won the heart and palate of modern wine drinkers—and their pocketbooks if they wish to taste Vega Sicilia, one of the world's great wines, at $100 or more per bottle.

If the Mediterranean heat, ancient tradition, and rugged reds sound Italian, think again. The wines taste of strawberries and cherries, likely smell of vanilla, and above all should be smooth. In that sense, Spanish wines seem to have a French Burgundian finesse (despite their Bordeaux connections).

The Spaniards prize mellow, supple texture over fruit flavor and achieve it by long aging, usually in oak barrels. Keeping wines in the winery for five years or more, a rare and expensive custom elsewhere, has been common here. Many bodegas choose to age their best wines until they are mature and mellow when released, ready for the customer to drink, not to stick in the cellar. Vega Sicilia did not release its 1970 vintage until 1995.

That long aging by the winery is why Spanish wines can always be found in much older vintages than those of other countries. If you want to see what a ten-year old wine tastes like without a connoisseur's budget, look for a Spanish label.

THE GRAPES

Given their range of hot and cold climates, Spanish vineyards display a wide variety of home grown and international grapes.

Of red grapes, tempranillo is the proud native that makes Spain's most distinctive wines. It grows best in the cooler regions and produces a wine with a delicate flavor and color. It is sometimes mixed with two bolder, hot-weather reds, garnacha and cariñena. (In France, they're known as grenache and carignan.) The more noble French reds—cabernet sauvignon, merlot, and cabernet franc—have grown in Spain since the mid-19th century and are planted more often today.

Most of Spain's white grapes are undistinguished and better off in blends, from oaky, dry whites to fortified whites, depending on local tradition. But there are a few with enough personality to be sold as largely varietal—malvasia, viura, and the especially fragrant albariño. By the way, one of the great sherry grapes, the Pedro Ximénez that sounds so Spanish, was named for Peter Siemens, who brought this riesling-like grape from Germany.

THE LABELS

The key to buying Spanish wines is to know the basic geography and wine regions of the country, the age of the wine, and a few producers you like. Many vineyards are still small and private, but the commercial and especially the export trade are dominated by large combines and cooperatives.

"For a bad night, a mattress of wine."

—Spanish proverb

Spain has a basic European system of appellations ranked by quality and then geography.

Most quality wine that you will see exported to the U.S. should be *Denominación de Origen* (DO), which corresponds to the French AOC and the Italian DOC. They refer to regions where the government has set distinct boundaries and requirements for the wines made there, such as La Mancha or Ribera del Duero.

An additional distinction of *Denominación de Origen Calificada* (DOC) is similar to the Italian DOCG—it's something of an honorary status, so far granted only to the Rioja.

Designation of age is a special concern of Spanish label laws. The youngest wines are sold as *joven* (young), *sin crianza* (without aging), or without any age specified. The age designations set the minimum years the labeled wine must have aged (although those years may be divided among oak or tank or bottle).

Words for Wine

Spanish labels rank wines according to the age, from youngest to oldest:

Joven, sin crianza

Crianza

Reserva

Gran Reserva

Crianza—Two years, including one year in oak. *Reserva*—Three years for reds, two years for whites. *Gran reserva*—Four years, at least two in oak, for red; three years for whites.

These distinctions are clearly reflected in price. You can buy a lightly oaked crianza for $10, many reservas for $15, and gran reservas for another $5 or $10. This is not only because of the costs of aging, but because most bodegas allot better grapes, more costly for each category, and will set aside grapes for a gran reserva only in good years.

And, of course, the age requirements are minimums, and Spanish wineries are patient and in no rush to release the wines. They'd rather hold the wine for seven, eight, or up to fifteen years than release a gran reserva before its time.

FINDING YOUR WAY

In Spanish wine country, it's a good sign if you have to have a glass of tinto to brace yourself against the morning chill. The best wines are in the northerly parts of the country, which, when you look closely at the map, stretch from Galicia all the way to Catalonia.

VINHO VERDE
(Region)

PORTO/DOURO
(Region)

DÃO
(Region)

PORTUGAL

ESTREMADURA
(Region)

LAGOS

PORTIMÃO

TAVIRA

LAGOA

NAVARRA
(Region)

LA RIOJA
(Region)

ARAGÓN
(Region)

CATALONIA
(Region)

Barcelona

CASTILLA Y LEÓN
(Region)

SPAIN

Madrid •

Tolido •

CASTILLA-LA MANCHA
(Region)

VALENCIA
(Region)

Borba •
• Évora

Beja •

Valdepeñas

ANDALUCÍA
(Region)

MURCIA
(Region)

RIOJA

The famous Rioja may be just around the corner of the Pyrenees from Bordeaux, but it was a remote area one hundred years ago. Modern highways and rail lines now link it easily to Bilbao in the Basque country. Head up into the high country forty miles from the coast and you'll see where the French crossed. It's also where far sighted Spaniards like the Marqués de Riscal and Marqués de Cáceres emulated the French techniques, using their small oak barrels and their grapes, as have more recent investors like the Domecq family. Blending tradition with imported ideas, they have upheld the region's reputation as Spain's most important source of red wines, made from both tempranillo and other local grapes, and the traditional Bordeaux reds.

They come from the giant CVNE co-op as well as a great number of other products. Of the Rioja's three regions, Rioja Alta and Rioja Alavesa are the best—and most expensive. The more prestigious wineries are located there, while the third region, Rioja Baja, is lower on most rankings. White wines here have never won as many fans; they are mildly flavored except for the oak aging, which in the best gives a richer color and fuller flavor.

Don't ignore Navarra, another DOC wine region, which lies just across the Ebro. While it lacks the Rioja's fame, its grapes and wines are similar, and its prices a better value; try Gran Feudo for proof. Look also for wines from Somontano farther east in the Pyrenees.

Rioja
Names to Know
(Compania Viñicola del Norte de España)

Marqués de Murrietta
Marqués de Cáceres
Marqués de Riscal
Marqués del Puerto
Campo Viejo
La Rioja Alta
AGE Bodegas Unidas

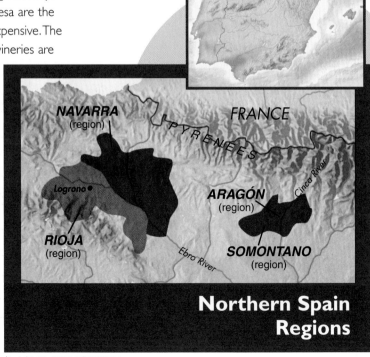

Northern Spain Regions

RIBERA DEL DUERO

The other great red wine region is the Ribera del Duero that sits almost as high, but 100 miles west of Rioja. The river here is the Duero, which will cross the Portuguese border and become the Douro, where the grapes of the great ports are grown. In Spain, the valley is part of Castilla y León, the heart of the old Spanish kingdom northwest of Madrid. It has been making wine for centuries, and here too the French influence was felt more than one hundred years ago. Its reds are often darker in color than those of the Rioja and have more berry flavors.

For years it was known simply as the home of the great Vega Sicilia that combined French grapes planted in the mid 1800s with the Spanish penchant for long aging. Its superb wines have been treasured for most of this century, some of them still reported to be drinking well at fifty years of age.

Today wine lovers know there's far more here, starting with the superb Pesquera tempranillo made by Alejandro Fernández. More names emerge on the American market with every vintage.

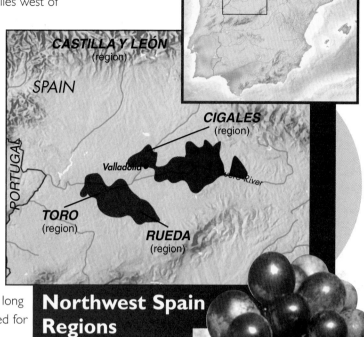

Northwest Spain Regions

Ribera del Duero
Names to Know

Alejandro Fernández (Pesquera)
Vega Sicilia
Condado de Haza
Ibernoble
Vega Sindoa

CATALONIA

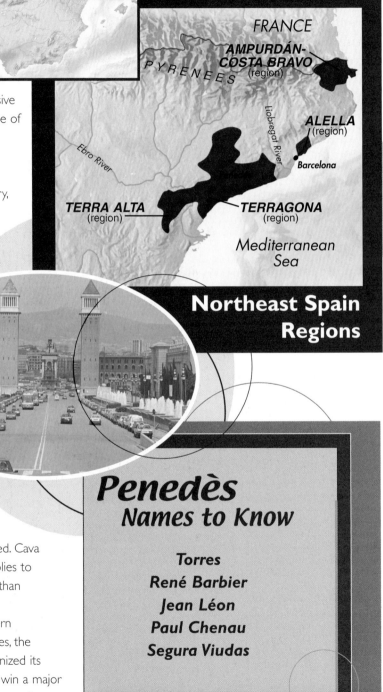

Far to the east, where the Pyrenees and the French border reach the Mediterranean, is a third major region known to wine drinkers for two reasons. Catalonia is the source of sparkling *cavas* that are a delightful, inexpensive alternative to Champagne and also the home of the Torres family, whose wines led the reemergence of Spanish wines on the world market.

The cavas began in the late 19th century, again to emulate a famous French wine. Although they used different grapes than those of Champagne, the winemakers of Penedès did something few other imitators bothered to do. They adopted the same, painstaking, labor intensive Champagne method of creating bubbles through secondary fermentation in the bottle, rather than in large bulk tanks. At first they even called the wines *champana*, but because of French complaints, switched to the term cava, referring to the cellars or caves where the wines were stored. Cava today is the only DOC designation that applies to wines made by a particular method, rather than geographic designation.

The Torres family made Penedès' modern reputation for still wines. Under Miguel Torres, the winery planted more French grapes, modernized its winemaking style, and by 1970 managed to win a major blind tasting against French competition. That quality was soon matched by aggressive marketing that firmly installed the family and its brands.

Northeast Spain Regions

FRANCE

AMPURDÁN-COSTA BRAVO (region)

PYRENEES

Llobregat River

Ebro River

ALELLA (region)

Barcelona

TERRA ALTA (region)

TERRAGONA (region)

Mediterranean Sea

Penedès
Names to Know

Torres
René Barbier
Jean Léon
Paul Chenau
Segura Viudas

GALICIA

Of the many other DOC regions of Spain, there are a few worth looking for. The nation's most interesting white wine comes from Galicia on the cold and rainy northwest corner of Spain. In Rías Baixas, these white grapes keep their acids and fragrance, so that albarino has a full bouquet of peaches and flowers, and good texture as well as crispness. Look for better-than-average whites from Murcia and chardonnays from Tarragona.

Atlantic Ocean

SPAIN

Rías Baixas

Miño River

RIBEIRO
(region)

VALDEORRAS
(region)

PORTUGAL

Galicia Regions

0   500   1000

SHOPPING 101

If you have a sense of adventure or a limited budget, you should explore Spanish wines. Spanish wines aren't competing in the bargain basement, but they're still good deals, especially on mature vintages. If you like dry reds, whether Bordeaux style or Burgundian, you should get some good Riojas and Ribera del Duero for $10 to $20. Keep your eye out for bargains from less well known regions like Navarra.

To get out of the chardonnay rut, try an albarino. Or take advantage of the affordable prices on cava to add some sparkle to an everyday dinner. You might even develop a taste for sherry.

Don't expect a big selection or much knowledgeable assistance on Spanish wines. But you may find more at a Spanish restaurant. Do remember Spanish wines when you're in a fancy restaurant that boasts a first-class wine list. There may be a Rioja or Ribero with an impressive fifteen or twenty years on it for $50 or so.

SHERRY, BABY

For all the obsession with aging in the north, it is in the heat of the Andalusian south that you can find the oldest vineyards and the oldest wines. Here's where the Phoenicians landed, where Columbus built his ships, and where the small town of Jerez de la Frontera is located. It gave its name to what the English speaking world knows as sherry. You'll know it too, when you get here, for the smell of sherry is in the air. So is the salt of the sea breeze, but you'll forget that, the closer you get to the great sherry bodegas. The distinct perfume of sherry— nutty, crisp, and sometimes sweet—is inescapable, as countless barrels stacked in hundreds of *solera* (racks for rotating barrels) exhale a tiny fraction of their wines. That evaporating profit is called the angels' share, but you can smell it for free.

The controlled evaporation is the most obvious distinction in the intricate process that makes sherry different from other wines. When winemakers put wine in barrels anywhere, they do so to allow a little oxygen to filter through the wood and mellow the wine, but without oxidizing it. To produce sherry, however, winemakers want to make the most of the aging effects of oxygen. They invite it in by using small, old barrels, filling them only two thirds full, and leaving the stopper loose. Then the wine ages for decades, and theoretically for centuries, through the solera system, by constantly adding old wine to younger wine. Sherries do not have vintages, just the year when the batch began.

Southern Spain Regions

This aging creates the mellow brown color of sherries, gives them luscious texture, and refines their taste. The main types, ranging from pale and crisply dry to caramel sweet, are: *fino, manzanilla, amontillado, oloroso,* and *cream.* Most begin life as palomino grapes, but at harvest are divided into different categories.

"If penicillin can cure those that are ill, Spanish sherry can bring the dead back to life."

—Sir Alexander Fleming

The fino grapes are crushed and fermented until all their sugar has been turned to alcohol. Then a neutral brandy is added to raise the alcohol level to 15 percent. This extra alcohol is what makes sherry a

fortified wine. (Port is also fortified by brandy, but it is added to stop fermentation when the wine has not converted all its natural sugars and still has some sweetness.)

Then nature adds a magical ingredient to the sherry, a yeast that blooms on the surface of the wine and continues to grow throughout its life; this is poetically called the *flor*.

Fino sherries made in the Sanlucar area closer to the sea often develop an especially thick flor. This gives fino here a delicate flavor, and it is called manzanilla.

If the flor fails to live beyond the first bloom in a fino, it becomes a third kind of sherry, an amontillado, still dry but with a richer taste.

What happened to the oloroso grapes? Not quite the same thing. The grapes are left out in the sun for a day so that some of the water

evaporates and the sugar concentrates more. They are then crushed, fermented, and fortified with brandy. Winemakers watch carefully to make sure no flor develops, and after about two years add more brandy to boost the alcohol to 18 percent.

The sweetest sherries depend on the Pedro Ximénez grapes. These grapes are sweeter than the palominos and sun-dried longer, almost to raisins, before they are made into wine. PX sherry is then added to olorosos to sweeten them further, or bottled as is for the richest of sherries.

This effort and tradition are ignored by many modern wine drinkers. Our ancestors, from George Washington to Edgar Allan Poe, loved the stuff; most American buyers pass it up for Port. A revived interest in sherry could happen, but you can have a sip of this elegant tradition anytime.

Try a crisp cold fino as an aperitif instead of a cocktail; nothing with gin or vodka can match sherry for delicacy. Manzanilla and amontillado are strong enough to go with snacks or light meals, and cream sherry or a PX could be all you wanted in a dessert or after dinner drink.

The main brands have been in sherry for decades, more often centuries: Gonzalez Byass, Pedro Domecq, and all the English houses, Croft, Harvey's, and Sandeman's. Many give proprietary names to the solera, but the labels will also designate the category, from fino to cream.

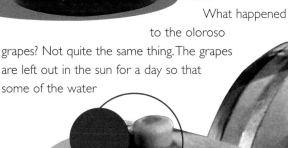

PORT & PORTUGAL

Perhaps the toast should be "There will always be a Portugal!" when we pass a decanter of vintage Port around the table. Clockwise, mind you, is *the* tradition, and Port is as rich in tradition as in taste.

If toasts and tradition sound English, they should in this case, for it is the British who invented the Port trade and inspired our love for it. Port is Portugal's greatest wine treasure, but not the only one. Portugal has grown grapes and, for centuries, made still and fortified wines, which cannot be found elsewhere.

Where else can you taste plums, chocolate, coffee, honey, and nuts in a glass? Even big spenders who used to insist they only drink dry wines have admitted Port's sweetness is luscious—and strong enough to accompany a fine cigar.

"That is why, in many ways, Port is so romantic, so spectacular. In the place that it's grown, in the way it's grown, in . . . the remoteness of it."

—Alistair Robertson, Port merchant

All those tastes are squeezed from the hot Portuguese sun and local grapes (more than forty varieties are allowed in Port). There's also the taste of time—decades and even centuries—that enrich the texture and flavor of Port and its cousin, Madeira. Despite a new fascination with Port, American-Portuguese wine trade has been sketchy. Oh, the colonists loved Madeira and many folks got their first glass of wine from Lancer's and Mateus (still one of the biggest brands in the world). Otherwise the Portuguese have been slow to join the global wine revolution.

The Portuguese have long held on to their native grapes, and still stomp them with their feet to get all the color and flavor they can out of the skins. That is starting to change and will inevitably produce a greater range of table wines from Portuguese grapes, a new diversity in vintage Port, and a revival in Madeira.

THE GRAPES

While the rest of the world has been busy trading grape varieties, Portugal has stood pat. Some are best in the cooler, wet northern sections of the coast, other thrive in the hot climates of the mountains and the south.

Portugal Regions

Because of the long British involvement in the Port and Madeira trade, English words like "Fine Old" are common on ports. Most table wines are labeled in Portuguese and knowing a few words may help. *Branco* means white, *rosado* rose, and *tinto* red. *Seco* means dry, *doce* sweet, *espumante* sparkling. *Garrafeira* is a term of value, like reserve, used on top-of-the-line wines that have had extra aging.

Vintages are of significant concern only when dealing with Ports and Madeira.

THE PRICES

Portuguese table wine on the U.S. market is generally under $10. Some basic versions of fortified wine can be found for $10 to $20; vintage Ports start around $35 and go much higher.

Only a few are shared with Spain: the white malvasia and albariño and the red tinta roriz, one of the most prized grapes in Port. Only recently have cabernet sauvignon and other international varietals been planted.

THE LABELS

Most table wines are sold under proprietary names for generic or vineyard names or by geography, rarely for the grape varietal. Geographically, Portugal's wine country includes several *Denominação de Origem Controlada* (DOC) designations for the most proven wine regions. *Vinho Regional* (VR) is a lesser category.

To Have & to Hold

Vintage Port lovers would prefer to have 1985, 1988, 1990, 1992, and 1994 in the cellar, and to drink 1983, 1970, and older.

Quinta do Vau

VINTAGE PORTO
SINGLE QUINTA

SANDEMAN
EST 1790

ALC. 20% BY VOL.   PRODUCT OF PORTUGAL
PRODUCED AND BOTTLED BY
SANDEMAN & CA., S.A., V.N. GAIA, PORTUGAL   750 ML

PORT

The story of Portugal's most famous wine started hundreds of miles away with the usual misunderstanding between the English and the French, both of whom seem to deserve each other. It was the 17th century and the English, by fussing with France, had again cut themselves off from the source of claret; London wine merchants started exploring Portugal. Traveling up the Douro River, they finally found the alternative in the rich red wines made in the hot highland country. Supposedly the best was made by an abbot who added a little brandy to his wine.

By 1700 the Port of Porto (Oporto) was full of English firms loading up wine to ship home, and adding brandy so that the wine would survive the voyage. It did. Three centuries later Croft, Warre, and Taylor still have Port lodges in Porto and the vineyards remain on steeply terraced hills up the Douro River. And, at least for nostalgia and tourism, workers stomp some grapes at harvest time and old-fashioned *barcas* (boats) hold races on the river.

The first secret to Port is not just adding brandy, but knowing when to add it. In Portugal, winemakers add brandy before the yeast has turned all the grape sugar to alcohol, only two or three days into the process. That kills the yeast and stops the fermentation while the wine still has a lot of residual sugar. The second secret is to know when to drink it, because aging is crucial, whether in bottle or barrel, at your house, the wine store, or the Port lodge.

All the various kinds of Port start out the same way, with red and white grapes grown, crushed, fermented, and fortified up in the hills. Although foreign wine buyers know Ports by the name of the shipper whose blend they like, Portuguese laws regulate the individual grapes and vineyards in detail. The six most famous grapes are touriga nacional and touriga francesca, tinta amarela, tinta barroca, tinta cão, and tinta roriz. The best vineyards are on rocky sites in the upper Corgo region, the center of the growing area. Government officials rank each of

Port Lodges

The great old names of Port are both Portuguese and English (and Dutch and French).

They include:

Cockburn	Noval
Croft	Offley
Delaforce	Ramos Pinto
Ferreira	Royal Oporto
Fonseca	Sandeman
Graham	Taylor, Fladgate, & Yeatman
Niepoort	

thousands of vineyards, or *quintas*, and set their production quotas and price. Vineyards are getting more recognition today as both Port houses and individual grower's market single-quinta Ports. Most wine is trucked down to Porto, where some of it is aged briefly, and then bottled and sold as ruby Port. It's a dark purple wine that tastes of fire and pepper, as well as sweetness and fruit, with tannins that are still a little leathery. Ruby Port and other Ports are sold with house brand names and sometimes called "vintage character," a term that has no meaning in Portuguese law (or often in the bottle). They are ready to drink and despite their richness can be served with food. Other inexpensive Ports, whether white or tawny, are often lesser efforts, but their nutty sweetness can be good aperitifs, especially cold.

"You see out of this dirty, dusty gray bottle, this beautiful red wine coming out, bright as a summer's day"

—Bruce Guimaraens, Port merchant

The rest of the wine will be aged in large wood casks and can become all different kinds of Port, depending on its quality and how it is aged. During the second year after harvest, when the wine is in casks, the Port house makes a big decision. If it believes that the wine of that year is good enough in quality and quantity (and that consumers will buy it), it can seek approval to declare it a vintage, the most sought after Port. Vintages are not declared every year and not always by every house. Only two or three years in a decade is a vintage widely declared.

SHOPPING 101

A thirst for Port can be expensive, but the price is usually justified in tastes as well as cost of production.

Still, you can sample ruby, tawny, and even some LBV Ports for $10 to $20. Aged tawnies, colheitas, and current vintage Ports will cost from $30 to $60. Best value is in LBVs and tawnies, but if you want to splurge on a vintage, go all the way and pop $80 for an older bottle. If that's too steep, try vintage Port someplace that offers good Port by the glass. You'll pay a hefty mark-up, but it'll still be cheaper than a full bottle.

By the way, the fabled match of Port with nuts and a blue-veined cheese like Stilton isn't just old fashioned, it's one of the great food and wine pairings.

Anyone who likes vintage Port should explore Madeira, say an 1845 Bual for $250, to see what history and money really taste like. The rest of us should keep an eye out for new Portuguese table wine. We'll be seeing more of the good stuff.

Beware that vintage Port is shipped when it is only two to three years old, and is designed to age in the bottle, and not to be drunk for at least ten years. That's why vintage Port is one of the wines available in older vintages. Most Port lovers are only now beginning to drink 1980 and 1985, and regard drinking anything younger some kind of abuse. You can drink the vintages of the '90s now; some can be chocolate-y and velvety, but that's just a hint of what they will be. Patience pays.

You don't have to wait a minute to drink other fine Ports if you let the Port house do the aging, which is the true glory of Port, turning it from the wild red youth into mellow, tawny maturity.

One type is called late bottled vintage Port, made from wine that was left in the casks for five to six years, at which time it has developed the richness to be bottled and drunk. They are still red, not as dark as a ruby or a young vintage Port, with intense, spicy flavors. Less expensive than vintage Ports, they are one of the best buys in Port. The best are crusted, made in a traditional style without filtration (and say so on the bottle). They will "throw a crust" of sediment and should be decanted and drunk like an aged vintage Port. They can also keep twenty-five to thirty years.

Another Port treat for immediate enjoyment is an aged tawny that showcases the value of decades in wood that slowly oxidize, and even caramelize, the wine. A ten-year-old tawny has become a deep orange, and picked up the nutty vanilla of the barrel; a twenty-year-old has turned copper, and developed into a luscious balance that can taste almost of macaroons. Even older tawnies that have spent thirty or forty years in oak are almost gold and even more mellow. Aged tawnies will also keep several months after opening.

While old tawnies can be blended from several vintages, a colheita Port is a single vintage Port that has been left in wood for seven years, so it is a deep red wine that has a little acidity and the caramel taste of a tawny. Many Portuguese winemakers regard the old tawnies as the height of their art, while the British and Americans revere the vintage Port.

HAVE SOME
MADEIRA, M'DEAR

Many wine drinkers who have fallen in love with vintage Port have yet to discover the equally rich and often older treasures of Madeira, made on a small island four hundred miles from the coast of Africa. Yet Madeira was once America's favorite wine, the toast of independence more than two hundred years ago. It's not just for cooking—in fact, it's already been cooked once.

Madeira

Portuguese explorers who settled on this outpost started making wine by 1600, and were soon provisioning ships on new trade routes to the Americas and the East with Madeira's fortified wines. On their way to Asia, the passing ships discovered something about wine too; the Madeira got better in the heat of the ship's hold after months in the tropics.

Although heat is exactly what winemakers and wine-drinkers try to avoid, the baking temperatures

TABLE WINE

While Portugal has exported Port and Madeira around the world, Portuguese table wine has stayed home. The Portuguese do grow grapes throughout the country by the ton, and make traditional wine the same as the rest of Europe, but the only successful exports most Americas have tasted are spritzy rosés.

The best known table wine is the *vinho verde* or "green wine," actually both red and white wines that are green only in the sense of their youth, tartness, and usually with a little sparkle. They are made in the Minho, the northern coastal region around Porto, and the lower Douro valley. If you visit Portuguese wine country, you can't miss the vines. They grow everywhere, on telephone poles and the sides of houses, as well as in vineyards. The wines can be thin and tart, and sometimes have a little effervescence that makes them refreshing.

Richer wines and the best reds come from the Dão south of Porto and coastal Estremadura. These include both huge co-ops and small family wineries with traditional methods, and a growing number of modernized firms, with the stainless steel and refrigeration equipment to make crisper, fresher wines.

Greatest progress has occurred around Lisbon in the wine regions of Bairrada, Ribatejo, Terras do Sado, and Alentejo. Some are planting vineyards with the grape varietals popular on the international market, but most are making a new generation of sophisticated table wine from native grapes, such as periquita and arinto. Expect more.

Island Shippers

Bareito
Blandy's
Cossart Gordon
Henriques & Henriques
Leacock

of the tropics so improved Madeira that island wineries started sending their wine on long sea voyages for the heat. When that became impractical, they found ways to heat the wine in Madeira, aging it in warm rooms, or practically cooking it in heated tanks. Somehow the heat made the wine resilient, and the most long-lived in the world.

Today Madeira fans can drink wines from rare soleras that began in 1792 and many that date from the mid-1800s. Modern blended Madeiras are sold after five, ten, and fifteen years of aging in barrels, and current vintages of Madeira must be held twenty years before release.

Madeira can be made from a range of grapes— tinta negro mole is most common and terrantez is the rarest—and Madeirans are more particular about varietal character than other Portuguese. The style of many fine Madeiras is identified by the grape used, ranging from pale, dry *Sercial* to golden *Verdelho*, and the sweetest *Bual* (Boal) and *Malmsey* (malvasia).

11
THE UNITED STATES, THE ABUNDANT

In wine, the United States is "America the Abundant"—so abundant that you start to see some of the complexity usually associated with European wines.

The first colonists imported as much Madeira, French claret, and German hock as they could afford, and gradually planted their own vineyards, in New York, Virginia, Ohio, and Missouri as they moved west. Yet northern California remains the place to start the story of modern American wine, with some of its most colorful characters at their rollicking best.

CALIFORNIA

California's tale is full of European immigrants and American originals.

There are Spanish friars and dons, Austrian counts, White Russian emigrés, and Italian peasants, freebooters from Gold Rush miners to venture capitalists, and plain old farmers gambling on nature and hard work. There are family feuds, literary lights like Jack London and Robert Louis Stevenson, adventurers like Jacob Sutter, and dance hall legends like Lily Langtry. They were all part of the wine business, as were the more tame Christian Brothers.

And in the last twenty-five years, add to this heritage some of Europe's great winemakers who have bought into the American action.

Winemaking started in earnest in the second half of the 1800s as the nation was knitted back together after the Civil War. More people came west, and they sent wine back to the more populous east.

The pioneering winemakers found the fertile land in the valleys north and east of San Francisco the most promising. General Vallejo, the last of the Spanish dons, had already planted vineyards in Sonoma.

Soon Count Agoston Haraszthy was importing European grape vines, and he and other immigrants were planting wineries all around the bay.

Some of their names remain today: Paul Masson, Haraszthy's Buena Vista, Chateau Montelena, Beringer, Inglenook, Charles Krug, Wente, Mayacamas (originally Fisher), Almaden, Beaulieu, and Seghesio.

By 1900, the Bay area vineyards had grown into sizable wineries. The valleys were full of vines and busy workers. The owners' majestic houses and sprawling wineries soon became landmarks. Even today, some of the old vines and olive trees they planted can still be seen. Grapes and wine had become big business throughout California, as small immigrant families and

big speculators had spread out from the Sacramento delta to the redwood forests.

From that beginning, the growth of American and California winemaking might have been a simple story, except for one thing: Prohibition. Allowed to sell wine only for religious purposes, the wineries cut production, workers left, vineyards were abandoned, and many of the lands turned to fruit growing. The repeal of Prohibition in 1933 gave birth to another wine generation.

This time, enterprising growers and winemakers, like the Gallo brothers, and large cooperatives, like the

Guild Winery, would create new brands and find new vineyard areas.

Others who returned to grape growing and winemaking set new goals for California wine. In 1939 André Tchelistcheff arrived to recommend to Beaulieu that it plant cabernet sauvignon.

Remember that fact for two reasons.

It means that Beaulieu and other big Napa wineries that followed suit—Krug, Inglenook, Beringer, and others—put Napa on the road to its current fame. Today they have fifty years experience with the great French grapes, which in wine time, like dog time, isn't very long.

Second, when you hear any winery invoke the name André, they're not talking about cheap champagne. Tchelistcheff advised many wineries on vineyard sites, grape varieties, and blends until his death in 1994, and his word is still gospel.

There were others who broke new ground in the years after Prohibition.

Parducci in Mendocino, Hanns Kornell, Martin Ray, and David Bruce in the Santa Cruz mountains. A few wineries and importers began to abandon the common practice of calling wines Chablis, Burgundy, Rhine, or Claret, the names they had borrowed from the Old World, often without justification. They instead began labeling the wine with the real name of the grape used.

SHOPPING 101

The diversity of California can fill a wine list of almost any budget. Don't sneer at the big producers. Almost all have steadily expanded their top of the line to show that they can make select wines worth $25 or more. They have the size, wealth, skill, and history to make good wines at the high and low ends. California makes the best jug wine in the world, and the best of the larger wineries make exceptional values in the $6 to $12 range. Beringer, Fetzer, Forest Glen, Geyser Peak, Gallo, Hess Select, Mondavi, and Napa Ridge all have lines of modest prices and good quality. When paying more for California varietals, keep geography in mind as you search for favorites.

For cabernet sauvignon, merlot, and red meritage blends, Napa is still king, on both the valley floor and the mountains. Oakville, Rutherford, and Stag's Leap are the best spots. In Sonoma, look to Knight's Valley and Alexander Valley.

For zinfandel look anywhere in Sonoma, the Napa mountains, Mendocino, the Amador foothills, and Paso Robles, even the central Valley, anywhere that can claim old vines. Rhône reds have so far proven themselves in Dry Creek, Santa Cruz, up in Mendocino and Lake, and farther south along the Central Coast down to Paso Robles. Expect them to spread. Pinot noir is more limited. The best come from Carneros, the Russian River of Sonoma and Edna Valleys, and other cool pockets along the Central Coast.

Chardonnay is everywhere, and while the best winemakers of Napa and Sonoma make exceptional ones, the geographic advantage goes to Carneros, Russian River, and the Central Coast. For more character, try sauvignon blanc from Napa and the Dry Creek Valley of Sonoma. For riesling and gewürztraminer, look to Alexander Valley, Mendocino, and the Central Coast.

Keep an eye on the experimenters. The new Cal-Italians are getting better and eventually cheaper. The Rhône clones have added spice to California's reds, and are slowly reinvigorating whites and rosés. For your cellar, find a cabernet or zinfandel you like at an affordable price; the 1997 vintage proves how well they age.

Despite the efforts to lead Americans to the best wines California could produce, the wineries couldn't make them drink the good stuff. Americans for years were more interested in jug wine than fine wine, until the wine revolution of the 1970s. The symbolic first shot is usually credited to young Robert Mondavi, who in 1966 broke away from the Charles Krug winery his family owned to start Napa's first new winery in decades.

A deluge followed. Where there had once been a few dozen wineries, by 1998 there would be more than 300 in Napa alone. They were started by college professors, doctors, and engineers, big business, and French Champagne firms, all encouraged by lenders who touted American wine as the next great investment.

As demand pushed up the price of land in Napa, eager new wine makers explored farther, turning to neighboring Sonoma, Mendocino, Livermore, and Santa Cruz.

Eventually the wine growing would spread to Monterey and much farther south—basically anywhere that grapes would grow.

But where the French concentrated on *terroir* (soil), the Americans focused on microclimates—not quite as romantic, but they measured such fundamentals as elevation, rainfall, temperature, and soil to match the right grapes with the right place. Consequently, many California wineries own vineyards in a half-dozen locations, growing different grapes in each one, and producing a dozen or more wines from them.

Yet the chief factor that subdivides the overall climate of the Golden State is not sunshine, so much as fog. Yep, similar to the stuff you saw at the last KISS concert. Fog is the tangible evidence of the ocean's influence, making some areas temperate and even cool. The clouds drifting in from the ocean and the veil of humidity can shield the vineyards from the sun. Mountains can hold the fog in a valley or block it off. Within these microclimates, wine makers are still exploring which areas make the best wines. For example, it's only in the last fifteen years they've established that the foggy flatlands of the Carneros region, and the cool weather, are perfect for grapes such as pinot noir. Again, in wine time, that's a hiccup.

THE GRAPES

You might think cabernet sauvignon, chardonnay, and merlot are the only grapes that grow in California, and it's true—they're the money grapes. Sauvignon blanc and pinot noir come next. Plantings of riesling, gewürztraminer, and chenin blanc have dwindled. Growth of minor French varietals has increased in small plantings of Bordeaux's red blending partners— cabernet franc, petite verdot, and malbec, as well as white sémillon.

There also are many less prestigious grapes, some European and some hybrid, that grow in California vineyards and were here long before the new wave of growers arrived. Thompson seedless, French colombard, gray, and green riesling were the base of many American whites. The list of red grapes is endless: carignan, grenache, gamay, Napa gamay, baco noir, charbono, barbera, and best of all, zinfandel.

After steady concentration on cabernet and chardonnay, however, California winemakers have begun to diversify again, looking through forgotten varietals at home and exploring further abroad. The two biggest sources for new-to-California grapes are Italy and the South of France. From Italy, winemakers have brought the sangiovese of Chianti, the nebbiolo of Barolo; from the southern Rhône, they have plucked mourvèdre, syrah, and viognier. They have also planted fragrant muscats, Spanish tempranillo, and the black grapes of Port.

THE LABELS

The most obvious features on most California labels are the name of the producer and the grape. The brand name of the line, such as Sebastiani Cellars, is hard to miss.

The switch from Euro-phony names to grape varietals made wine buying easier for the American public (and it has since been copied by all of the New World and much of the Old that chooses to sell here). And it has taught many consumers the names of the grapes, although many might not have known that chardonnay referred to a grape. To be honest it may have scared them away from some wines that were easy to drink but hard to say, such as gewürztraminer.

There are some exceptions. Some wineries do not name the grapes used, preferring a trademarked brand name such as Hearty Burgundy or fanciful names like The Flying Cigar. The other distinction made by most U.S. labels is geographic, agreeing with European tradition that place is important—especially if the place name they can put on the bottle is Napa. The general thinking is that the smaller the area named, the more distinctive and better the wine.

Although winemakers and their statisticians have long preferred certain areas for grape growing, actual geographic designation, like the European AOCs, began only in 1978. They're called American Viticultural Areas (AVAs). Unlike European appellation systems, the U.S. is not administered by a wine bureaucracy, but by the Bureau of Alcohol, Tobacco, and Firearms (ATF). (Yep, same guys who gave you Waco.) So these names are not hallowed by centuries of experience, readily recognized by the public, or always justified on quality as much as

in a distinctive marketing plan. Still, they can be very useful if you find an AVA that makes a style you like, say Alexander Valley zinfandel or Rutherford cabernet.

The largest geographic designation is by state, as in California wine, which can come from anywhere in the state but usually the central valley. Then the designations drop down to groups of counties and gradually get smaller (and often overlap). Wine labeled Coastal must come from any of the designated counties along the Pacific, from Mendocino down to Santa Barbara. North Coastal would be from Sonoma, Mendocino, or Napa. Napa Valley wine is smaller still, and far more prestigious. Even smaller is a sub-appellation, such as Stag's Leap.

In each case, ATF requires the same 75 percent minimum for use of a place name as a grape name. Of course many wineries, no matter where the winery is located, buy grapes from all over the state, and make wines from a variety of districts, which often accounts for a winery's many labels. One winery might make four chardonnays, one in an inexpensive line from coastal grapes, and one from Napa grapes. At the top of the line, they could sell a reserve wine chosen from its best grapes, and a wine made from the grapes of a single vineyard. So always check to see the source of the grapes. And if you don't see a familiar geographic place name, look closer. Many wineries, from Robert Mondavi to Bonny Doon, have imported wine from Europe and South America as California crops fell short during the 1990s. These wines always disclose the source of the grapes, in type large or small, and carry a variety of labels, which generally look quite American. (Remember, it wasn't so long ago that every U.S. winery wanted a French name!)

Reserve, a term seen on some bottles, carries no official meaning, although it ideally means the winery culled out its best grapes or wines, gave them special handling, and extra aging, usually in oak. *Dry* on U.S. labels, however, does mean dry.

U.S. wines also carry mandatory warnings from the Surgeon General. These warnings, plus UPC codes and other information, have led in many cases to a back label that is almost as big as the front. There you may also find a touching family story, incomprehensible data about the harvest, or a parody of all the above. But the label may include some helpful information about the source of the grapes, additional varieties in the blend, aging techniques, and fanciful descriptions that strike you as right or wrong. Don't hesitate to turn a bottle around in the store, but don't be gullible enough to believe every word.

The vintage to remember for the next few years in California is 1997, a rare combination of quality and quantity, very welcome after a string of short harvests in the mid-1990s. The first whites taste superb and some winemakers expect the reds to be better after they have aged a little. Given the weather, only a few California vintages are stinkers; most California vintages range between good and great. The best ones were 1985, 1987, 1989, and 1990.

FINDING YOUR WAY

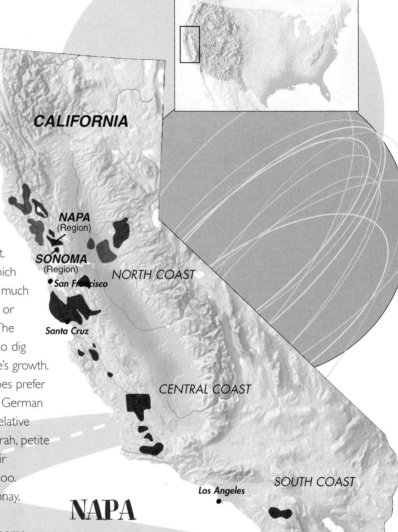

California wine geography can get as intricate as you want. Given five minutes, any good grape grower will take at least an hour describing a vineyard. Details will include where geographic faults exposed limestone, where river beds left gravel, the exact time the fog reaches what point, the angle of the spring sun on the west slope of a mountain, and the precise number of acceptable degree-days, not to mention the style of trellis or canopy management.

Or the geography can be fairly simple, which is where we're going. Grapevines do not need much rain (much of the wine country is rather arid) or what most farmers would call good, rich soil. The soil's ability to drain and allow the vine roots to dig deep in search of water is important to the vine's growth.

The main determinant is heat. Certain grapes prefer different levels and react differently. Pinot noir, German whites, and the reds from northern Italy like relative coolness; dark and thick skinned grapes like syrah, petite sirah, and grenache like the heat similar to their homeland in southern France; zinfandel does too. Other grapes, especially cabernet and chardonnay, adapt to both.

Looking at the map, there's Napa and Sonoma, which you may already know, and the coastal counties north and south of San Francisco, which you should get to know. There's also the Central Valley, which you might insist you don't need to know about, but you'll probably be drinking wine from there. There are other place names worth knowing, from the Russian River to the Santa Cruz mountains.

The obvious starting point is San Francisco, so let's cross the bay and head north.

NAPA

The Napa Valley is the first stop for most explorers of California wine, and it's a very instructive one—a learning experience with a buzz.

For once you have crossed over the salt flats above San Pablo Bay, you begin a step-by-step tour through climatic zones in a classic wine valley. Here at the far south of Napa and Sonoma is the Carneros region, which straddles both counties. The fog is thick, and the breeze is cooling. Pinot noir does exceptionally well here, and most Napa pinot makers buy their grapes here. So do many of the wineries that make sparkling wine. Pinot noir's cousin, chardonnay, grows well here too.

Drive through the town of Napa, head north, and you are in the heart of the valley, a broad flat alluvial plain with mountains on each side. It's similar to Burgundy in France, except that the mountains are higher and the vineyards and wineries seem to cover every inch—the flatland on both sides of the river and much of the mountains on either side. It's expensive property.

Follow Route 29 up the middle, dodging tractors and tourists (hey, you're a wine connoisseur, not some gawking visitor), and you'll go through a string of small towns and a succession of steadily warmer zones on the valley floor—Yountville, Oakville, Rutherford, St. Helena, and Calistoga—each with its own specialty. This is where the Napa River rages in the winter, but most of the year it's a thin, quiet trickle. Its stony floodplain provides excellent drainage for vines.

Napa is the perfect thirty-mile microcosm for understanding California wine. When you reach Yountville, you might think the southern valley is undistinguished, yet Cosentino and Trefethen are here with good chardonnay as well as cabernet (as is Thomas Keller's fabled French Laundry restaurant). Once you hit Oakville and Mondavi's huge Spanish mission winery, you are probably close to the heart of Napa's cabernet sauvignon. Oakville and what geologists call the Rutherford "bench" to the north make the most Bordeaux-style cabernets and Napa's best sauvignon blanc, which indicates the temperatures and soil here are similar to France's. Wines from slightly cooler vineyards hint of mint, while those to the north brag on the earthiness of Rutherford dust. This is the historic home of Beaulieu and Inglenook, and an honor roll of today's most famous producers, Cakebread, Caymus, Grace, and Heitz.

Joseph Phelps,
Proprietor, Joseph Phelps Vineyards

Moving north in St. Helena and Calistoga you will see geysers and boiling springs. There's also a slight rise in temperature. Here, Schramsberg champagne cellars and Chateau Montelena started more than one hundred years ago, and it was the modern revival of Montelena that produced the first U.S. cabernet to beat the French in a tasting contest in the 1970s.

Okay, back on the road. Start again in the south on the western side of the valley where the Mayacamas mountains divide Napa from Sonoma, and you'll likely find yourself alone on a long twisting road up to Mt. Veeder. Though most wine stalkers miss it, this area has wine growers galore. Eventually you'll reach the Oakville grade, the pass that connects the two counties. Go back up on the west side to Spring Mountain and Diamond Mountain, above St. Helena and Calistoga, and you'll find some exquisite vineyards, like Newton and Diamond Creek.

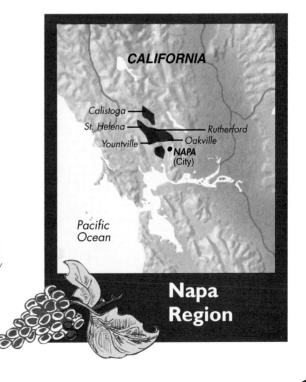

CALIFORNIA

Calistoga
St. Helena
Yountville
Rutherford
Oakville
NAPA
(City)

Pacific
Ocean

Napa Region

On the eastern side of the valley floor, the Silverado Trail provides a peaceful alternative to Route 29. Make your way up the hillsides, and you'll find another fabled vineyard area, Stag's Leap. Here is where Warren Winiarski made the cabernet that upset the Bordeaux first growths in a 1976 competition. He's not alone. Silverado, Shafer, and Frenchman Bernard Portet's Clos du Val all make exceptional wines here. Beyond and up high are Atlas Peak, a mountain top that's now home to the biggest planting of Italian sangiovese grapes.

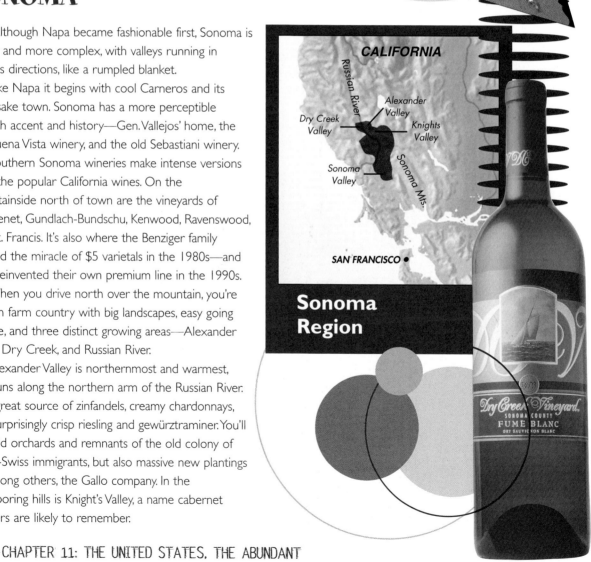

SONOMA

Although Napa became fashionable first, Sonoma is bigger and more complex, with valleys running in various directions, like a rumpled blanket.

Like Napa it begins with cool Carneros and its namesake town. Sonoma has a more perceptible Spanish accent and history—Gen. Vallejos' home, the old Buena Vista winery, and the old Sebastiani winery.

Southern Sonoma wineries make intense versions of all the popular California wines. On the mountainside north of town are the vineyards of Carmenet, Gundlach-Bundschu, Kenwood, Ravenswood, and St. Francis. It's also where the Benziger family created the miracle of $5 varietals in the 1980s—and then reinvented their own premium line in the 1990s.

When you drive north over the mountain, you're truly in farm country with big landscapes, easy going people, and three distinct growing areas—Alexander Valley, Dry Creek, and Russian River.

Alexander Valley is northernmost and warmest, and runs along the northern arm of the Russian River. It's a great source of zinfandels, creamy chardonnays, and surprisingly crisp riesling and gewürztraminer. You'll find old orchards and remnants of the old colony of Italian-Swiss immigrants, but also massive new plantings by, among others, the Gallo company. In the neighboring hills is Knight's Valley, a name cabernet drinkers are likely to remember.

To the west and closer to the ocean, Dry Creek runs hot and cold. Wineries make near-prefect zins and sauvignon blanc, but can also grow Rhône reds. When the Russian River turns west and heads straight to the Pacific it lets in cool breezes that make this superb, sparkling wine country. Korbel started here before the Civil War, and Iron Horse and Piper-Sonoma have raised the reputation. Even without bubbles, the chardonnay is exceptional (this is the home of Kistler). And the zin is great, too.

MENDOCINO

As you head north the most noticeable inhabitants of the nearby ocean tend to be whales, so it seems fitting that you're in the "big" (as in flavorful) wine country of Mendocino. It's an old source of California grapes (and hops) and now is finally winning attention again.

Mendocino was home to pioneering Italian immigrant families like Parducci, whose winery is still active and now the nation's biggest producer of petite sirah. It's also the base of operations of Fetzer, one of the great modern success stories.

Its most distinct and coolest region is Anderson Valley, which favors grapes like riesling, pinot noir, and chardonnay, especially for sparkling wine. That's why Roederer, the makers of Cristal, put its U.S. operations here. Pioneers like Ted Bennett and Deborah Cahn of Navarro came here to make gewürztraminer, and found vineyards that could grow a wide range of grapes as well.

LAKE

Moving east and higher across four thousand-foot-high mountains and north of Napa is Lake County, the most rugged corner of California's wine regions. You expect to see John Wayne on a horse sliding down a rocky hillside, and if you could look back in time far enough, you would see Lilly Langtry escaping the music hall and concert tour to start a vineyard with her French winemaker.

It's warmer and drier here. The giant winery is Kendall-Jackson, which makes the popular chardonnay for much of America. Actually, the best grapes that grow here are sauvignon blanc, cabernet, and syrah.

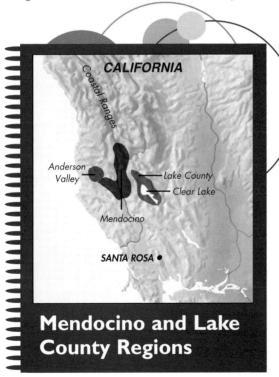

Mendocino and Lake County Regions

CALIFORNIA
Coastal Ranges
Anderson Valley
Lake County
Clear Lake
Mendocino
SANTA ROSA •

SOUTH OF SAN FRANCISCO

Even if you head directly away from wine hot spots like Napa and Sonoma, you're still in great wine country. California winemakers have spread out, down, and across the state for more than 150 years, and some of the biggest producers and the most creative winemakers, past and present, can be found here. Very early, Wente, Concannon, and other wineries and vineyards bloomed in the area east of San Jose, a region with the least appetizing of California wine names— Livermore. They make a wide variety of wines with the benefit of their vineyards, which are ancient by New World standards. Yet today, it's also home to newcomers like Rosenblum, the zinfandel specialist, and keeps attracting new entrepreneurs, particularly those who want to raise grapes like those grown in France's Rhône valley.

The rugged Santa Cruz mountains that separate Livermore from the Pacific Coast intimidated many winemakers, but those who ventured here were often the geniuses and visionaries who shaped twentieth century winemaking.

Martin Ray came here after he sold Paul Masson, so did David Bruce, each producing wines of legendarily

Central and South Coast Regions

intense flavor. Ridge Winery with its Stanford engineers and scientists like Paul Draper, arrived in 1959 with the modern analytical tools that produced great wines. At Bonny Doon in 1981, Randall Grahm began endless experimentation with Mediterranean grapes and Monty Python-style marketing that gave Rhône varietals a boost up in recognition, and a send-up of wine tradition. Grahm is now moving to Livermore.

By the mid 1970s, Monterey and especially the Salinas Valley across the mountains from Big Sur and Clint Eastwood's Carmel, was the site of big vineyards and bulk wine production. But the coast was also beginning to reveal vineyard sites of exceptional quality, especially for the cool-weather grapes of France's Burgundy. There was Chalone sitting high on a mountain top forty miles inland above Soledad, and farther south around San Luis Obispo and Santa Barbara, a wealth of pinot areas, thanks to fog and mountains.

Less than one hundred miles north of Los Angeles are some of the best U.S. sources for pinot noir and chardonnay: Edna Valley, Arroyo Grande, Santa Ynez, and Santa Maria. No surprise that there is good riesling here; yet nearby parts of Santa Maria and Paso Robles make great zinfandel and Rhône reds too.

CENTRAL VALLEY

The heart of California's wine business is in the far less glamorous Central Valley, the great vast fields that lie between the coastal ridge and the Sierras, the center of California's agri-business and its wine basket.

The weather is hot, the production is huge, and the grapes include the likes of colombard, ruby cabernet, rubired, and even table grapes and raisins. The wine centers are Sacramento, Modesto, and Fresno. Not wine-country-quaint or prestigious, its big vineyards

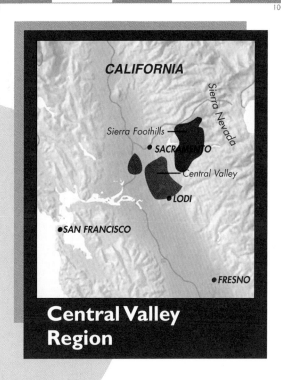

Central Valley Region

produce most of the wine Americans drink, which may be the best inexpensive wine in the world. This is the land of giants, and not just Ernest and Julio; if you drink Robert Mondavi's Woodbridge label, you've tasted the wine of the Central Valley. With so many grapes, and so much wine, however, there's plenty of room for innovation. This is where you'll find America's best Port and dessert wine makers, Quady and Ficklin, and another of the great Rhône innovators, R.H. Phillips.

PACIFIC NORTHWEST

Washington and Oregon were the first states to join the wine revolution and prove that California was not the only place to make fine wines in the European style. Indeed, as their partisans point out repeatedly, the Northwest is geographically closer to the latitudes of France's great regions than their neighbor to the south. Although there were some vineyards here after Prohibition, this was vegetable and fruit territory until the 1960s. That put the Northwest behind California in experience. But today Washington's Château Ste. Michelle is the largest producer of varietal wines made from vinifera grapes, and Washington is second to California in total production.

Add the emergence of Northwest cuisine with its salmon and oysters, mushrooms and berries, and Washington and Oregon clearly aim for the same reputation as California in food and wine.

THE GRAPES

Northwest wineries never planted grapes like Thompson seedless or carignan, or made jug wines. From the start, they concentrated instead on the good stuff, only the European varietals. Given their pockets of cooler climates, they have done particularly well with pinot noir and chardonnay, and German grapes such as riesling. Washington does have two unique specialties, the red Lemberger that also grows in Austria and the local loganberry, which is used in liqueurs.

The climate picture ranges both hot and cold, yet the shorter growing season does have longer days with more sunlight. That and the emergence of a Northwest style of winemaking give freshness and flavor to almost all of its wines.

WASHINGTON

If your image of Washington is lush and wet, a cool coastal rain forest with giant trees set against giant mountains, you'll be surprised in Washington's wine country. It's on the other side of the Cascades. Remember those maps that show half of Washington dark green and half dull brown?

A few wineries are in the green around Puget Sound but most of the grapes grow in the brown half, on the eastern side of Cascades, far from Seattle. The Yakima flows here and so does the mighty Columbia, but most of eastern Washington is desert and wouldn't be farm country if it weren't for irrigation. But it is full of the apples, cherries, pears, and sweet onions for which the state is famous. And now Washington has made the desert bloom with grapes.

At first skeptics said the state's only strengths would be in white wines, but Château Ste. Michelle's stock now has reds of twenty years of age that prove otherwise. Indeed Washington was one of the early leaders in merlot and continues to make exceptionally flavorful examples, as well as strong cabernets. There's also some experimentation with other red grapes from the Rhône and Italy.

In white wines, Washington makes good chardonnay, and does even better with almost every other white grape—crisp sauvignon blanc, fresh chenin blanc, creamy sémillon, and aromatic rieslings.

OREGON

Oregon is a great source of pinot noir. The Willamette Valley below Portland is the Burgundy of the East Coast. Its wines are fruity, sleek, and dry. You can probably guess that these vineyards are cooler than those of Washington to the north. It's because most of Oregon's vineyards are much closer to the Pacific. It is wet here, of course, and rain can be a problem. The weather is close enough to Burgundian standards that Joseph Drouhin of Beaune has planted vineyards here. Besides Drouhin, the pinot noir stars are Adelsheim, Eyrie, Knudsen Erath, Rex Hill, and Sokol Blosser.

Oregon chardonnay also sticks close to the French model, not so oaky or lush; more interestingly Oregon vineyards are experimenting with pinot blanc and the pinot gris of Alsace.

SHOPPING 101

The Northwest may have caught your attention with inexpensive varietals. They're still well made, easy to drink, and good values, but don't be afraid to pay good money for fine reds, especially merlot, pinot noir, and single-vineyard or reserve cabernets.

Shop the Northwest for white alternatives to chardonnay, from sauvignon blanc and sémillon, to full bodied chenin and aromatic rieslings, and dessert wines. There's a great range of choices from $10 to $15. Don't forget the bubbly: Ste. Michelle's is one of the best. Similarly, sparkling wine from Ste. Chappelle, right over the border in Idaho, is excellent.

Turn to Washington for merlot and Oregon for pinot noir. It's more consistent and less expensive than Burgundy, but pinot noir is never cheap: Expect to pay $15 to $20 for most Oregon pinot. Oregon's best vintages were 1990 through 1993.

12
AUSTRALIA, THE INNOVATIVE

Wine from Australia arrived in U.S. shops about the same time the oh-so-clever *Crocodile Dundee* premiered, big cans of Foster's debuted, and lucky Australian sailors in the America's Cup won. The wine was refreshing, friendly, and good value. Meaning, in America, the wines were well-made, easy on the taste buds, and cost only $5 to $10—a price point many popular California brands were abandoning.

With Dundee thankfully gone and New Zealand the latest sailing threat, the Australian wines remain popular. They embody its national character—sun-tanned, big-flavored, open-handed, and independent, yet eager to travel the world. It was only logical to think of Australia as the California of the old British Empire (it had its own Gold Rush—and many of its vineyards are nearby), or a bit like Chile, another come-lately from the Southern Hemisphere to offer us an inexpensive drink. And Australia's wine names sounded right, alternating between aboriginal words like Coonawarra, and plain-spoken English like Margaret River.

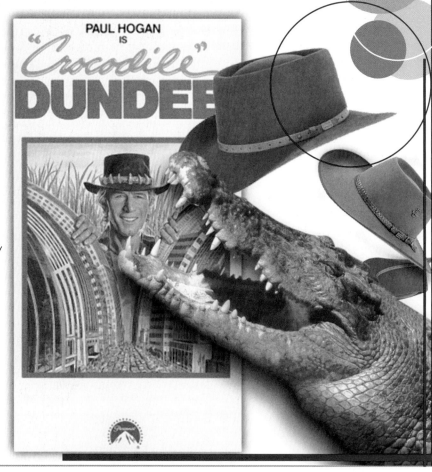

QUINTESSENTIAL
NEW WORLD
WINEMAKER

Australia is a quintessential New World winemaker like the U.S.—and maybe more so.

Shortly after the first British colonists and convicts arrived in the 18th century, they too set about making the Old World wines they missed. The difference between Australia and the U.S. is that *serious* winemaking—*and* wine drinking—have been a big part of Australian national life for two hundred years, not just a trendy taste of the last decades of the 20th century.

Still, no one can deny that Australia's greatest strides in wine have been since 1950 and, most spectacularly, since 1970, much as in California. Ten thousand miles from Europe and in a very foreign climate, Australians were forced to improvise from the start, and they have remained among the most innovative winemakers in the world.

Like the rest of the New World, their goal was to replicate the wines of Europe, especially France and Germany, and to indulge their special thirst for fortified wines, like those from Portugal and Spain. In the heat

"I never drink wine."
—Count Dracula,
in Dracula

of Australia they found that the noble grapes that grew best were the shiraz of the Rhône, the sémillon of Bordeaux, Germany's riesling (surprise), and countless lesser grapes that could be made into something strong and sweet. They took these grapes and slowly added cabernet sauvignon, chardonnay, and a few others, and blended them in just about any way that worked.

Perhaps the Old World never tasted sémillon and chardonnay together, or cabernet and shiraz; it was right enough in Australia.

And people liked it. For all the beer Australians consume, they drink wine at a greater rate than any other English speaking country, more than twice the consumption in the U.S.

In restaurants, they bring their own favorite bottles. At the barbie, Aussies drink wine by the box, big plastic-lined containers that fit in the fridge. Yet they also admire fine wines so much that wine judging is practically a national sport.

For most of its history, Australia's wine was good enough for local consumption, but hardly a world-beater. That changed after World War II; in 1950 work began on what would become the greatest of all Australian wines, Penfolds Grange Hermitage. It was supposed to be a Bordeaux style red blend, but Rhône grapes were better, so the Australians borrowed the grapes and the name Hermitage instead. Today, due to pressure from the European community and Australian pride, it is simply Grange, but there is no mistaking it, or the renaissance it started.

In the last 50 years Australian wineries have planted many new European varietals, found cooler hillside vineyards, and pioneered better techniques, especially with vineyard mechanization, and refrigeration during fermentation.

Eventually they decided to give it a go in export, and took their wine back to the Old World that had inspired them. It was a bust: Australia gave England a taste of "Kanga rouge" in the 1970s, and its only redeeming quality was its cheapness.

Ten years later Australia was back with the good stuff, and the world was impressed. Winemakers had mastered modern techniques, hot weather, and most important, a user-friendly way to please the palate. Wineries across the Old World hired flying squads of Aussie winemakers to head north in their off season, and share their expertise all around the Mediterranean.

If you have found yourself liking Australian wines, it is a deliberate result of their unique style. They have put their fruit forward, full of juicy flavor, and minimized the tartness of white wines, and softened the harsher tannins of the reds. They have been so successful and original, Australian wine writer Oz Clarke claims Australia's chardonnay is a brand new strain, a fruit cocktail that's spicy *and* easy to drink.

It's just as true of Australia's reds, especially the shiraz, which can be almost as sweet as it is spicy, and the cabernets that are as soft as merlots. In some areas, Australia hasn't had as much luck. A lot of pinot noir has been planted, but it has not yet found many happy homes here, and sauvignon blanc doesn't seem to do well (although it is superb in New Zealand). Australia has one success unique in the New World: Its ports are the most luscious wines outside of Portugal, and that is a credit to years of effort, not innovation.

The secret is partly in the oak, but more in the exceptional care of the grapes from vineyards to very modern wineries, several hours distant.

Australia already had a heritage of big wines, whites brawny enough to go with steak, and reds you could have instead of meat. Now they've added a newer style as tropical as a fruit salad.

THE GRAPES

Australia is now best known for growing the full international range of grapes such as cabernet sauvignon and chardonnay. Its greater contribution may have been in keeping alive less popular grapes such as shiraz, sémillon, riesling, and muscat. Australians did more than make do with these grapes, they showcased them.

THE PRICES

There's still plenty of under-$10 wine from Australia, but the smaller wineries command higher prices. Penfolds Grange will cost $40 or more for the current vintage.

THE LABELS

As in the U.S., Australian wines were once named after the European region or style they emulated, such as claret or Burgundy. Australians have since become more straightforward, and have the most plain-spoken of labels. They state the varietal used and region of origin

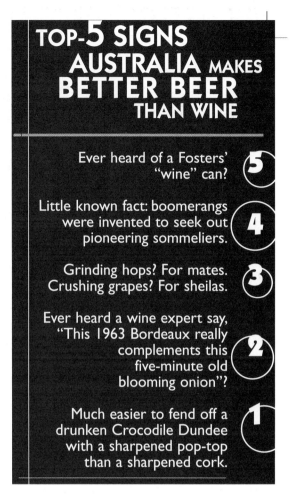

(if 85 percent of the grapes are of that origin—an Australian requirement that is stricter than the U.S.'s 75 percent). The Australians are also happy to spell out a blend's components in specific mathematical formula, or just designate the wine by the vat or bin number used at the winery.

The wine industry is divided between two groups. At the top, four large firms with vineyards all around the country make most of the big labels you see. Below them are hundreds of boutique wineries, some quite old family firms, and many started in the last 30 years.

So if you don't know a producer, look for the place.

Many wines are identified by place names, although in such a vast, largely empty country, wine pioneers are still finding infinite climate variations and redefining boundaries. All the more reason wine lovers should show Australia the respect of learning some geography. You'll be glad you did if you want to drink the best.

A reminder about vintages: In the southern hemisphere, harvest is in the spring, six months ahead of the crush in the U.S., or Europe. Six months is not a long time in the life of a wine, but you should not dismiss an Australian wine out of hand as too young. You may see 2000 whites before the year is over, for instance. Most Australian wines are made to be drunk when released, but the bigger reds, better whites, ports, and muscats are long-time keepers.

FINDING YOUR WAY

Remember there's a reason it's called Down Under. In the southern hemisphere, the weather gets cooler as you head south, not north. Australia's vineyards, like most of her people, are found almost entirely above the 35th parallel in the southern third of the country, most in the southeast, and some in the far west.

In each of the southern states, the wine geography follows a similar history. The first colonists soon planted vineyards wherever they could, though not too far from what would become a big city (Sydney, Melbourne, Adelaide, Perth) more than one hundred years ago. Later generations took advantage of improved irrigation and transportation to expand into massive vineyards for bulk wine production. Modern quality-conscious winemakers pioneered prestigious new vineyard areas in cooler locations.

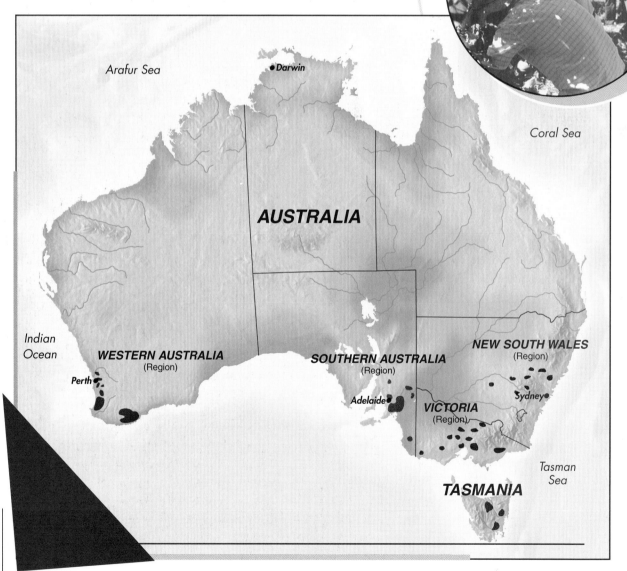

EASTERN AUSTRALIA

Take New South Wales on the eastern side of the continent to start with. This is where Sydney and its fabulous Opera House perch on the harbor, and where the first English colonists settled. They planted their first vineyards one hundred miles north of the city in the relative cool of the Hunter Valley two hundred years ago. Maybe it wasn't the best place, but it's still active, and not just as a historic site for tourists: its old faithful shiraz and sémillon have new style. The newer and more exciting vineyards are in Mudgee, northwest of Hunter.

The bulk wine of New South Wales is produced in an area laced with a system of canals and rivers that form a great watershed, watering vineyards in three states. Here at its eastern end they include the Riverina or Murrumbidgee areas. You won't see many labels bragging about those names, but you'll find their grapes in many a bottle.

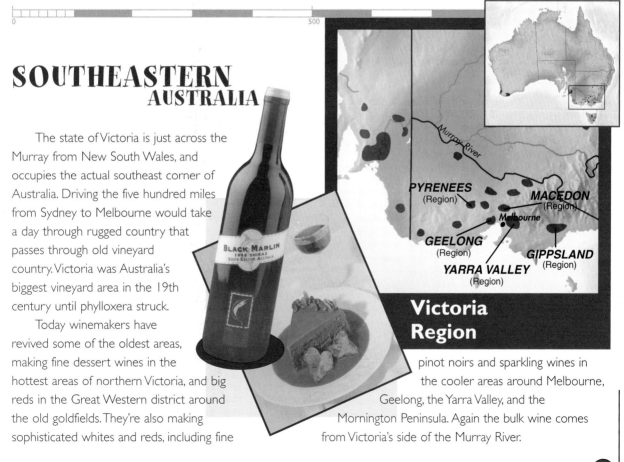

SOUTHEASTERN AUSTRALIA

The state of Victoria is just across the Murray from New South Wales, and occupies the actual southeast corner of Australia. Driving the five hundred miles from Sydney to Melbourne would take a day through rugged country that passes through old vineyard country. Victoria was Australia's biggest vineyard area in the 19th century until phylloxera struck.

Today winemakers have revived some of the oldest areas, making fine dessert wines in the hottest areas of northern Victoria, and big reds in the Great Western district around the old goldfields. They're also making sophisticated whites and reds, including fine pinot noirs and sparkling wines in the cooler areas around Melbourne, Geelong, the Yarra Valley, and the Mornington Peninsula. Again the bulk wine comes from Victoria's side of the Murray River.

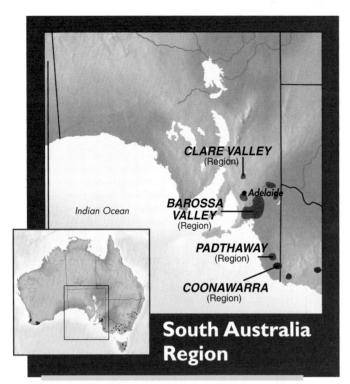

SOUTH AUSTRALIA

Heading west for another day, we cross into South Australia, which is today the country's biggest source of wine, almost all of it grown in the eastern quarter of the state. The bulk of it comes from the area where the Murray River crosses the border and heads to the sea at Adelaide. Here are the massive vineyards of Riverland and the big wineries of the Barossa Valley. Grange is assembled here from grapes grown throughout the state; the best whites are full-bodied, citrusy rieslings that can live for decades. Newer names to know for good cabernets and good whites are Clare Valley to the north of the Barossa, and McLaren Vale and Coonawarra to the south of Adelaide.

South Australia Region

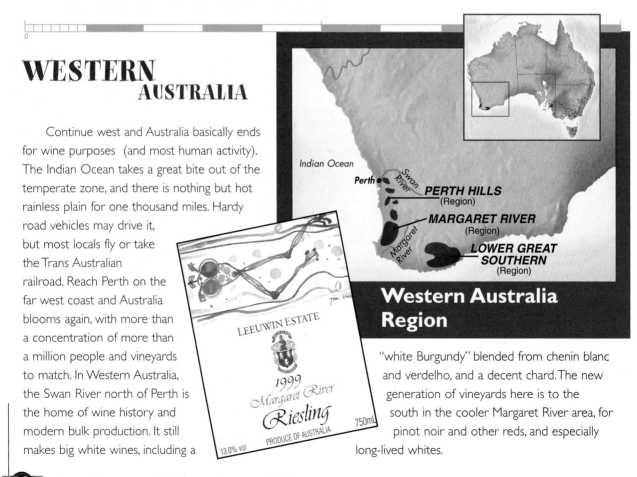

Western Australia Region

WESTERN AUSTRALIA

Continue west and Australia basically ends for wine purposes (and most human activity). The Indian Ocean takes a great bite out of the temperate zone, and there is nothing but hot rainless plain for one thousand miles. Hardy road vehicles may drive it, but most locals fly or take the Trans Australian railroad. Reach Perth on the far west coast and Australia blooms again, with more than a concentration of more than a million people and vineyards to match. In Western Australia, the Swan River north of Perth is the home of wine history and modern bulk production. It still makes big white wines, including a "white Burgundy" blended from chenin blanc and verdelho, and a decent chard. The new generation of vineyards here is to the south in the cooler Margaret River area, for pinot noir and other reds, and especially long-lived whites.

TASMANIA, AUSTRALIA

The ultimate new vineyard area for all of Australia is Tasmania, which contrary to the cartoons is not devilishly hot. A big beautiful island two hundred miles south of Melbourne, it is generally cooler. Wineries that have grown up there in the last thirty years produce the most European-style, near-Burgundian chardonnay and pinot noir, and excellent sparkling wines.

GOLDERS
Pinot Noir 1997
PIPERS BROOK, TASMANIA.
12.5% Vol   Produce of Australia   750 ml

Tasmania Region

0 — 500 — 1000

SHOPPING 101

No question that Australians make some of the most drinkable $5 to $7 wine in the world, but please don't consign Australia to being one more source of cheap cab and chardonnay.

You should taste what they can do if you give them a few dollars more. You don't have to pop for a bottle of Grange, but spend $12 to $20 on a shiraz or cab-shiraz blend and see what great wines can be made with old traditions and new imagination. And get this: the whites can be just as big; the sémillons and chardonnays of Oz are the best-aging dry whites in the world. Australia's rieslings are a superb tropical version of this under-appreciated grape. Ignore the ports and muscats at the peril of your own pleasure.

Pay attention, too, to Australia's varied and somewhat confusing geography. A new labeling term "South Eastern Australia," is an absurdly broad area that includes South Australia, New South Wales, plus Victoria, or virtually all the wine-growing portions of the continent except the far west. For the better stuff look instead for more specific addresses such as Hunter Valley, Geelong, Yarra, McLaren, and the Southern Vales, Coonawarra, and Margaret River.

WINE DIARIES

(GOOSE) DOWN UNDER

See, this is what you get for acting like a tourist.

Sure, you didn't blow a few grand traveling all the way to Australia *just* for the express purpose of an authentic winery tour, but it was certainly among the Top-10 List of things you wanted to accomplish before you traveled back to "sunny" Seattle.

After all, you're no wine snob. You know better than to think the "only" wine worth swilling, ehhr, sipping comes from France. Or even California. After all, what about Germany? Spain? Chile? Sure, Australia wasn't your *first* choice to start your "Wondrous Wines of the World" tour, but here you were and you certainly weren't going to pass up the chance to appreciate what was definitely an *under*-appreciated region.

And, now that it's your last day "down under" and you haven't quite gotten around to experiencing the unique joys of a great Australian winery, you guess it's about time that you did. Therefore, waddling down the short flight of stairs (you need a little exercise after a steady diet of Anzac biscuits, Crown mints, muesli bars, and, of course, Caramelo koalas) you head straight for the front desk and ask the perky "sheila" behind the counter for a little help.

"We make wine?" she retorts, after informing you, albeit politely, that her name is Audrey, *not* Sheila. And, nudging her stunningly tanned co-worker in amazement, she continues: "In Australia?"

Hoping that your current blush can pass for a wicked sunburn, you continue to wait patiently as they consult a phone book for what seems like an eternity until finally they shout, "Aha" in unison and write down directions to a quaint little winery not too far from Sydney.

Jumping in your compact rent-a-car and heading north on Elizabeth Drive, you wind your way through Penrith, turning east at Camden, and finally finding the sagging sign for Wallaby's Winery right where it should be. Sighing contentedly that the folks at your "quaint" Aussie hotel were as friendly as the brochure had bragged, you park in a sandy lot (more "quaint") and walk up a cobblestone (even "quainter") drive to an ancient Woolshed that bares a fading plaque.

Squinting your eyes in the Australia sunshine, you read that the "…Woolshed itself was constructed sometime around the 1890s with the facilities for shearing about 2,500 sheep." Hmm, you wonder.

Interesting, but … what about the winery?

Finding a map next to the plaque, you try to mentally calculate the distance between the koala bear shaped "You are Here" icon to the winery, located, from what you can tell, just past the flea market, picnic tables, craft stalls, petting zoo, and driving range. Grabbing a complimentary koala sticker from the basket in front of the Woolshed (you can never have too much koala memorabilia), you set out on a good old-fashion "walkabout" to find the "oldest continually operated winery" in the North Sydney region.

Naturally, it takes a while to get there. Well, you've come this far, why rush it? After all, where in Seattle do you get the chance to pet a furry, if overly friendly, goat? Or feed wild geese from a gumball machine containing what look suspiciously like rat pellets? Or ride a merry-go-round?

"A hard drinker, being at table, was offered grapes at dessert. 'Thank you,' said he, pushing the dish away from him, 'but I am not in the habit of taking my wine in pills."

—"The Physiology of Taste" by Anthelme Brillat-Savarin

Then, of course, there are all those tempting Aussie snacks at the crafts fair. Who could pass up a few of those scrumptious pouches crammed with steamed onions and spicy beef? Amateurish blooming onions twice as tasty as the ones they serve at the Outback back home. And you couldn't leave Australia without buying a few homemade sock kangaroos, now

could you? What would the folks back home think? And what's a driving range without taking a whack at a bucket of balls?

Eventually, however, you do wind your way to the famed cellars, where you catch the last half of a vineyard tour already in progress, only to learn that they had the complimentary tasting at the start of the tour! Oh well, you were a little full anyway. Besides, there were plenty of bottles of Wallaby's winningest for sale at the gift shop.

Of course, after hearing the over-theatrical (perhaps he'd enjoyed the preliminary wine tasting a little too much) tour guide ramble on about the supremacy of Australian wines, you were ready to buy a whole case!

Naturally, however, his rambling diatribe on the blight of the vine louse "Phylloxera vastatrix," which devastated Australian vineyards at the turn of the century, brought you right back to reality. In the end, you purchased a darling bottle of vintage Shiraz and called it a day.

After all, you'll have plenty of time tonight, after your meandering Aussie odyssey, to enjoy a little local flavor and see what all the hubbub is about. Now, if you can just avoid that much-too-friendly goat on your way back to the car.

13

THIRTEEN

AROUND THE
NEW WORLD

Grapes and wine spread outside the Old World long before western Europeans set out to explore the planet. From its ancient base in the Mideast, wine moved west through Persia into Uzbekistan, and eventually India, China, and Japan, and also south into Africa. Yet, in wine terms, outside of Europe, it is pretty much the New World, whether it be the birthplace of man, Africa, or some other ancient culture. A handful of New World countries are joining the U.S. and Australia in the international arena.

CHILE, THE CHALLENGER

Almost anyone who's been in a supermarket in the last ten years knows that Chilean vineyards in the shadow of the Andes make fine cabernet sauvignon of high quality and low price.

The Spanish knew that long ago. They were drinking wines made by their colonists on the other side of the world 400 years ago. Other colonists planted vineyards around Santiago. The French caught on in the mid-1800s when they found it was one of the only wine regions in the world that was phylloxera-free (and still is). That began a century of cooperation and mutual interest.

Chile waited until late to join the wine revolution, but it came on with a bang as the first big exporter in South America. Like other Latin American countries, Chile had used its vineyards primarily for brandy, Pisco, and heavy, tasteless wines from sweet, cheap grapes for domestic consumption. As Chile's economy revitalized in the 1980s, a retooled wine industry made Bordeaux-style reds part of a new line of high-end food exports. Besides wine, there's everything from sea bass to raspberries, and an orchard of tree fruits.

The first brand many U.S. wine drinkers remember is probably Concha y Toro, but we got an earlier clue of Chilean wine know-how. If you had watched California's wine revolution in the 1970s closely, you might have noticed that two of its great innovators were Chileans who knew how to make wine that people enjoyed drinking. Augustin Huneeus shaped Franciscan, Mt. Veeder, and Estancia in Napa and Monterey, while Sergio Traverso revived Concannon, and recently opened Murrietta's Well in Livermore.

Much expertise and investment has come from the U.S., Europe, and elsewhere. Robert Mondavi is now in a partnership that bottles large amounts of Chilean wine under the Caliterra label, and similar international ventures by French (Lafite-Rothschild) and Spanish (Torres) wineries are common. Mondavi and Errázuriz are also making a luxury meritage wine called Seña.

Chile's record rise to its new status as a significant producer and exporter of varietal wine carries risks and challenges. Simply, its wines must continue to be good as well as cheap; Chile's initial success has now produced a number of wines that are only cheap. And presumably, Chilean winemakers want to follow Australia up the market so that their better wines command better than bargain prices. Chile now has the money and the talent to refine and improve on a great beginning. That means making sure it has the best grape varieties, finds the best places to grow them, and keeps the yield per vine modest to avoid overproduction. It had better; plenty of other winemaking countries are eager to take the cheap spot, but few wish to win it for long.

THE GRAPES

Chile's domestic wines depend on old Spanish standards; but her export wines are all made from the internationally popular fare. The great successes so far are cabernet sauvignon, merlot, sémillon, and chardonnay. Syrah and zinfandel have been good, but sauvignon blanc is a very weak link.

THE LABELS

Name of the grape variety is first and foremost on Chilean labels, as they are with almost any New World entry bidding for the international market.

Place can be confusing. It seems like all wine comes from the Maipo or Rapel Valleys, and since most wine is made in those two areas, it's no guarantee; so look for more specific, smaller locations.

Remember that Southern Hemisphere vintages are slightly earlier than ours. Look for "reserva" and on the back label for information on aging.

THE PRICES

Chilean wines have steadily pushed up well above the $5 range, sometimes because of quality, sometimes because of marketing budgets and popularity. Prepare to spend more for reserve or prestige products from the big producers (Concha y Toro has several high-grade lines).

ShoPpINg 101

Chile still makes fine bargain-priced varietals through big names like Concha y Toro, Santa Carolina, and Santa Rita. You can rely on them, but do give some support to better labels and smaller vineyards too. Look for more wines from Curicó, Colchagua, and Casablanca. Top producers to know are Cousino Macul Canepa, Errázuriz, and top lines of the big outfits like Concha y Toro.

FINDING YOUR WAY

A map shows Chile is a very long, very skinny country. It's barely 200 miles wide and more than 2,500 miles long, and hugs the west coast of South America between the Andes and the Pacific Ocean. It runs from the Atacama desert in the north all the way south toward Antarctica (thus the "upside-down" temperature patterns of south being cooler).

As you might guess, the people and the vineyards were and are in the middle. They stretch from the desert to Santiago and farther south, covering a lot of latitude and climates. From the north, the chief areas are Aconcagua, Maipo (Santiago), Rapel, Curicó, Maule, and Bío Bío.

Most of the vineyards and wine making started in the Maipo centuries ago. The modern rebirth remains concentrated here and in the Rapel, which lie in a flat north-south valley between the Andes and a much lower mountain range on the coast. These are relatively warm areas, where the versatile cabernet sauvignon and chardonnay can do well. There are grand old names and quality wines here, but big yields for export are the rule.

More variety, especially in whites, and greater delicacy is found in cooler sections, specifically the southern half of the Rapel called Colchagua. This is where Lafite-Rothschild's Los Vascos and other new premium vineyards are.

Other promising new wineries are farther south in cooler locations in Curicó and Maule. One of the most talked about new areas is, however, in the opposite direction, Casablanca. This area is officially in Aconcagua, north of Santiago, which is generally the hottest of the wine regions. But Casablanca lies on the coast, where it gets the same kind of fog that creates so many cool spots in California; Franciscan and other quality wineries are planting here.

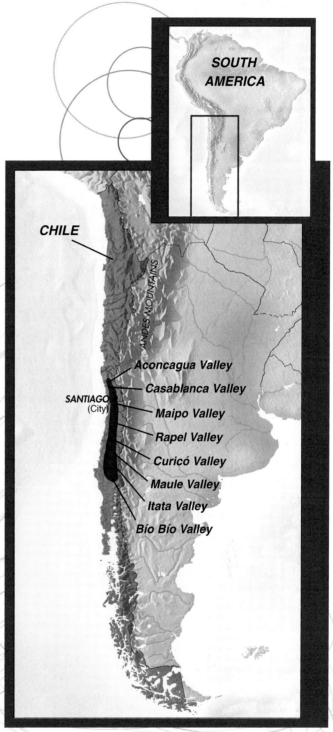

Chilean winemakers are just beginning to explore the potential of their landscape and its infinite microclimates. Expect the wine map to change radically in the coming years.

ARGENTINA

The biggest wine producers in South America, Argentineans are also big wine consumers, and never bothered to export much until Chile took the lead. Grape growing and wine making goes back to early Spanish days, and modern times have brought in new money and ideas from Spain and France, so you'll see more of them. Long-time specialty is big reds made from Bordeaux's malbec, but look for more international varieties and Argentina's own white torrontes. Big labels: Bosca, Catena, La Rural, Norton, Santa Ana, Trapiche, and Weinert.

Argentina Regions

CANADA

A smaller wine revolution is a foot north of the U.S. border. Canadian vineyards are centered in the Okanagan Valley in British Columbia and southern Ontario, which is only a little bit north of Washington state, and just across Great Lakes from the Ohio vineyards. Canada's best wines are white, a few from hybrid varieties such as vidal, more from chardonnay, pinot blanc, rieslings, and other German grapes. And since it does get cold, Canadians make respectable ice wine for dessert.

Canada Regions

MEXICO

The Spanish made the first wine in America here centuries ago and then took their vines into California, but today most Mexican grapes make raisins or brandy. With the help of California and Spain, however, Mexico's vineyards have been getting better. The weather in Baja, California, Ensenada, and Zacatecas can be good for cabernet sauvignon and for darker, spicier red varieties such as petite sirah, zinfandel, and Italian nebbiolo. Best names to look for are Bodegas San Antonio, Santo Tomas, and L.A. Cetto.

Mexico Regions

NEW ZEALAND

Maybe because of a depressingly long spell of temperance, New Zealand got into the wine game quite late and made a horrible false start at that: Growers planted Müller-Thurgau, Germany's least-exciting white grape. All was forgiven once New Zealand hitched its star to sauvignon blanc in the 1970s. It's as good and as expensive as sauvignon blanc gets, often better than French Sancerre: tart, austere, steely, and delicate at the same time. These plus fine pinot noir, chardonnay, riesling, and sparklers come from the cool valley of Marlborough on the South Island. Cloudy Bay is the most famous Marlborough sauvignon blanc, but there are many others. For bigger reds, look north to the warmer regions of Hawke's Bay and Waiheke Island on the North Island. Like Switzerland, New Zealand wineries can't afford to make cheap wines, but they're worth it. As in most cool climates, vintages can be chancy, but 1994 through 1996 were good ones; 1991 is considered exceptional.

New Zealand Regions

SOUTH AFRICA

Out from the dark shadow of apartheid, South Africa is rejoining the modern wine world and the export trade. It has much to offer and much to learn. An initial burst of varietal wines with wild-animal labels and novelty names on the U.S. market gives a poor sample of the nation's 300 years of wine tradition. Given the heat, South Africa put most of its vineyards on the southwest corner of the Cape just outside Cape Town in the Paarl and Stellenbosch areas. Originally wineries relied on hardy varieties like chenin blanc, called steen, and pinotage, a local cross of pinot noir and cinsault, and made sturdy wines, dessert drinks, and brandies. Over the last century, many reached European quality with cabernet sauvignon and sauvignon blanc and now aim for Australian-style progress and success. KWV and SWV are huge co-ops; many fine smaller wineries should show up on U.S. shelves.

South Africa Regions

14 FOURTEEN

KNOW THY GRAPES, GREAT WHITES

T he "great whites" all have a distinct personality of their own, one that is as evident to the casual drinker as it is to the hardcore aficionado. Some describe white wine as "casual and light," others declare it "sweet and breezy." Like everything else, white wine has its own unique style and appeal. Yet that shouldn't limit its place at mealtime or cocktail hour. The distinction between white and red wine is in the pallet of the drinker. After all, you've seen that the old rule of "white with fish and fowl, red with beef" doesn't quite stand up to the diversity of today's lunch and dinner menus. Neither should those other old stand-bys: "white at the bar, red at the table," "white with friends, red with family," etc.

No, today's wine drinker knows better. Wine is an accessory to complement a meal or an occasion, much like a colorful scarf or favorite pair of go-go boots. Sometimes you're in the mood for solid colors, some time you're in the mood for tiger prints. Either way, the color of wine you choose is much the same. When it feels right for white, you'll know it. All right?

Chardonnay. Chenin blanc. Gewürztraminer. Muscat. Pinot grigio. Riesling. Sauvignon blanc. Sémillon. When it's time for a great white wine, these are the names to know. (Not to mention, love and cherish.) And whether the particular vintage you're partaking of is oaky or crisp, tropical or buttery, tart or sweet, you'll still know you're drinking a white even if your eyes are closed. But all great white wines have to come from great white grapes, and to get a feel for the best, we've picked the sweetest off of the vine for you.

CHARDONNAY

Why does chardonnay seem to be everyone's favorite white wine? Because it is so easy to say, so easy to grow, so easy to drink, and so easy to make? Or because there's so damn much of it?

All of the above are true, but chardonnay's long-term status rests on its beginnings as the source of the great white Burgundies of France, such as Puligny-Montrachet, and as the elegant heart of Champagne and other fine sparkling wines. Chardonnay is the real grape of Chablis.

However, it does grow happily in a variety of climates, although many feel best in cooler areas, because it does bud early and at picking time heat can

CHAMELEON OF FLAVORS

rob its acidity. Because it is so flexible in the hands of winemakers and so susceptible to oak, it is a chameleon of flavors, although the key flavor ranges from apples to melon, ideally a pear, but that can be a crisp fresh d'Anjou or a canned Bartlett.

Today there are at least three groups of chardonnay styles. The classic Burgundian tastes of pears and toast, which you should try at least once. If the Chablis are too expensive, look for a Mâcon around $20.

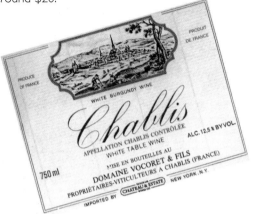

Then there is the style refined by the best Australian and California winemakers in recent years, that tastes of pineapples and tropical fruits. It has a rich buttery texture that comes from oak and/or malolactic fermentation. Too much oak and it can taste like drinking butter, but the Aussies have had special success with a tropical fruit style.

The third is the crisper, green apple style with lots of fruit, citrus flavors, and tart acidity. It often comes in less expensive wines from the stainless steel tanks in Italy, the U.S., and Chile.

Good quality reserve chardonnays should keep ten years. Some of the best American chardonnays come from cooler regions such as Carneros, Anderson valley, and the central coast of California.

CHENIN BLANC

The finest white grape of France's Loire valley and a favorite of no less a wine lover than Rabelais, chenin blanc gets little respect in the U.S. That's probably because it was used as the basis of so much jug wine.

Too bad, because it has good acidity, even in hot weather, honey and musky flavors, and a wealth of potential. In Vouvray in the Loire valley the French make it as a long-lived dessert wine and as a bright sparkler, sweet and dry. It is also one of the most popular grapes in South Africa where it is known as steen. In the U.S., some of the best chenin is made in Washington State.

Château de Montfort

VOUVRAY

APPELLATION VOUVRAY CONTROLÉE

contents 750 ml

Alc. 12% by vol.

MIS EN BOUTEILLE AU CHATEAU
par SCI CHATEAU DE MONTFORT- CHANCAY - 37210 VOUVRAY - FRANCE
PRODUCT OF FRANCE

GEWÜRZTRAMINER

The most deceptive of all wine words: Behind its intimidating looks lies absolutely enjoyable wine. If you can't manage the whole thing, just say the first two syllables, gewürz, which is German for spicy, for it is the gewürz strain of traminer. Whatever you call it, lift a glass to your nose and give your sense of smell a work out: flowers from roses to gardenia, spices from cinnamon to honey, fruits from peaches to raisins. If you're skeptical about wine talk about bouquets and aromas, try this. The taste usually follows through with a matching peachiness, only a touch sweet, balanced by a delicate crispness with a deep gold color and surprisingly full body. It's perfect with Thai and other Asian foods or Caribbean dishes and rarely expensive.

It is a somewhat difficult grape to grow and requires cool weather. In Germany gewürz is far behind riesling. Best producers are in Alsace where they make a very dry style. In California and the Pacific northwest gewürz ranges from dry to late-harvest lusciousness. It is also blended with riesling and other white wines by winemakers with imagination.

MUSCAT

Possibly the oldest grape in Europe and beloved since ancient times, this grape in its various strains can be colored, white, pink, or deep red, but it always has a very bold, musky perfume, that makes for delicious sweet wines, both still and sparkling.

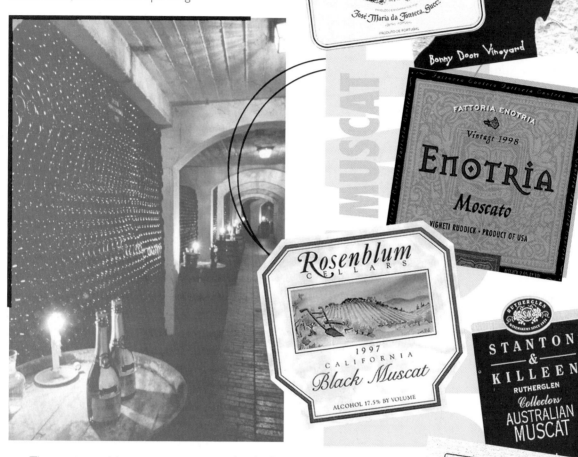

The most prestigious muscat grape carries the jaw-breaking last name of blanc à petits grains rond. It is the peachy base for muscat de Frontignan and Beaumes-de-Venise in France, the Asti spumante and moscatos of Italy, the brown muscat of Australia. The Alsatians use it too, but of course, it's crisp and dry there.

The second most common is muscat of Alexandria, sweet grapes found in hot climates around the world from Spain and Portugal to the Middle East, South Africa, and Australia. It is used in the Pisco brandy of Peru and Chile.

PINOT GRIS/ PINOT GRIGIO

The gray, sometimes blue, sometimes pink cousin of pinot noir, it is still grown and sometimes used in Burgundy, but you probably know it better as a crisp Italian white wine. Actually pinot gris can be soft, relatively low in acid, and with a little spice. It's made as a fine varietal in Alsace, but in Germany it is known as ruländer and used mostly in blends. Pinot blanc is a whiter version with a full body and mild aroma that can be a little like chardonnay. It's popular in Alsace and especially in Austria and Eastern Europe.

RIESLING

This is a significantly underappreciated grape, not just a good grape that can't get any respect, but possibly the greatest white grape of all. If you think it makes flabby sweet wine, taste again, and this time try a good riesling from the Moselle.

It is a grape with remarkably intense flavor and perfume. It has a crisp acid that is immediately pleasant and refreshing. Compatable with all kinds of food, it's the most long-lived of white wines, capable of lasting thirty years. Rieslings can be vinified from dry, all the way to incredibly sweet botrytised dessert wines; don't say you don't like them if you get a chance to taste one.

The best vineyards are in the Moselle-Saar-Ruwer, Rhinegau, and Pfalz districts of Germany. Best American growers are in cooler sections of Sonoma and the Central Coast of California and the Pacific Northwest. German vineyards have tried many hybrids because riesling is not easy to grow—the small berries take all summer and part of the fall to ripen—but the real thing in a good vintage is superb. It's going to make a comeback soon, so get in on it early.

SAUVIGNON BLANC

Sauvignon blanc is the second most famous white grape in France, a mainstay of both Bordeaux and the Loire, and now popular around the world.

Sauvignon blanc is more difficult to grow and has maintained a more distinct personality than chardonnay. It makes a wine that is green, crisply tangy, and dry but not neutral. Its aromas range from citrus, especially lemon and grapefruit, to herbal, grassy, and, in the worst of times, cat spray. Depending on whether aging is done in stainless steel or oak, it can be almost smoky.

In the Loire, unblended sauvignon blanc makes the great wines of Pouilly-Fume and Sancerre, steely in texture and powerful of nose. In Bordeaux, sauvignon blanc is more often blended with sémillon to make the dry wines of Graves and the grand dessert wines of Sauternes and Barsac.

Sauvignon blanc, a popular varietal in California where Robert Mondavi coined the term fumé blanc (and added more oak), reaches its greatest heights outside France in New Zealand. In the recent global expansions of plantings for the American varietal market, sauvignon blanc is also coming from Italy, Chile, Australia, and in surprisingly good form from the Languedoc region of France.

SÉMILLON

This is the modest partner of sauvignon blanc in Bordeaux, a grape whose secret weapon is a low-acid texture so creamy you can almost smell it, and an oiliness among the honey and melon and figs. It adds a lushness to the white wines of Graves and is a key part in the dessert wines because it is susceptible to noble rot.

It was once used on its own to make somewhat soft, bland wines in Australia and other parts of the New World, but today Australians make it into a fine varietal as well as using it in innovative blends with chardonnay. U.S. winemakers are making more use of sémillon all around, in blends as dry table wine, and in dessert wines.

WINE DIARIES

CHAMPAGNE WISHES AND CAVIAR SCREAMS

Well, it's been nearly a week now and you're getting a little tired of your girlfriend's cold shoulder routine. The silent treatment, the smoldering stares, the un-returned phone calls, the rejected advances. They're all adding up to equal something you can't quite understand.

Backtracking through the last week, you try to uncover the source of this sudden frigidity. Indeed, the majority of the past week has been the uneventful stuff of most long-term relationships: nightly phone calls to bitch about work, some take-out Chinese on the porch, the mid-week dinner and a movie, a flurry of business-like e-mails. Routine. Safe. Simple.

Of course, there was that impromptu celebration you'd thrown for her just this past weekend in honor of her recent promotion at work. As soon as you'd heard the good news, you'd gone out and bought the best bottle of champagne you could find, a box of chocolates, a sappy greeting card, and enough roses to keep every killer bee in Africa busy for the next thousand years.

Naturally, she'd been surprised, thrilled, and… quiet? Thinking back, you realize that her reaction was not quite what you had expected. After all, when you'd been promoted earlier in the year, she'd treated you to dinner and that was about it. You'd thought your "champagne celebration" was much more personal and thoughtful. After all, anyone could make a dinner reservation. What you'd done had stepped up to the plate, taken the bull by the horns, and gone the proverbial "extra mile." You'd planned. You'd hypothesized. You'd fretted. You'd mulled it over. You'd followed through.

Why, you'd even shopped!

Now it's *you* who's steaming! Calling her new office number at work (a promotional perk), you ignore her cool, "Oh, it's just you," and ask her to, scratch that, insist that she meet you at your place after work. Sighing, she agrees and hangs up promptly, feigning some lame excuse about an annual corporate shareholder's meeting or some other such nonsense.

Waiting impatiently, you tap your loafers on the foyer linoleum until her car pulls up before leaping onto the couch to look appropriately bored and indifferent. She announces her arrival with clacking heels and dropping keys as she comes to sit as far away from you on the couch as humanly possible.

"All right," you say before her searing gaze can wither your courage any more than it already has. "Just exactly what is your problem? You've acted like a stranger all week, and for the life of me I don't know why."

Rolling her eyes, she gives you the obligatory, "Oh please. It's you who's been acting strange."

"Actually," you admit, "for once—it isn't."

This newfound honesty seems to surprise her, and after a few minutes of stunned silence she responds, "All right, then. If you really must know, I was a little surprised that you

than you, emasculated by my sudden rise up the corporate ladder, and, as a result, you subconsciously sabotaged what should have been a celebration with that dollar store domestic champagne!"

Stunned, you have to pick your jaw up off the floor before human speech is possible once again.

"If you must know," you explain, your voice shaking with emotion, "that 'bogus bubbly' you're bitching about was a nearly $150 bottle of Pol Roger Cuvee Sir Winston Churchill, circa 1986.

"First made in 1975," you continue, mentally replaying the snooty salesman's spiel and passing it off as your own, " it wasn't released until 1984. I found it to be pale, even, bright gold with a very fine mousse. In fact, it had a fat, toasty nose of baked apples, which was both ripe and complex. It was full bodied with rounded, sweet, ripe fruit, creamy acidity, and a luxurious, long finish. All in all, I found it to be complex with superb balance!"

Out of breath, you collapse back onto the sofa, wearily triumphant. Your girlfriend, awed by your recent recitations, rushes to apologize.

"But it just looked so—plain and boring," she reasons, running her fingers through your hair soothingly. "I mean, it wasn't even a name brand."

"What," you scoff with sudden superiority, "you mean like Cook's or—Welch's sparkling cider? Of course it wasn't some off-the-rack bottle. It was a special bottle for a special occasion."

"Well why didn't you say so?" she asks, looking embarrassed, as if she too should have known about the champagne's persnickety pedigree.

"I thought the superior, refined taste would help clue you in," you insist.

"Well," she murmurs tentatively, "nothing personal, but—I didn't taste all that 'nutty fruitiness and the mousse and the acidity,' like you said. I just sort of tasted a mediocre bottle of sweet champagne."

Shrugging, she sits back to await your reaction. When you smile slyly, she is obviously surprised.

"Me either,"

weren't happier about my promotion at work last week."

"WHAT?!?" you exclaim. "I couldn't have been more proud. You work so hard and so well, it was just what you deserved. And too long in coming, if you ask me. I know how long you've wanted this promotion, that's why I went all out."

"Humph," she snorts in that superior way she has. "You call that cheap bottle of champagne you picked up on the way home from work 'going all out'? I think you're threatened by the fact that I make more money you admit sheepishly, relief flooding your nervous system after seven days of living a liquored-up lie. "I just pieced together what the salesman told me and memorized the little pamphlet they included in the box."

You share a good laugh until she stands up abruptly and reaches for her keys.

"Where are you going?" you ask. "I thought we were both due some heavy duty 'making up', if you know what I mean."

"Oh, we are," she says sultrily from the doorway. "But I thought I'd run up to 7-11 and get some champagne to celebrate our little misunderstanding. What are you in the mood for? Vanilla? Nutty? Fruity? Moussey?"

"Actually," you admit, "If they've got a cold bottle of Cook's, I'd prefer that."

"And if not," she smiles knowingly.

"Welch's sparkling cider will do just fine..."

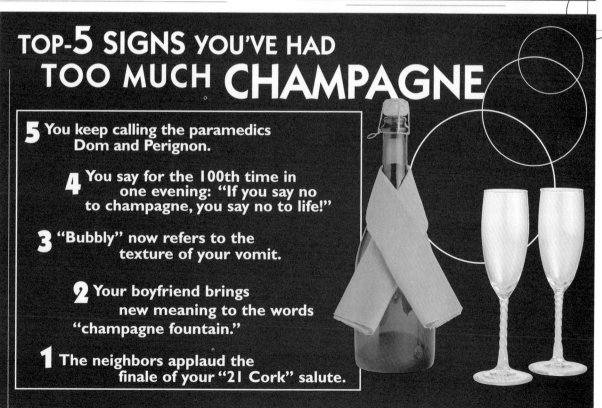

TOP-5 SIGNS YOU'VE HAD TOO MUCH CHAMPAGNE

5 You keep calling the paramedics Dom and Perignon.

4 You say for the 100th time in one evening: "If you say no to champagne, you say no to life!"

3 "Bubbly" now refers to the texture of your vomit.

2 Your boyfriend brings new meaning to the words "champagne fountain."

1 The neighbors applaud the finale of your "21 Cork" salute.

15
FIFTEEN

KNOW THY GRAPES II, GREAT REDS (AND THE REST OF THE BUNCH)

Like all that is noble and good about wine (and those who drink it, of course), red wines tend to rise to the top when brought up in casual, or even serious, discussion. It may be the historical factor, as most wine in the Bible (or at least on those televised versions on TNT) has the deep, evocative portrayal of being red. On the other hand, perhaps red wine's reputation precedes it. After all, white wine is what you drink on a blind date when you want to appear cultured but not too snooty. Red wine is what you sip provocatively three weeks later when you've finally gotten him to invite you over to his artsy loft and show up ready for action, candles lit, glasses poured, white curtains flowing, etc.

Or perhaps it's just the whole color wheel thing. After all, white stands for purity, virginity, chastity, and a fresh, clean page to write on. Red is passion, fire, brazen, and bold. Now, which would you prefer to have in your mouth?

Cabernet sauvignon. Gamay. Merlot. Nebbiolo. Pinot noir. Sangiovese. Syrah/shiraz. Tempranillo. Zinfandel. When the menu calls for red, bring in one of the troops from above to save the day. While each has its own individual style and personality, all can provide certain tastes the whites only hint at. (And vice versa.) Yet just like great food comes from great ingredients, great red wines must come from great red grapes. To find out what those are, we've gathered a selection from the best of the vineyard for you.

CABERNET SAUVIGNON

The best varieties of wine grapes are called noble, and all the nobility yields to cabernet sauvignon as king, because of its power, longevity, and popularity. Its texture can be royal velvet, its flavor generous with plums and cherries, violets and cedar, or mint, with enough acidity and tannin to give it rich color, formal structure, strong backbone, and a long reign, thirty years or more for the best.

Its real strength is not its flavor but the small size of the individual grapes and their thick, blue-black skins, both of which put more strength in the juice. This is what enables it to improve so handsomely while aging in the bottle.

Although enthroned in Bordeaux for more than five hundred years, cabernet sauvignon may have once been considered "savage" and could have been around as long as 2000 years ago.

While cabernet does well in both hot and cool climates, it takes a long time to ripen, is not particularly productive, and prefers well-drained gravelly soil.

It remains one of the most flexible of red grapes and has grown easily in almost any region that aspires to fine wine status. Cabernet sauvignon is a key part of the greatest reds of U.S. and Australian vineyards as well as prestige wines of Spain and Italy and a mainstay of the Chilean wine industry. Originally limited to the Médoc and the west bank of Bordeaux, it is now grown in most of southern France and the rest of the world.

One secret of Bordeaux's cabernets that has spread more slowly to the rest of the cabernet-growing world is that it works well, possibly best, in blends. In Bordeaux vineyards, there are four other grapes used: cabernet franc, petit verdot, malbec, or merlot to fill in the wine—or the crop. However, outside winemakers have come up with two handsome cabernet blends, with shiraz in Australia and with sangiovese in Tuscany.

NOBILITY YIELDS TO CABERNET SAUVIGNON AS KING

SEVEN PEAKS
CABERNET SAUVIGNON

GAMAY

A light red grape that has gotten little respect for centuries, gamay is still the charmingly impetuous heart of Beaujolais. It grows in a hurry and can be harvested early and made quickly into wine that

has bright strawberry and cherry flavors, light aromas, crisp acidity, and low alcohol.

That wasn't good enough for the duke who kicked it out of Burgundy's better vineyards five hundred years ago. And that's not good enough to justify the annual hullabaloo and hyped-prices every November for Beaujolais nouveau, the least of gamay.

Taken on its own terms, given a little respect and a few more months in the winery, gamay makes quite respectable wines in various villages in Beaujolais. These are fine, affordable wines, the best of which can last fifteen or twenty years. Gamay also grows in the Loire Valley and in neighboring Switzerland. Some cousins of gamay have red flesh and are used to "dye" inexpensive wines darker red.

Forget the nouveau hype and try gamay in a Beaujolais the rest of the year. It's been given a bad rap.

MERLOT

Once hidden in the shadow of cabernet sauvignon as the blending partner that put softness into Bordeaux blends, it has since come well into its own. Its taste is more lush and less tart than cabernet sauvignon because its tannins are softer, its bouquet is of plums, chocolates, and violets, and its color lighter. What mattered as much, if not more, in Bordeaux hundreds of years ago is that merlot bloomed and ripened earlier, providing "insurance" for the years when bad weather cut the cabernet sauvignon crop.

Merlot was, however, the dominant crop (with cabernet franc) in Pomerol and St. Émilion on Bordeaux's right bank, where it made the lusciously famous wines such as Pétrus. Look for ample and forceful merlot in the larger region labeled Lalande-de-Pomerol or Libourne.

Merlot wines were also made in northeast Italy, but it was only recently that it was widely planted in California. It became a popular varietal in the 1980s and the dominant phenomenon of the 1990s. The first U.S. producers, such as Louis Martini, Clos du Bois, Rutherford, Clos du Val, Newton, and Duckhorn still make fine Bordeaux-style wines. But merlot's faddishness as a softer alternative to cabernet led to overpricing; eventually overproduction may correct the balance.

Washington State may prove to be the best U.S. source of varietal merlots. Merlot is increasingly exported from Chile, Italy, and Australia to the U.S. market.

NEBBIOLO

An ancient grape that is the most noble of Italy's great reds, nebbiolo grows only in the Piedmont in the northwestern corner of the country. Even there it does best only on hillsides with special soils. Still, it does not ripen until quite late in the year, usually in October. It

has deep color, full flavor, high acidity, and substantial tannin, all of which give its wines exceptionally long life, indeed it often needs ten years, preferably twenty, to mellow into drinkability.

It is the grape behind the great big reds of Barolo and Barbaresco and the more affordable spanna or gattinara. It has also been planted in California in the recent fascination with Italian varietals.

PINOT NOIR

Pinot noir is a precious and fragile grape that makes the treasured reds of Burgundy and gives body and color to many great Champagnes. It can be sleek in texture, brilliant in color, and full of delicate cherry, strawberry, and pepper in the nose, and subtle on the palate.

Unfortunately a great Burgundy is a rare and expensive thing; so-so pinots from Burgundy are more common and often no less expensive, because production is both limited and difficult.

Pinot noir is one of the few red grapes with an affection for cool climates, but it is not an easy relationship. It suffers from late frosts and fails to ripen fully in many vintages so it is often ameliorated with added sugar to boost its alcohol content. Pinot is equally difficult in the winery, where the length and temperature of fermentation, the amount of aging, is a risky decision. Even the French get it wrong in many vintages, and even the best years age more quickly and less predictably than cabernet sauvignon. Odds on great Burgundy are long, however, they don't discourage red wine lovers from gambling; the risk makes victory exciting as well as sweet. Pinot noir is also grown more affordably in Alsace. Outside of France, it is known as pinot nero in Italy and as spätburgunder in Germany and in Eastern Europe.

Making good pinot noir in the U.S. was especially difficult and expensive: In the 1980s, one winery conducted a tour of tastings of its pinot noirs candidly showing failed vintages as well as signs of hope. By the end of the 1990s, Americans were much better with reliable pinot noir production concentrated in cooler areas, especially Oregon, Carneros, and the Central Coast in California. Australians are mastering the beast as well.

Given pinot's low yield in most areas, it is only rarely seen as a cheap varietal, but good quality can be had in the $15 to $20 range. If you only know cabernet and merlot, try a pinot. You may find it a tasty alternative and a better buy.

SANGIOVESE

The other great Italian red grape, sangiovese is planted quite widely in Italy, but achieves its greatest success in the hill towns of Tuscany. Sangiovese is quite a chameleon and can be made in all grades of quality, but it is at its best as the primary red grape in Chianti, and the dominant one in the better Chianti Classico. Special clones of sangiovese are responsible for two other fine wines in the region, the famous Brunello di Montalcino and Vino Nobile di Montepulciano.

It has also been a big player in the Super-Tuscan category of table wines created by Italian winemakers in the last thirty years. Freed from traditional recipes, they found sangiovese could be blended with a wide variety of non-Italian grapes from cabernet sauvignon and merlot to shiraz, or made into a lovely wine by itself.

Sangiovese is enjoying new popularity in the U.S. too. Winemakers researching the roots and vines of their Italian-American ancestors have planted sangiovese in California; the Antinori family of Tuscany has planted some in Napa too.

Primary red grape in Chianti

SYRAH/SHIRAZ

Twenty years ago few wine drinkers could have identified this grape or known if they liked it; we're luckier today.

Syrah is a dark, spicy, hot-weather grape that has always been part of France's Mediterranean, especially the northern Rhône vineyards, and may have roots in the famous wines of Persia. It was a member of the Châteauneuf-du-Pape blend, but sometimes considered more rustic and less sophisticated than pinot noir or cabernet. Its flavors are strong too, plums and blackberries, with a tingle of pepper or mint.

It was winemakers from Australia and California searching the Rhône and the Mediterranean who really brought it to our attention. Down Under it changed its name to shiraz and became one of Australia's great reds, which could waltz gracefully with cabernet sauvignon or by itself. Many Californians make syrah as a varietal or blended with other Rhône reds. A distant cousin

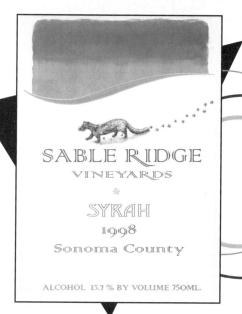

planted in California decades ago and often neglected, makes a similar, even bigger wine, ironically named petite sirah.

This is the wine that stands up to the boldest food flavors, like lamb and barbecue, and defines spiciness in red wines without losing a soft texture.

TEMPRANILLO

The most noble red grape of Spain, it has grown best in the hillside vineyards of the Rioja, but is increasingly planted in other regions aiming to make fine wine. It has medium body and color, the flavor of strawberries and cherries, and a faint aroma of leather. It is generally easy to drink because it is relatively low in acid and traditionally got long aging in wood. New styles of winemaking, however, have produced young wines with more fruit without

...better grapes for Port

losing the smoothness. Tempranillo is also the star in Ribera del Duero and Navarro; the Portuguese call it tinta roriz and consider it one of the better grapes for Port. Vineyards in other countries are experimenting with tempranillo.

ZINFANDEL

This is a distinctly American grape, which means we really don't know where its ancestor came from, but it has a strong distinct character, lots of charm, and a significant place in California winemaking history. The best can taste like blackberry jam or be made into a sleek Bordeaux style claret.

Current theories of its origin trace it to the Adriatic, either Croatia, where it is known as plavac mali, or Italy as primitivo. Someone brought it to California where it became one of the basic ingredients of sturdy red wine and a fixture in Italian-American vineyards. When wine started to boom in the 1960s, sage advisers predicted Americans would love red wine and still more vineyards were planted with zinfandel. Bad idea until another mistake twenty years later: Someone removed zinfandel juice from its skins before it had picked up enough color to turn red and was still pink. White zinfandel was born and so was a whole category of blush wines and a generation of consumers who discovered wine could be light, fun, and pretty.

While the white zin craze gobbled up many of the grapes, true zinfandel fans feared the real thing, zin the red, might disappear. Thankfully, Gresham's Law was suspended before a great element of America's wine heritage was lost.

Zinfandel vines have the same diehard character as their fans, and are among the oldest in California. They can be fifty to ninety years old, still producing small lots of grapes with intense color and flavor, and growers and vintners who cared have kept them going. While the most expensive wine land has long since been converted from zinfandel to cabernet and other more profitable grapes, some of America's best reds are zinfandels. Some are young and fresh and perfect for pizza, others are big, highly alcoholic, and will live for thirty years or more (the dividing point is around 13 percent alcohol). Best zin growing is in the high mountain vineyards of Napa, Santa Cruz, Amador County, and the Alexander and Dry Creek Valleys of Sonoma.

a distinctly American grape

88 Zinfandel, Howell Mountain, bottled May 90
Zinfandel on Howell Mountain set a better crop in 1988 than was typical on the North Coast. The cool climate moderated late August's extreme heat, and the grapes ripened normally. We increased the percentage of uncrushed and unstemmed clusters in the fermentation, and the resulting wine shows considerable spicy fruit, with rounder tannins than usual. Accessible now, this complex zinfandel will continue to develop over the next five to seven years.
PD (5/90)

Founded in 1959, Ridge was one of the first of today's small, fine California wineries—limiting production to achieve the highest quality. Close adherence to traditional techniques—including use of natural yeasts, racking for clarity, and filtering only when necessary for stability—have set Ridge apart. Our winery and estate vineyards are located above 2300 feet on Monte Bello Ridge in the Santa Cruz Mountains overlooking San Francisco and the Bay Area. To order wines or visit, write or call (408) 867-3233.

NET CONTENTS 750ML

CONTAINS SULFITES
PRODUCT OF CALIFORNIA, U.S.A.

RIDGE
CALIFORNIA ZINFANDEL HOWELL MOUNTAIN 1988

HOWELL MOUNTAIN, NAPA COUNTY   ALCOHOL 14.3% BY VOLUME
PRODUCED AND BOTTLED BY RIDGE VINEYARDS, INC. BW 4488
17100 MONTE BELLO ROAD, P.O. BOX AI, CUPERTINO, CALIFORNIA

WINE DIARIES

SEEING RED

You don't know why you ever agreed to his little, "Tuesday Night Taste Test" request in the first place. Number one, you're strictly a margarita and banana daiquiri girl yourself. Number two, about the most you've ever had to drink on a Tuesday night is that extra ounce of Lactaid you use to wash down your nightly fat-free Fig Newton.

But, your four-month relationship had grown pretty stale of late, and he thought this was the perfect idea to liven it up. Naturally, he frowned on *your* idea to at least hold your weekly taste test at your place, citing the fact that you didn't have the right "equipment." By this, he meant his new $200 corkscrew, the one that looked just like Captain Kirk's stun gun and the reason you'd been paying for dinner all month!

Fine. Sure. Whatever. It's not bad enough you're buying into his vino variation, but, come Tuesday night, you slog yourself up to his snooty downtown high-rise after a long workday to find him seated at the bar wearing a pair of silk pajamas and smoking a new pipe contentedly.

"Oh, I'm sorry," you stammer at the front door. "I didn't realize you'd relocated the Playboy mansion, Mr. Hefner."

He doesn't even crack a smile.

"You're late," he reminds you soberly. "I specifically requested that you be here precisely fifteen minutes after I open both bottles. If they breathe much longer, their delicate tastes will be suffocated."

You'd like to tell him that, if he keeps

talking to you this way, "the taste" is not going to be the only thing being "suffocated" around here, but instead you make some lame excuse about the traffic and manage to approach the bar without smashing both bottles over his head.

"This evening," he intones seriously, as if he were the master of ceremonies at Borefest 2000, "we will be sampling the Ata Rangi Pinot Noir, 1996. You will be well served by noticing the deep red color, fading slightly to pink. As you sample the aroma, please consider the lightly stewed black fruits on the nose with some smoked oak and a hint of corruption, truly lovely!

"As you taste, be sure to notice the medium to full-bodied texture with ripe black fruits, candy and nut flavors, some underlying oak, and a rich, long finish. After sampling this superior specimen, I am sure you will agree with my vino verdict that it is excellent now but should develop over the next couple of years and beyond."

"Good God," you think to yourself as he hands you the tiny sip of Ata Rangi nestled in one of his obnoxious, poser bowl-sized wine glasses. Tasting under his watchful eye, you try with all your taste buds' limited might to seek out the fruit, candy, and nut flavors, but instead find a tight tartness not unlike an aspirin that's gone down the wrong chute.

When you swallow it without ceremony, the little vein alongside the left side of his skull pulsates and he nearly freaks out.

"What do you think this bowl here in the middle is for?" he practically shouts, pulling at his thinning hair.

"Potato chips?" you ask tartly, secretly enjoying the way his pale face explodes in a brilliant red. No, scratch that, a lovely rosé.

"We spit the wine out after we taste it," he informs you after a quick demonstration, one that makes him look more like a ball player than a wine expert. "That way it leaves our palate unsaturated and more . . . alert."

"Fine, fine," you sigh. "Next time, I'll spit."

"Thank you," he grunts, displaying the second bottle of the evening as if it were a newborn child. "Now, on to our challenger, the Fery Meunier Pommard Epenots, circa 1995."

"Circa?" you think to yourself as you mentally castrate your soon-to-be ex-boyfriend. After all, the last time you heard anyone say "circa" you were still sporting a sorority-girl sweatshirt and dozing through World Religions 101.

"Notice," he goes on sternly, perhaps reading your wandering mind, "that this hue is a much paler red, almost fading to pink. Smell the restrained nose showing ripe, sweaty fruits, and just the slightest hint of oak. Enjoy the medium body with flavors of strawberries, raspberries, and cream and, perhaps, some oak as well.

All in all, a fresh clean style with some complexity."

Again, he hands you yet another humongous glass with a tiny sip of wine at the very bottom. Straining your neck to get at it, you sip and, remembering his recent tirade, spit the sip out indelicately into a bowl after swishing it around in your mouth like some actress in a Listerine commercial.

Sighing, he insists that you couldn't possibly decipher the wine's "subtle nuances" or "piquant personality" in such a short amount of time, and instructs you to "soak it all in" next time and not spit it out quite so quickly.

You want to scream at him that there won't be a next time until, instead, you get an intoxicating inspiration and thank God that you were blessed with being left-handed.

As he berates you about your Merlot manners and French faux pas, you reach for your wine glass and, quite accidentally (wink, wink, nudge, nudge) knock not only the bottle of Pinot Noir off the thoroughly modern kitchen counter, but the crystal glass and elegant "spittoon" as well. As if in slow motion, you watch the triumphant trio spill across his brand new living room rug.

His shrieks and cries, gasps and moans follow you into the hallway as you leave your Hefner-clad, crybaby ex-boyfriend and his

one and only Tuesday Night Taste Test far, far behind. "What fool with a taste for red, red wine buys an imported white carpet in the first place?" you smile to yourself as you head home for a little Lactaid and fat-free Fig Newtons. Who knows, tonight you might even have an Oreo as well. After all, it was a taste test, right?

THE REST OF THE BUNCH

RED AND WHITE GRAPES

Albariño - A very fragrant white grape from Galicia in northwest Spain; known as alvarinho in Portugal. A pleasant alternative to chardonnay. You'll see more of it.

Baco noir - A red hybrid from France that has been one of the best grapes to grow in the eastern United States, especially New York.

Barbera - A red grape from the Italian Piedmont where it is a decided second to nebbiolo. It is high in acid, fruit, and can be rustic or rich and complex. One of the old Italian grapes in California.

Cabernet franc - One of the secondary red grapes in Bordeaux blends. It ripens early and has more alcohol but less flavor than the preeminent cabernet sauvignon. In St-Émilion it's usually blended with merlot. In the Loire Valley of France and Italy it often stands on its own as a full-bodied, earthy wine. In U.S. wineries it has been blended with cabernet sauvignon and sometimes made as a varietal.

Carignane - A prolific red grape in California's Central Valley, the French Rhône, and Spain but never highly regarded. It's a key ingredient in good jug wines and can also make good hearty reds in the south of France and in the hands of U.S. Rhône rangers.

Charbono - A fruity red grape, once popular with California's Italian wine growers in the early part of the century. Could be related to dolcetto. Some vineyards still make it. Try it if you find it.

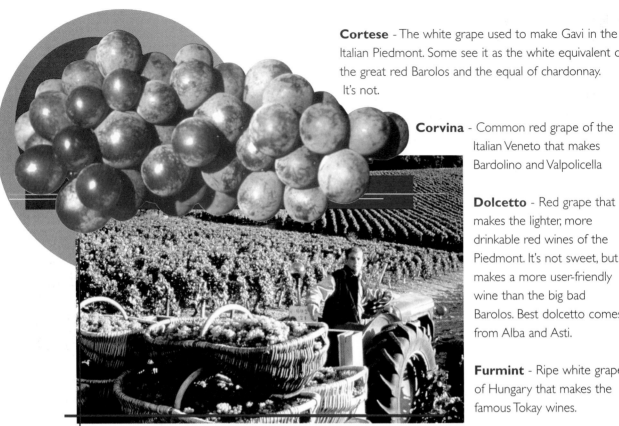

Cortese - The white grape used to make Gavi in the Italian Piedmont. Some see it as the white equivalent of the great red Barolos and the equal of chardonnay. It's not.

Corvina - Common red grape of the Italian Veneto that makes Bardolino and Valpolicella

Dolcetto - Red grape that makes the lighter, more drinkable red wines of the Piedmont. It's not sweet, but it makes a more user-friendly wine than the big bad Barolos. Best dolcetto comes from Alba and Asti.

Furmint - Ripe white grape of Hungary that makes the famous Tokay wines.

Chasselas - A white table grape sometimes drafted into wine production for bulk wines. It is known as fendent in Switzerland where it is widely planted.

Cinsault - A productive, but unimpressive, red grape in the south of France and hot-weather vineyards around the world. You'll probably only see it in blends.

Colombard/French Colombard - A tart white grape that has only recently been displaced by chardonnay as California's top white grape. You might not have heard of it except on a few jug wines. Most goes into blends or brandies, which are its chief uses in France too. Its chief assets are high alcohol and high acidity, not flavor.

Concord - The great native American grape, red and white, used in jellies and sweet wines like Mogen David and Manischewitz. Although it is adapted to grow in much of the U.S., it's a member of *Vitis labrusca*, not *V. vinifera*, and is unlikely to be used in a fine wine, even for patriotic purposes.

Grenache - Gutsy red grape in the hit vineyards of Rhône and Provence, California, and elsewhere. It makes fine rosé and also plays a role in more robust Rioja Port and Sicily's cannonau. Also known as garnacha and tinto. Makes better wine than many realize.

Grignolino - A tart red grape from the Italian Piedmont that also grows in California. It makes great rosés.

Kerner - One of the more unusual and successful modern German hybrids, crossing riesling with a red grape. It has a floral nose and good acidity.

Lambrusco - A light red grape with little distinction that produces a lot of wine in Central Italy.

Lemberger - A peppery red grape from Germany and originally Austria. Rarely seen in the U.S. except Washington State.

Malbec - A near-black Bordeaux blending grape, valued for deep dark color. Only recently added to a few American meritage blends, it stands on its own as the "black wine" of Cahors in southwest France and has long been a varietal in Argentina and northern Italy. It won't replace merlot but it's surprisingly good on its own.

Malvasia - A white grape with good sugar and sweet aromas of orange blossoms. It has been made as a semi sweet wine in many countries. Under the name Malmsey, it is one of the greatest of the fortified wines of Madeira.

Marsanne - A white grape with more body and color than flavor. It's used in ordinary bulk blends in the Rhône and in the great whites of Hermitage. It's getting more use in the southwest of France and in the U.S.

Montepulciano - An up-and-coming red grape, very common in the Abruzzo region on Italy's Adriatic coast. It makes a spicy but easy drinking red there and is showing up in new blends with sangiovese. Look for it. (Not to be confused with a winemaking town of the same name in Tuscany.)

Mourvèdre - A red grape of rich aromas, strong tannins, and deep color that's tough in the sun and harvests late. A traditional favorite in the Rhône and the south of France, many U.S. and Australian vineyards are growing it for blends and varietal wines. It's big in Spain as monastrel and mataro. Done right, it can have merlot softness with a kick of Rhône spice. You gotta try it.

Müller-Thurgau -
Most common white
grape in Germany, a
disappointing hybrid
responsible for too much
liebfraumilch. Crossing the
good sylvaner with the great
riesling created a grape that
produces a lot of dull flabby
wine. Also used to make bulk
wine in Eastern Europe and in unfriendly climates like
England. Best wines probably are from Italy.

Muscadine - The tough and thick skinned branch of
American grapes; scuppernong is the best known. Not
particularly good for wine or out of hand eating, but a
Southern favorite.

Palomino - Pale white
Spanish grapes used for
fino sherries.

Pedro Ximenes -
Richest and sweetest of the
sherry grapes, sometimes
blended into cream sherries. A
pure PX sherry can be eaten on
ice cream.

Petit verdot - Most difficult of the
red blending grapes of Bordeaux. Petit
verdot ripens late and can add extra sugar and color to
a cabernet or merlot blend. A few California wineries
determined to have all five Bordeaux varieties grow it.

Petite sirah - A little black grape with big flavor and
tannins that grows well in hot climates. It made
California's most stout-hearted red wines for decades. It
is high in alcohol and long-lived, and still gives muscle to
many red blends. It fell into disfavor and now enjoys a
modest revival. Origins are possibly in the Rhône Valley
of France, but it's very distantly related to the syrah.
Best comes from the hotter zones of California.

Pinot blanc - A full bodied cousin of chardonnay that
can have a lively bouquet. It's grown in Germany,
northern Italy, and other parts of Europe, but gets the
most respect and best showing in Alsace; American
vineyards are experimenting with it, especially in the
Pacific Northwest.

Pinot meunier - Red grape that is the main grape of
Champagne. Chardonnay and pinot noir get the

attention but this one provides much of the body and bouquet.

Pinotage - A red hybrid grape in South Africa made by crossing pinot noir and cinsault. Can be tart or very plummy. Worth a try for its uniqueness.

Roussane - A sweet white grape with nutty aromas. This grape adds the richness and wonderful smells to the great whites of the Rhône such as Hermitage and Châteauneuf-du-Pape. It's hard to grow but U.S. wineries are trying.

Ruby cabernet - A U.S. hybrid of cabernet sauvignon and carignane created to grow well in extreme heat. Most of it goes into bulk wines.

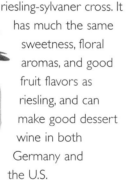

Scheurebe - A white German hybrid that is the best modern riesling-sylvaner cross. It has much the same sweetness, floral aromas, and good fruit flavors as riesling, and can make good dessert wine in both Germany and the U.S.

Scuppernong - A variety of the thick-skinned muscadine grapes native to North America. Makes a heavy sweet wine, sometimes fortified. Was commonly grown in the South and also grows in Mexico.

Seyval blanc. - A white grape created by French hybridizers. Seyval blanc has been most successful in the eastern United States where more traditional varieties have proven difficult. Try it if it grows in your state, just don't expect great crispness or aroma.

Sylvaner - A white grape that is Germany's second-best behind riesling. It has high acids and sugars and reliable production but lacks the aroma and balance of

riesling. Often used in high-quality blends, best from Franken and Rheinhessen. Also made as a varietal wine in Alsace and northeastern Italy.

"Red wine with fish. Well, that should have told me something."

—James Bond

Thompson Seedless - The most common white grape in California. This is the main grape in the vast Central Valley of California, where it makes raisins, bulk wine, and brandy.

Touriga Nacional - Red Portuguese grape that is considered the best grape in Port. Also used for table wine in Portugal but rarely seen in the U.S.

Trebbiano - A common white grape of northern and central Italy. Trebbiano is the grape of Italy's best known white wines, such as Soave and Orvieto, and can make crisp wines but they have little flavor or aroma. In France, it's called ugni blanc and used primarily in brandies.

Viognier - Aromatic white grape from the Rhône Valley. A grape with a soft texture, bright gold color, and pleasant aroma of apricots and peaches that is a traditional favorite in the northern Rhône, especially in Condrieu. It's one of the best white grapes that the Rhône rangers brought back to the U.S.

GLOSSARY

Abariño: A white wine grape of the Galicia region of Spain; known as the alvarinho in Portugal.

Acidity: The combination of tartaric, malic, lactic, and citric acids in the wine give it its zing. Too little acidity and the wine is flabby or flat; too much of it causes the wine to taste sour.

Alcohol: The result of yeast fermentation; helps to preserve the wine, and contributes to the wine's body.

Alsace: A French province bordering the Rhine north of Switzerland; riesling, gewürztraminer, sylvaner, and pinot blanc are the most common varieties of grape cultivated in Alsace.

American Viticultural Areas (AVAs): Geographic designation of regions within the United States.

Anbaugebieten: The thirteen large wine regions of Germany, such as Rheingau or Franken.

Appellation d'Origine Contrôlée (AOC): The highest-ranking French designation of wines; sometimes shortened to Appellation Contrôlée and abbreviated AC.

Aroma: The smell of a wine.

Auslese: A German wine containing as much as 15 percent alcohol. It is made

from a select late picking of the most ripe grapes, some of which may have botrytis cinerea.

Baco noir: A red hybrid from France that has been one of the best grapes to grow in the eastern United States.

Balance: The combination of the elements of wine: acid and sweetness, fruit and wood.

Barbera: An Italian red wine varietal grown in the Piedmont region; also abundant in the San Joaquin Valley of California.

Barolo: A fine red wine of Italy made from the nebbiolo grape in Piedmont.

Barrel: A relatively small wooden container for fermenting/aging wine, usually made of oak and about sixty gallons in size.

Beaujolais: A district of Southern Burgundy, which produces a lively, popular red wine from the gamay grape.

Beaujolais Nouveau: A popular category of Beaujolais red wine that is released for sale within weeks of the harvest and is best when consumed within a year.

Beerenauslese: A rare QmP German wine made from a late picking of the ripest individual berries, often affected with botrytis. A very sweet wine with a high alcohol content.

Bereich: The division of German wine regions a little more specific than Anbaugebieten. This division contains many groupings of smaller vineyards.

Bodega: A Spanish winery or building where wine is stored.

Body: A wine's weight in your mouth. Generally described as light, medium, or full.

Bordeaux: An ancient port city in southwestern France with a tradition of red wine (the British call this claret) blended from up to five grape varieties including cabernet sauvignon, cabernet franc, merlot, petit verdot, and malbec.

Botrytis: A fungus that attacks grapes grown in moist conditions; can be detrimental to many grapes, and vineyards are often treated to prevent it; however, it is desired for some white wine varities because it softens the grape's acidity and concentrates its sugars, lending a honeyed aroma/flavor.

Bouquet: The combination of aromas in the wine.

Burgundy: A region of eastern France stretching from Dijon to Lyons, and including Chablis (ninety miles southeast of Paris, removed from the rest of the region); famous for whites as well as red wines.

Cabernet franc: A red wine grape used in the blends of Bordeaux; also grown extensively in northern Italy producing a wine simply called cabernet; a more recent addition to California vineyards intended to blend with cabernet sauvignon.

Cabernet sauvignon: A small blue-black grape that ages well in the bottle; a key component of Bordeaux's blends and now a varietal throughout the world.

Carignane: A key ingredient in good jug wines, grown in California's Central Valley, the French Rhône, and Spain.

Cask: A relatively large wooden or steel container for making or storing wine.

Cavas: A Spanish alternative to Champagne that uses different grapes but the same process of creating bubbles through secondary fermentation in the bottle, rather than in large bulk tanks. Cava is the only DOC designation that applies to wines made by a particular

Chardonnay: A white grape, used in the finest wines of Burgundy and throughout the world.

Chasselas: A white table grape, known as fendent in Switzerland where it is widely planted.

method, rather than geographic designation.

Cellar: A cool, dark area for storing wine. The ideal temperature is between fifty-five and sixty degrees.

Chablis: A small town in the Burgundy region known for its fine white wine, although the name of the town is applied generically to many white wines.

Charbono: A fruity red grape, could be related to dolcetto.

Chateâu: A French name for a grand winery estate.

Chenin blanc: The finest white grape of France's Loire valley; makes fruity, dry to medium-sweet wines.

Chianti: A famous Italian red wine made in Tuscany.

Cinsault: A red grape used primarily in blends.

Claret: A British name for the red wines of Bordeaux.

Classico: An Italian term applicable to

certain DOC or DOCG wines whose vineyards are situated in the original, classic part of the territory.

Colheita: "Vintage" in Portuguese.

Colombard/French Colombard: A tart white grape that, until chardonnay, was California's top white grape; used primarily in blends and brandies.

Complex: Not simple! A complex wine has many aromas, flavors, and nuances.

Concord: The great American grape, red and white, used in jellies and sweet wines.

Cortese: The white grape used to make Gavi in the Italian Piedmont.

Corvina: Common red grape of the Italian Veneto that makes Bardolino and Valpolicella

Cosecha: "Vintage" in Spanish.

Crianza: A Spanish age designation, which means the wine was aged two years, including one year in oak.

Cru: This indicates that the wine came from a "classified" growth, meaning it's an exceptional wine. Premier Cru is the top rank for Bordeaux; Grand Cru is the tops for Burgundy.

Crush: The month or two every fall when grapes are harvested.

Decanting: The process of pouring the wine out of one bottle into a decanter or another bottle to allow the wine to breathe or to pour a red wine from its sediment.

Denominação de Origem Controlada (DOC): Designations for the most proven wine regions of Portugal.

Denominación de Origen (DO): Spanish geographic appellation that corresponds to the French AOC and the Italian DOC. An additional distinction of Denominación de Origen Calificada (DOC) is similar to the Italian DOCG; it's something of an honorary status, so far granted only to the Rioja.

Denominazione di Origine Controllata (DOC): The Italian law that governs using place names for wines; Denominazione di Origine Controllata e Garantita (DOCG) is a higher quality designation.

Dolcetto: Red grape that makes the lighter, more drinkable red wines of the Piedmont.

Eiswein: An exquisitely flavored, crisp German wine made from grapes left on the vine until January or February when they are frozen raisins.

Fermentation: The process by which yeast converts sugars into alcohol.

Finish: The aftertaste of a wine when it has been swallowed.

Fortified: A wine to which additional alcohol has been added to raise its alcoholic strength.

Furmint: Ripe white grape of Hungary that makes the famous Tokay wines.

Gamay: A light red grape used especially in Beaujolais wines with bright flavors, light aromas, crisp acidity, and low alcohol.

Gewürztraminer: A spicy German grape that requires cool weather and varies from dry to super sweet. Sometimes blended with riesling.

Grenache: Red wine grape grown in the Rhône and California; makes better wine than many realize.

Grignolino: A tart red grape from the Piedmont; makes great rosés.

Kabinett: The lightest and most common category of QmP German wine, usually at least nine percent alcohol. This is the most common category of good German wine served in America.

Kerner: A modern German hybrid—a cross between a riesling and a red grape; has a floral nose and good acidity.

Lambrusco: A light red grape with little distinction that produces a lot of wine in Central Italy.

Landwein: A German country wine from a particular region similar to vin du pays.

Lemberger: A peppery red grape from Germany and originally Austria.

Malbec: A Bordeaux blending grape valued for its dark color; surprisingly good on its own.

Malvasia: A white grape with good sugar and sweet aromas of orange blossoms. Called Malmsey, it is one of the greatest of the fortified wines of Madeira.

Marsanne: A white grape used in blends.

Merlot: A red wine grape grown as the dominant grape in Pomerol and St. Émilion and often blended with other varietals. After wide-spread plantings in California in the 1980s, merlot began to earn respect as a varietal itself.

Montepulciano: A red grape that makes a spicy but easy drinking red, and it is showing up in blends with sangiovese.

Mourvèdre: A favorite red of the Rhône, and becoming popular in the United States and Australia.

Müller-Thurgau: A disappointing German hybrid responsible for a lot of dull flabby wine.

Muscadine: An American grape that is not particularly good for wine, but still a favorite in the South.

Muscat: An ancient favorite grape, known for delicious sweet wines, both still and sparkling.

Nebbiolo: An Italian red grape, grown only in the Piedmont; it often needs ten years, preferably twenty, to mellow into drinkability.

Nose: The collection of smells associated with a wine, similar to the bouquet.

Palomino: Pale white Spanish grapes used for fino sherries.

Pedro Ximenes: Richest and sweetest of the sherry grapes, sometimes blended into cream sherries.

Petite sirah: Red grape grown in California; not the same as syrah.

Petit verdot: Blended with cabernet sauvignon and merlot for color; small amounts grow in Australia.

Phylloxera: A tiny louse that attacks and eventually kills a vine through its root system.

Pinot blanc: A whiter version of pinot gris with a full body and mild aroma that can be a little like chardonnay. It's popular in Alsace and especially in Austria and Eastern Europe.

Pinot gris/pinot grigio: The gray, sometimes blue, sometimes pink cousin of pinot noir, it is still grown and sometimes used in Burgundy, but most familiar as a crisp Italian white wine.

Pinot noir: A precious and fragile grape, used in dry red wines and sparkling wine; the most important grape of Burgundy.

Pomerol: The smallest appellation in Bordeaux. Pomerol has no official classification system and doesn't really need one; its wines are few and expensive.

Port: A wine fortified with brandy.

Qualitätswein: Quality German wine, divided into two categories.

Qualitätswein bestimmter Anbaugebiete (QbA): The largest and most basic level. QbA wines come from within one of the thirteen large regions and have some of the characteristics of that region.

Qualitätswein mit Prädikat (QmP): Quality wine with special character. These are Germany's best wines and are further ranked by sugar and alcohol content.

Reserva: A Spanish term for wines that have aged three years for reds, two years for whites.

Reserve: A term seen on some bottles, carries no official meaning, although it ideally means the winery culled out its best grapes or wines, gave them special handling, and extra aging, usually in oak.

Roussane: A sweet white grape with nutty aromas. This grape adds the richness and wonderful smells to the great whites of the Rhône.

Ruby cabernet: A hybrid of cabernet sauvignon and carignane created in the United States; most of it goes into bulk wines.

Sangiovese: Another great Italian red grape, planted quite widely in Tuscany as the primary red grape in Chianti.

Sauternes: A region in Bordeaux that produces some of the world's greatest white wines.

Riesling: Possibly the greatest white grape of all; principal grape of Germany and also important in Alsace and Austria.

Riserva: Italian for "reserve," applies to Italian wines that have met aging requirements.

Sauvignon blanc: A white wine grape grown principally in France and California.

Scheurrebe: A white German hybrid that is the best modern riesling-sylvaner cross. Makes good dessert wines in both Germany and the U.S.

Scuppernong: The most common of the muscadine grapes; it makes a heavy sweet wine, sometimes fortified.

Sémillon: This is the modest partner of sauvignon blanc in Bordeaux; U.S. winemakers are making more use of sémillon all around, in blends as dry table wine and in desserts.

Seyval blanc: A white French hybrid; it has been most successful in the eastern United States.

Sherry: A fortified wine from southern Spain (around the city of Jerez de la Frontera from which the English speaking world took its name).

Shiraz: The Australian name for the syrah grape.

Sommeliers: Wine specialists, usually in restaurants.

Spätlese: A QmP German wine made from a late harvest of grapes. High in sugar and alcohol, but a good food wine nonetheless.

Sulfites: Sulfurus acid compounds used widely in winemaking.

Syrah: A dark, spicy, hot-weather grape that has always been part of France's Mediterranean, especially the northern Rhône vineyards.

Tannins: Acids derived from the skins, seeds, and stems of the grape and oak barrels; the astringency tasted on the tongue; tannins help preserve the wine.

Tempranillo: A red wine grape that grows best in the cooler regions and produces a wine with a delicate flavor and color. It is sometimes mixed with two bolder hot-weather reds, garnacha and cariñena.

Tinto: A Spanish word meaning red when applied to wine.

Touriga Nacional: Red Portuguese grape that is considered the best grape in Port.

Trebbiano: A common white grape of northern and central Italy. It makes crisp wines with little flavor or aroma. In France it is called ugni blanc and is used primarily in brandies.

Trockenbeerenauslese: A very rare, and consequently expensive, German wine. This wine is made from the ripest grapes, individually picked, and only in certain years. This wine can be more than 21 percent alcohol.

Varietals: A wine named after a grape; under U.S. law, 75 percent of the grapes in a varietal wine must be of that variety named. Some wines have 100 percent of the same grape; most will have some other kind of grape added for extra taste, aroma, or color.

Vin de Pays: Wine made from a wide but specific region, with the region named; it's of better quality and should show some regional character.

Vin de table: The lowest grade, which can come from anywhere in France and is rarely seen in the U.S.

Vin Délimité de Qualité Supérieure (VDQS): The French classification just below AOC.

Vintage Date: For a wine to be considered vintage, 95 percent of all grapes used to make the wine must have been picked that year.

Viognier: A white grape—a cross between chardonnay and gewürztraminer.

Zinfandel: A significant California red wine grape.

DE LOACH

SONOMA COUNTY
RUSSIAN RIVER VALLEY

ZINFANDEL
ESTATE BOTTLED
1992

YOUR PERSONAL WINE DIARY

A

Accessories, 62, 64
Acidity, (defined), 197
Aftertaste, (defined), 32
Aging wines, 69–70
Albariño, 192
    (defined), 197
Alcohol levels
    detecting, 17
    reduced, 58
Alsace region
    (defined), 197
    German grapes, French accent, 92
    map of, 92
American Viticultural Areas (AVAS), (defined), 197
Appellation d'Origine Contrôlée (AOC), (defined), 24, 75–76, 197
Argentina, 8, 163
    map of, 163
Aroma, (defined), 32, 197
Aroma wheel, 17, 42
Astringent taste, (defined), 32
Australia, 8, 149–158
    down under, 157–158
    Eastern Australia, 154
    finding your way, 153
    grapes, 151
    labels, 152
    maps of, 153–155
    prices, 161
    quintessential New World wine maker, 150
    South Australia, 155
    Southeastern Australia, 154
    Tasmania, 156
    Western Australia, 155

B

Baco noir, 192
Balance, (defined), 32, 197
Barbecue, wine with, 58
Barbera, 192
    (defined), 197
Bargain wines, 6, 117–118
Barolo, 114
    (defined), 197
Barrels, 69–70
    (defined), 197
Basics about wine, 15–28
    corkscrews, 25–28
    knowing the grapes, reading the label, 22–24
    sipping, 18
    speak or shut up please, 19
    swirl and sniff, 16–17
Beaujolais nouveau, 87
    (defined), 197
Beaujolais region, 33, 87
    (defined), 197
    map of, 87
    more than a one-night stand, 87
Bennett, Ted, 66
Benziger (winery), 143
Beringer (winery), 137
Best wines, 29–36
    tasting, 30–33
Blanc de noirs, 95
Bodega, (defined), 197
Body, (defined), 32, 197
Bond, James, 196
Books and magazines about wine, 70, 84, 96
Bordeaux bottle shape, 33
Bordeaux region, 11, 31, 33
    come to the Cabernet, 78–82
    (defined), 197
    maps of, 78, 82
    vintages of, 5